LONDON'S
UTILITY
BUSES

LONDON'S UTILITY BUSES

KEN BLACKER

Capital Transport

First published 1997

ISBN 185414 198 8

Published by
Capital Transport Publishing
38 Long Elmes
Harrow Weald
Middlesex

CONTENTS

AUTHOR'S NOTE

When I was a boy, London Transport's utility buses were very much part of the everyday scene. To this day I remember the sound and smell of Guys when they were brand new. I travelled to school on them each day, and utilities were still in the fleet – though numbers were beginning to decline – when I started work with London Transport in 1951. I was sorry to see them go. In researching and writing this book I have been able to revive many personal memories, some of them half forgotten with the passage of time, and I hope that by recording as thoroughly as I possibly can a fascinating but fleeting era in London's bus history, the result will prove as interesting to readers as it has been nostalgic to me.

It is impossible to write detailed fleet histories of this sort without calling on friends and colleagues of many years for their assistance, for no single person can have a monopoly of knowledge on such a subject. There are a number of people to whom I am particularly indebted for their help in providing or confirming material for this volume both recently and over the years, and I would especially like to mention the assistance given by Alan Cross, Frank Davis, John Gillham, Geoff Morant, Alan Nightingale, John Shearman and Reg Westgate, not forgetting others such as Alan Goodey from the diminishing band of those who once worked on the utilites. I must not forget the contributions made by three friends who are with us no more, Peter Aldridge, Ron Lunn and Prince Marshall. I am also indebted to the PSV Circle for allowing me to quote from their records of vehicle movements after leaving London service, and I must also thank the many photographers who have given permission for the use of their material which is so essential to bring a narrative of this nature to life.

I have endeavoured to make this story fully comprehensive but it is inevitable that, after a lapse of so many years, there will be omissions. All the facts which are quoted have been double checked as far as possible and where uncertainty exists I have indicated this. Almost inevitably the odd error will have crept in; long experience has shown that even official records quoted in good faith can sometimes prove incorrect. For any errors that you may find, I apologise.

This volume is dedicated to a friend from years ago who showed many of us, when we were young, the importance of recording London's buses and their movements, either in written detail or photographically, so that with the passage of time their history would not be lost. Alan Smith set an example which I am glad we followed. After his tragic and untimely death much of his huge photographic output was lost, but some of his work remains in the care of Alan Cross and is used in this book. A rare shot showing Alan Smith himself appears on page 56.

Lowestoft, March 1997   KEN BLACKER

INTRODUCTION

For several decades from 1933 onwards the nation's capital city and a large area surrounding it, often referred to as Greater London, was served exclusively and efficiently by the comprehensive bus network organised and operated by London Transport. From the sound base constructed by two of the great names in British public transport history, Lord Ashfield and Frank Pick, London Transport gained world renown and was visited from many points of the globe by those wishing to see urban public transport at its best.

London Transport's impact upon bus design, and its pursuit of engineering superiority through large scale standardisation of vehicles and parts are legendary. This is the story of a short but interesting era when, because the world was at war and London Transport temporarily ceased to be master of its own destiny, it was forced to abandon its high engineering design standards and to purchase a hotch-potch fleet of more than seven hundred double deck buses which it would not have touched at any price in normal times. These were the infamous 'utilities' which, though much maligned and undoubtedly inferior to what Londoners had come to expect, nevertheless served the network well over a few difficult years. When their London days were deemed to be over most found a new life elsewhere, which is also recorded here. Some were modernised mechanically and rebodied to create nearly-new vehicles at a cost far below that of purchasing new buses complete. Examples of these operated for many years in two major British cities and in other places, a fact which did not go entirely unnoticed by the inevitable critics who asked why could not London Transport have saved money by doing like-wise? However London Transport, perhaps wisely, was not to be dislodged from its goal of maximum vehicle standardisation which, through its magnificent RT family, it at last achieved.

The fleeting passage of time means that more than forty years have elapsed since the utility buses ran in London, and those who can remember them represent today's older generations. These same generations can also recall the days when the British bus manufacturing industry flourished and a plethora of indigenous chassis and body builders, such as those who contributed towards London's utility fleet, filled the market. Now all except one of the manufacturers mentioned in this book have gone; even the 'great' names whose demise would once have seemed unthinkable – such as Bristol, Daimler, Leyland, Park Royal, Duple, Weymann – grace the bus scene no more. A salutory lesson as to the great tragedy that has befallen the British bus industry during the intervening years is that today's only survivor is Northern Counties, a company which in the war was a comparatively insignificant manufacturer who London Transport, of its own free will, would never have patronised. After the demise of the utilities many years were to elapse before Northern Counties was asked to build buses for London service once more, but now their well-respected products are found in several of the fleets which run, in a multitude of liveries, where once London Transport reigned supreme.

CHAPTER ONE

THE BARE NECESSITIES

War engulfed Britain in September 1939 and, though no-one could have been aware of it at the time, almost six long years of upheaval, shortages, gloom and danger lay ahead. Work and leisure patterns changed abruptly and manufacturing emphasis quickly switched from peace-time priorities to the production of military aircraft, warships, tanks, guns, armoured vehicles and all their supporting paraphernalia. Against this background, the basic essentials for civilian life had somehow to be procured and maintained too. From the outset, effective public transport was rightly viewed as being vital both for the war effort and for the continuation of at least a semblance of normal civilian life. Priorities changed, of course, as leisure travel inevitably lost ground against the burgeoning need for maintaining mobility of labour to ensure full output of essential supplies, both military and civilian. Bus operators faced many new problems apart from the obvious operational difficulties posed by the night time 'blackout'

and by the requisitioning of many modern and serviceable vehicles for military use. Experienced staff soon began drifting away to serve in the armed forces, fuel and parts supplies became increasingly less dependable, and – above all – the long term availability of new and used buses became increasingly in doubt. During the early months of the war the supply of new buses continued much as before because most of the component parts had already been made or were in course of production, but as the various manufacturing concerns turned their output increasingly to the war effort, the flow of new buses became ever more erratic and finally ceased completely. London Transport's last motor bus built to a peace-time order, RT 151, was not completed ready for service until January 1942 after over a year's delay waiting for components, but by this time vehicles of a very different breed had become the norm.

For the duration of the war the task of ensuring that the country's manufacturing

resources and material supplies were conducted as effectively as possible lay with the Ministry of Supply which had powerful authority over all sections of industry, and this Ministry was one of two which, between them, controlled all aspects of bus manufacturing, heavy repairing, sales and scrapping during the war years. The other was the Ministry of Transport (later renamed the Ministry of War Transport) which in July 1940 issued an Order controlling the sale of new public service vehicles, and goods vehicles too. A year later this was extended to bring the acquisition and disposal of second hand vehicles under the same control. Operators could not make any changes to their fleets without permission. The system which operated right through the war and into 1946 was that the Ministry of Supply would procure the manufacture of new vehicles whilst the Ministry of War Transport would allocate them to operators on the basis of need as perceived by the Ministry.

Facing Page **Many wartime buses were delivered to operators in plain grey paintwork which served to emphasise the austere lines of the austerity body. This 'unfrozen' Leyland TD7 was, in fact, London Transport's Park Royal bodied STD 101 and carried the first utility body to be built. Park Royal constructed more bodies of this type than any other manufacturer and their design, with its crisp front profile forming a continuous straight line from bonnet top to roof, could be regarded as the classic of them all.**
Park Royal Vehicles

Above **The archetypal wartime double decker was undoubtedly the Guy Arab which embodied the roughness, ruggedness and total freedom from embellishment for which the era is best remembered. The classic out-turned front mudguards and protruding bonnet of the famous Arab Mark II are demonstrated on Park Royal bodied G 74. An anachronistic feature was the bulb horn; this was fitted to meet Metropolitan Police requirements which still pertained in the earlier years of the war.** LT Museum

By mid-1941 the situation had become very gloomy. Many buses had been destroyed in London and elsewhere by enemy bombing, increasing numbers were becoming time expired, and on all vehicles irrespective of age maintenance standards were declining because of the departure for the armed forces of many skilled fitters and the ever-worsening spare parts supply situation. The need to maintain public services was fully acknowledged and it was clear that something would have to be done to resume the manufacture of new buses which had now all but ceased. An obvious first step was to complete several hundred vehicles upon which manufacture had come to a halt when production for war purposes had taken top priority, and which lay in differing states of construction, or even as sets of parts, at various chassis and body builders and component suppliers throughout the country.

The Ministry of Supply gave the order for this material in stock to be – in its own word – 'unfrozen', and assembled into complete vehicles for allocation to those operators whose need was judged to be the most critical. When the go-ahead was given neither the manufacturers nor the Ministry were totally clear how many new buses could be achieved by this means. AEC, for example, found on taking a full stock inventory in July 1941

that it could produce 54 more vehicles from unfrozen materials than the figure it had originally notified the Ministry. Eventually over four hundred unfrozen vehicles, the great majority of them double deckers, were supplied to operators in 1941/2 of which London Transport received the largest single share. In recognition of the heavy toll taken on its rolling stock during the enemy's Blitz over London, the Board was allocated 54 comprising 34 AEC Regents, 11 Leyland Titan TD7s and 9 Bristol K5Gs.

In authorising the unfreezing of partly built rolling stock the Ministry of Supply secured a breathing space in which to organise an ongoing manufacturing programme for new passenger vehicle chassis. This proved to be a far from easy task as most of the nation's chassis production capacity was already fully committed to the war effort, but programmes were drawn up for Leyland and Guy to construct chassis for double deckers, with Bedford acting as the sole manufacturer of single deck chassis and Sunbeam likewise for trolleybuses. It was acknowledged that the total output of which these four manufacturers were capable would fall far short of normal peace-time production levels and so, as in the case of the unfrozen stock, all new vehicles continued to be allocated by the Ministry of War Transport according to need.

Whilst it was possible to concentrate chassis manufacture on just a few key firms, the supply of bodies could not be similarly concentrated. The number of passenger vehicle body building companies had always far exceeded the number of chassis suppliers, and even under the tightly controlled wartime contractural arrangements it was inevitable that a similar position would continue to apply. Body construction was a time consuming and labour intensive task which the Ministry of Supply was quick to realise would have to be greatly simplified to take account of wartime shortages of labour and materials. In July 1941 the Ministries of Supply and War Transport set up a committee on which they were joined by representatives of the National Federation of Vehicle Trades representing manufacturers, and members of the Joint Passenger Transport Operators' Organisation representing the various operators' federations, to produce a standard specification for double deck bus bodies. Their objective was to facilitate production and effective economies in labour, time and materials, with the emphasis on simplification of

design and standardisation of fittings. Two double deck designs were in fact produced, one for normal height and another for low-height vehicles, with seating capacities of 56 and 55 respectively. Drawings were issued to all approved bodybuilding concerns, and the era of the wartime austerity bus was born.

The Standard Wartime Specification for Double-deck Bodywork, as the design was officially designated, resulted in a vehicle which to the trained observer was unmistakably spartan and angular, although the normal passenger may have been less aware of the difference had it not been for the elimination of side and rear destination boxes, the reduction in opening windows to only one per side in each saloon, and the use of a steel panelled emergency door at the rear of the upper deck in place of the usual glazed variety. To compensate for the paucity of opening windows two narrow hinged ventilators were fitted above the upstairs front windows with a similar one on the nearside of the lower saloon bulkhead; designed to hinge inwards from the bottom, these were officially described as 'adjustable intake flushing ven-

tilator windows'. There were also four fixed ventilators in the upper deck roof. The ventilator windows were very much a feature of the austerity body, as was the elimination of double curvature panels from the front and rear roof domes. This was particularly noticeable at the rear where the angular arrangement was very prominent and immediately became known in the industry as the 'lobster back'. Elimination of unnecessary curves was ordered to minimise the amount of work required by skilled panel beaters who were needed on aircraft production. No provision was made for an illuminated rear registration plate, it being deemed sufficient to paint the number on to the bodywork or the platform rear window.

Working drawings provided by the National Federation of Vehicle Trades showed clearly the 'no frills' specification of the wartime standard double deck body, but left interpretation of the final contours to each individual manufacturer's whim. This drawing shows the normal height version; a similar one was produced in respect of lowbridge bodies.

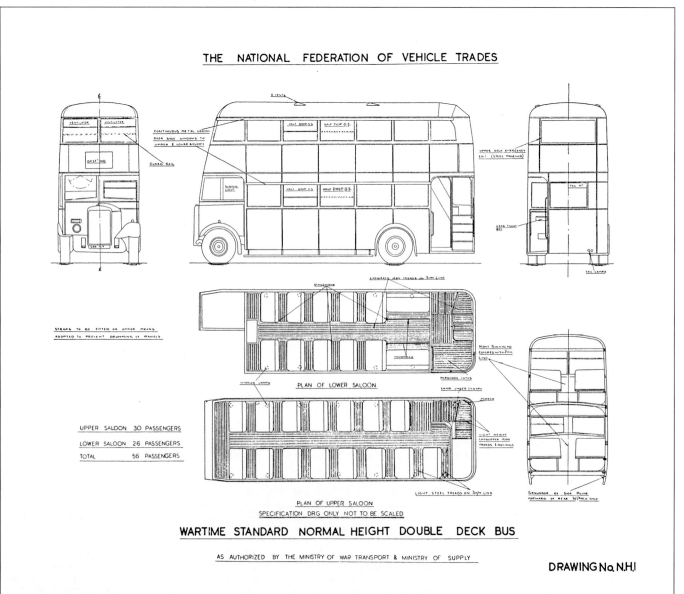

THE NATIONAL FEDERATION OF VEHICLE TRADES

UPPER SALOON 30 PASSENGERS
LOWER SALOON 26 PASSENGERS
TOTAL 56 PASSENGERS

PLAN OF LOWER SALOON

PLAN OF UPPER SALOON
SPECIFICATION DRG ONLY NOT TO BE SCALED

WARTIME STANDARD NORMAL HEIGHT DOUBLE DECK BUS

AS AUTHORIZED BY THE MINISTRY OF WAR TRANSPORT & MINISTRY OF SUPPLY

DRAWING No. N.H.I

Although comparatively rare in London, low height bodywork was essential for many operators. The wartime version achieved a seating capacity of 55 within the standard format employing a sunken offside gangway in the upper saloon, and vehicles of this type were often used as replacements for hard pressed single deckers. Duple's interpretation of the utility concept is seen on D 4 based on a Daimler CWA6 chassis. C F Klapper

The specification stated that the body should be of composite (ie wooden) construction with framings of ash, oak, mahogany or teak except for longitudinal rails which could be of pitch pine. The normal steel flitches and gussets could be used and the front bulkhead could be strengthened and braced with steel plates if desired. Roof hoops on both decks would be of ash and floors – of deal or hardwood – would be covered in 3mm linoleum with light steel treads in the gangways and between seats. Interior side lining panels were omitted from both saloons so that the outside panelling served as the inside skin too, suitably painted to match the interior decor. Similarly the upper deck ceiling was only single skinned but, in order to eliminate dust traps, internal cove panels were permitted running from the seat rails down to the floor and covered in linoleum. The main lower deck ceiling panels were of pressed wood. The use of aluminium was prohibited, all external panelling being of 20 gauge sheet steel. Entrance grab rails and internal stanchions were cellulose-acetate covered, a white finish being used for visibility at night, and the grab handles on the transverse seats were similarly plated although not necessarily in white.

It was estimated that a considerable saving of some 550 direct man hours could be achieved per body besides further savings in ancillary industries, although the actual saving depended to some extent upon each individual company and its construction methods. In the case of two manufacturers (Northern Counties and East Lancashire

Coachbuilders) the use of steel for body framing rather than timber was permitted as these companies had abandoned composite construction before the war and could not easily return to it. Although the official drawings were supposed to be followed fairly closely, in fact each manufacturer placed his own interpretation upon them with the result that the output from any particular factory was instantly recognisable. A small number of builders, though incorporating some of the specified austerity measures, did so within a body which still outwardly resembled peacetime practice, a major exponent of this being London Transport itself who built 46 such bodies at Chiswick (26 highbridge and 20 lowbridge) for its STL fleet in 1941-3. The diverse way in which the great majority of bodybuilders interpreted the basic theme was in complete contrast to the system which applied with the single deck Bedford OWB where the four main body contractors were all required to build a completely identical design and the bodies were, in fact, assembled in jigs even though they were timber framed. In fact the earliest recorded use of the word 'utility' as a generic term for wartime bodies appears to have been in respect of the Bedford OWB when, at a conference of Regional Transport Commissioners in October 1944, it was described as the 'Bedford utility bus'. Thereafter the name stuck and before long it was common practice to describe all wartime austerity bodies as 'utilities'.

The first manufacturer to commence construction of utility bodies was Park Royal.

This was not surprising as the company's Director and General Manager, W. R. Black (later Lord Black), was President of the National Federation of Vehicle Trades and took a leading role in drawing up the specification. As the number of unfrozen chassis exceeded the supply of part-completed bodies it was inevitable that the earliest utility bodies would be placed on the balance of these chassis, and the very first to be completed in October 1941 was a Leyland TD7 destined to become London Transport's STD 101. In the latter part of the month this vehicle, along with an AEC Regent comprising one of a batch of three for Rhondda Transport Co. Ltd, were demonstrated to the press before delivery to their new owners. In the all-grey livery in which most early utilities were delivered, pigment for coloured paint becoming scarce, the two bodies looked almost identical apart from differences in the indicator box, the positioning of the side lights, and the use of green moquette on the Rhondda bus as against the brown leathercloth on the London vehicle.

The utility bus was a novelty at first, but by the end of 1945 there were few places in the country where it could not be found in one form or another. London Transport alone amassed over six hundred. Naturally the original specification underwent modifications as time went by in line with swings in the availability of materials and manpower, but the basic theme remained the same throughout. These variations, and the features which distinguished one builder from another, are described in the chapters which follow.

CHAPTER TWO

THE LEYLAND TITANS – STD 101-111

On 4th September 1941, almost two years to the day after war commenced, London Transport was allocated its first utility bus by the Ministry of War Transport. Taken into stock on 2nd October, Leyland Titan chassis No. 306715 was despatched on the 10th to Park Royal's coachbuilding factory where its body was to be fitted. It had initially been ordered as one of a batch by the West Riding Automobile Co. Ltd in whose service it would have carried a Roe lowheight body and fleet number 567. In London Transport's books it became STD 101 and when, on 20th October, licences for a further ten identical vehicles were issued these brought the class up to a new peak at STD 111. Following on from its trade and press debut, STD 101 arrived at Chiswick on 24th October 1941. The projected purchase price for STD 101 was £1,200 (plus £8.5s.0d delivery charge!) for the TD7 type chassis plus £859.10s.0d for the Park Royal body, but higher construction costs than originally anticipated along with modifications carried out upon receipt at Chiswick brought the body cost to about £966.12s.0d, this being the actual outlay for each of the ten bodies on STD 102-111. However on the credit side each chassis worked out about £80 cheaper than anticipated at £1120.

The choice of STD as the class type was an obvious one since it perpetuated the designation given to the earlier batch of one hundred 1937-built TD4 type Titans which, apart from ten with less than satisfactory 'Gearless' transmission, had proved successful beyond all expectation. The TD7 model, first introduced in 1939, was a natural follow-on from earlier Titans, but whereas STD 1-100 had been heavily modified from Leyland's standard specification to meet London Transport's special requirements, the wartime ones were not. There were several points common to the two models and the visible parts of the TD7 certainly looked much as before except for a new, slimmer front hub cap. Both employed Leyland's superb and smooth-running 8.6 litre direct injection engine mounted as a unit with the single dry plate clutch and crash gearbox. Another common point was the worm and nut type steering, although this had been present on the earlier batch only as a special London requirement for harmonisation with the STLs and had not become standard Leyland practice until much more recently. However there were many differences apart from one which may have been apparent to the driver, if to no-one else, in that the driving position was slightly higher

on the later model. The wheelbase was now 16ft 3ins, a reduction of 3ins on earlier Titans, the brakes were now of the triple servo type with Clayton Dewandre servo operating through Lockheed hydraulics, and the road springs were longer. The TD7 employed fully flexible engine mountings which, in order to avoid excessive oscillation upon them, required a larger and heavier flywheel to provide steadier idling. This arrangement gave one of the smoothest and, despite the spartan nature of the utility body, almost certainly the quietest ride achieved on a London diesel-engined bus up to that time. From the road-side the passing TD7 seemed to emit just a little less of the distinctive, deep-throated engine roar always associated with pre-war Leyland diesels, but a new sensation was an unusual siren-like sound given out by the fly-wheel which no other London buses have ever emulated.

Above **Another pre-delivery shot of STD 101, this time at the Park Royal factory where another, very different example of wartime output is just visible in the shadow of the doorway. At this stage the still unlicensed vehicle carries its original grey primer livery although the mudguards are in gloss black, whilst white wartime markings adorn the front wings, dumbirons, lifeguards and rear body lower edges.**

Above **The same vehicle is seen resplendent in full London Transport livery. The photograph is a posed one, and STDs never operated from Camberwell (Q) garage or on night route 297. The side lamps have been repositioned to a higher level and built into the bodywork, and approved wartime masks have been fitted to the headlamps. The anti-blast netting on the windows is of the earliest type without the distinctive diamond-shaped inserts to aid visibility.** LT Museum

Left **A rear view of STD 101, taken at Kew Green before entering service, shows the metal panelled rear emergency door typical of early utilities and the registration number just visible above the platform window. The nearside indicator box has not yet been fitted.** LT Museum

STD 101 was licensed for service on 1st December 1941 at Victoria where it was joined, between May and August 1942, by STD 102-111. This association with Victoria garage turned out in due course to be permanent, so much so, in fact, that the eleven Leyland utilities never operated in public service from any other location. Before they entered service, however, there were items of work which needed to be carried out on each vehicle in the central works at Chiswick. An aspect of the design with which London Transport was particularly dissatisfied was the positioning of the small side lights which were located on the driver's dash and on the nearside bulkhead at a level only slightly higher than the headlamps. To improve effectiveness these were raised to a position just below window level and at the same time they were built into the bodywork instead of being mounted upon it. Although the utility specification permitted a single indicator box with dimensions to the operator's requirements at the front only, London Transport was reluctant to place vehicles into service without a supplementary box on the nearside above the platform in which to list intermediate points served. This screen was installed at Chiswick on the STDs (and also on 127 utility bodies on Bristol and Guy chassis received subsequently). London Transport was rare amongst purchasers of utility bodies in specifying that the front destination box should be capable of being opened from the outside for the purpose of inserting or removing blinds and their rollers; in fact the front destination equipment was supplied to Park Royal by London Transport as 'free issue' material for incorporation into the new bodies during construction. A little handle was subsequently added at Chiswick to assist in lifting the flap when access to the box was required. When in service the front blind was changed from inside the driver's cab but as there was no periscope the conductor's help was needed to ensure that the correct display was shown. Having been delivered in grey primer the vehicles had to be put into fleet colours before entering service. The livery chosen was the standard one of the time with red main pan-

els and broken white window surrounds. The customary black band running around the centre of the vehicle was omitted, there being no suitably prominent moulding to accommodate it, but mudguards and lifeguards were black as usual and wheels were in the standard brownish shade called Indian Red. An innovation was the use on STD 101 of a brown (officially bauxite) roof, this having just been adopted as standard because Chiswick was unable to obtain the shade of grey previously used.

STD 101 was the first new double decker in London service since the era of the independents to feature a grained wood internal finish with brown leather-type (actually leathercloth) seats. London Transport, and General before it, had been happier with rexine or painted finishes and moquette upholstery. However the highly polished mahogany and other wood finishes of the 'pirate' buses were not quite reproduced here; in fact the grained effect was achieved simply by applying clear varnish over the body frame which was left exposed wherever possible to avoid the manufacture and fitment of separate wooden cappings. Another un-London like feature, but one which again had been favoured by the independents, was the white (rather than cream) lower deck ceiling with varnished wooden mouldings running the length of the saloon to separate the centre section from the cove panels. Despite being single skinned below the windows, the interiors of the utilities did not look particularly spartan when new, and the worst feature of the bodies aesthetically was that the upper saloon ceilings, which were not lined internally, were very prone to hold condensation and quickly became marked with nicotine and rust stains.

London Transport had always maintained an internal system of chassis and body coding to help in reference purposes and to denote interchangeability, etc. The unfrozen STDs marked the third type of modern Leyland Titan chassis (the first two comprising STD 1-90 with crash gearboxes and STD 91-100 with 'Gearless' transmission) and were thus coded 3STD; the bodies were the second type to be

carried by the STD class and were thus coded STD2, the complete vehicle being known as type 3STD2. A few were mistakenly referred to on internal documentation as 3STD3/2 when new but this was rectified on paper in 1946.

Operationally the unfrozen STDs were not as successful as their illustrious predecessors, in fact they were not far short of a disaster. Despite having more than adequate power they were totally unable to keep time except at the quietest periods. It was not entirely their weight which slowed them down, for despite the absence of aluminium from the body structure they weighed, at exactly 7 tons, only 5cwt more than the TD4s. Most of the extra body weight added by the use of steel panelling was presumably largely compensated for by the absence of interior lining. The problem lay with the flexible engine mounting and the large, heavy flywheel which went with it, making gear changing painfully slow. Coupled with high gearing, this made the vehicles very difficult to drive, and the only way to achieve any degree of success was to build the engine revolutions up to their very peak in each gear in the hope that, by the time the upward change was achieved, the road speed would not have fallen so drastically as to render the higher ratio inappropriate. In truth the TD7s were totally unsuited to in-town work with frequent stops and would have fared better had they been allocated to the Country Bus & Coach department where stops were far fewer and their top speed potential would have been better appreciated. Possibly resistance by the country bus staff to a proliferation of vehicle types prevented such a move, but it was always surprising that the eleven vehicles were not at least transferred to a quieter, suburban garage within their own Central Bus department; understandably they were always deeply unpopular at Victoria.

A standard pattern of modification was applied to the bodies of these and other early-type utilities which subsequently joined the London fleet. As early as April 1943 a programme was approved for the replacement of the plain glass forming the driver's cab win-

STD 107, seen at Victoria shortly after its final overhaul in February 1949, demonstrates the additional opening windows fitted shortly after the war and the smaller headlamps with which these vehicles were also subsequently equipped. The bulkhead nearside ventilator has been removed and a plain glass window has taken its place.

dows with the toughened variety. Two months later another programme commenced, this time to install a quick release emergency exit for the driver on his nearside to provide an escape route over the bonnet, thereby bringing the utilities into line with pre-war practice. During the early months of 1945 a conventional inset registration plate was fitted at the rear which involved a fair amount of dismantling and reconstruction. The small number of opening windows in the passenger saloons caused much adverse comment each summer and the Board determined to augment them as soon as the opportunity arose. In August 1945 sufficient new half drop windows were ordered to provide each bus with six extras, four upstairs and two down, and from October onwards a programme of fitting these commenced, sometimes coinciding with the Chiswick works vehicle overhaul programme but not always. In some cases at first overhaul in 1945, but otherwise at the second in 1948/9, the opportunity was taken to glaze the emergency window at the rear of the upper deck, this being achieved by removing the steel outer panel and inserting two panes of glass. On most if not all of the utility STDs the lower saloon front nearside ventilator was removed and it is probable that the front bulkhead was strengthened at the same time.

Because their work was on routes serving central London, the unfrozen STDs maintained a fairly high profile except that they seldom if ever ran on Sundays when diminished schedule requirements ensured that adequate numbers of more acceptable vehicles were available. They led a totally uneventful life and were the first complete class of utilities to be taken out of passenger service. Withdrawals commenced on 5th February 1951 when six out of the eleven were delicensed, and ended with the demise of STDs 108 and 111 on 1st May. All were later used for a short while as staff buses from which most were subsequently demoted to humble 'learners'. The last were removed from stock in September 1955 but, unlike all the other London utility classes, they found no useful afterlife with other operators.

Above **A rather battered STD 111, photographed in October 1948, demonstrates the revised positioning of the rear registration plate adopted in 1945. The repanelling of the lower rear end necessary to accommodate it has resulted in the loss of the secondary moulding which formerly ran below the window line. The white wartime disc still shows through the red paint which had presumably been applied to hide it without using undercoat first.** Alan B Cross

In the final stage of its London career as a learner bus allocated to Muswell Hill, STD 107 carries the glazed rear emergency window which all of this class received, in some cases on overhaul in 1945/6 and the remainder in 1948/9. John C Gillham

CHAPTER THREE

THE FIRST BRISTOLS – B 1-9

In November 1941 the Ministry of War Transport informed London Transport that it had in mind allocating nine new double deckers which were shortly to be constructed from unfrozen stock by the Bristol Tramways & Carriage Co Ltd. The identity of the body supplier had not been finalised but at the time it appeared likely that utility bodies by Strachans would be fitted. Acceptance was not automatic; London Transport had never purchased anything remotely like the Bristol K5G and this was a big decision to take. Lord Ashfield himself finally gave the go-ahead, probably mindful that, with war conditions likely to exist for quite some time, it would be foolhardy to refuse any offer of new vehicles however non-standard they may be.

Introduced in 1937, the Bristol K5G was noted for its simplicity and economy. It was a product of the Tilling group and was highly regarded by the many operators within that group who had standardised upon it. The family connection between Bristol, as a bus manufacturing unit, and Tilling operators was not unlike that between AEC and London Transport. The K5G had been primarily designed around the Tilling group's requirements in the same way that the design and subsequent development of the AEC Regent

had been dominated by the needs of the LGOC and, later, London Transport, who between them had taken the lion's share of production output. However any similarity stopped there for in vehicle development terms the two groups followed diametrically opposed lines. London Transport had become convinced of the need for large engines to provide long life, coupled with sophistication in general design terms; Tilling found merit in small engines for fuel economy and sought maximum design simplicity. To glide along in an RT was as far removed from travelling in a K5G as it was possible to get. Now, though involuntarily, London Transport was to sample the K5G for itself.

Confirmation that the nine new Bristols had been allocated was received on 7th January 1942 and the necessary orders for them were placed with the manufacturers a few days later. The first two chassis were received on 31st of the same month and all nine were in the Board's possession by 14th March. It had now been established that the bodies would in fact be built by Park Royal, and in the event they were identical to those on the STDs except where modifications were necessary to suit the different chassis characteristics. The purchase price per vehicle was

almost identical to that of the Leylands but delivery was accomplished much more speedily. The first complete Bristol arrived at Chiswick from Park Royal on 26th March 1942 by which time STDs 102 and 103 were already in stock, though not yet in service, but when the final Bristol was delivered on 12th May the Leylands had still not progressed beyond STD 103. Originally it was intended to number the Bristols in the series STB 1-9. This would have been a fairly logical step following on from the STL and STD, but after the first two had received their STB numbers, on paper at least, the simpler code B (for Bristol) was decided upon. On 1st May 1942 the first four (B 1-3 and 6) entered service at Hanwell marking the start of a link between this garage and Bristols which was to last for nearly eleven years.

Though the Park Royal bodywork resembles in most respects that of the STDs, the sounds emitted by B 2, and its riding qualities, are totally unlike anything that Londoners have grown used to. Anti-shatter netting had not been applied to the windows of Hanwell's Bristols when they were first pressed into service. C F Klapper

The lower saloon of B 4 shows the basic but adequate upholstered seats with white grab handles, and the lamp masks fitted to ensure that only the very minimum of light was visible from outside the vehicle after dark. The varnished wood window frames and ceiling mouldings give a pleasant finish to an otherwise spartan design. LT Museum

In the upper saloon of B 4, where even the roof is single skinned, trunking above the windows is necessary to accommodate the internal lighting cables. The unusually slim appearance of the window pillars arises because no cappings are provided to cover the basic body framework. LT Museum

B 4 photographed in July 1942, two months after entering service, shows a rear end aspect identical to that on the Leylands. On some members of the class – including B 4 – the lower horizontal mouldings were half-round in profile whilst on others they were flat, probably reflecting availability of materials at the time. LT Museum

Hanwell was an unsurprising choice of garage for the Bristols as it was the only one in the whole of London Transport to operate buses with Gardner engines. True the handful of Bluebird LTs on route 105 were equipped with 6LWs whereas the Bristols carried the smaller five cylinder unit, but there was much commonality of parts and the accumulated expertise was probably also useful. It was fortunate that Hanwell was physically able to accommodate the vehicles. The standard wartime specification was for a body giving 14ft 6ins unladen height which was greater than London Transport's peace time standard. The Board had always insisted, when ordering bodies from outside manufacturers, that the overall height should be no more than 14ft 3¼ins and it was always written into contracts that 'the overall height is most important and must on no account be exceeded'. This was not just a case of being pedantic for the sake of it, for the fact was

that doorway clearance at many garages was very tight and higher vehicles could not be accommodated. Later, as utility Guys joined the fleet in ever increasing numbers, the selection of suitable garages was by no means a straightforward matter when 32 out of the 52 in the central bus fleet were unable to accommodate them. After the war the problem was resolved when a general programme of raising doorway heights was undertaken.

The Bristol factory at Brislington traditionally numbered batches of chassis in series known as 'sanctions' and B 1-9 comprised part of the 87-strong 57th sanction. This was the company's last for the time being, the works now being under the control of the Ministry of Aircraft Production for manufacturing nose, rear fuselage and tail sections for fighter planes. The unfrozen vehicles of 57 sanction had the standard Bristol features including Gardner 5LW engine mounted as a unit with the Borg & Beck single dry plate clutch and

Bristol constant mesh gearbox, Clayton Dewandre triple vacuum servo braking system, and worm and quadrant type steering. The wheelbase was 16ft 3ins and the complete vehicle, with its Park Royal body, weighed in at 7 tons exactly. The components on the K5G were all tried and tested and were intended to last without major overhaul for a mileage of about 100,000.

Compared with normal London standards, the ride on a K5G was rough despite the fitment of Luvax hydraulic shock absorbers on both axles. The real cause of the roughness lay in the three point mounting arrangement of the five cylinder engine which was bolted solidly into the chassis with no attempt at providing rubber buffers or anything else to relieve vibration. This was present most of the time but particularly when the engine revolutions were high, and it was not unknown for passengers seated just behind the engine to receive a kind of back massage from vibrations transmitted through the seat. The solid mounting also rendered the vehicle noisy, and particularly so in the cab. However despite these drawbacks the vehicles were not unpopular with drivers. They benefited from Bristol's traditionally light but positive steering, the smooth clutch and very reliable brakes. Gearchanging was not difficult to master and, thanks to Gardner's excellent low speed torque characteristics, was not required quite as frequently as the small capacity of the engine might suggest since the vehicle would chug away happily down to about 12mph in top gear. The Bristol was sometimes described as the 'busman's bus' and such was the performance of B 1-9 at Hanwell that they built up a grudging and lasting respect.

From 1943 onwards the bodies on the nine vehicles were subjected to the same programme of modifications as those on the STDs. At their second, and as it turned out their last, overhaul a major change took place. Twenty more Bristols had joined B 1-9 at Hanwell in December 1945 and January 1946, but these were of the K6A model with AEC 7.7 engines and it was decided to bring the original nine into line by converting them into K6As too. London Transport had a huge stock of suitable engines from vehicles currently being withdrawn for scrap and regarded the Bristols' 5LWs as being of greater value as spare units for its large fleet of Guys. The conversion itself was not especially difficult but it necessitated replacing the 12 volt electrical system with which B 1-9 had originally been fitted by one of 24 volts, including making provision to house two more batteries. As a result of the modifications the unladen weight of the vehicles rose by 10cwt and their official classification was amended from 1B1 to 1/1B1. They were dealt with in two groups. Bs 1, 2, 4, 5, 8 and 9 emerged from Chiswick with their AEC engines between October 1948 and January 1949, with the remaining three following between May and August 1949. In the case of the earlier conversions the front bulkheads were rebuilt at the same time to remove the nearside ventilator window, as had been done on the STDs, but the final three were not dealt with in this way and remained in their original condition. The last of the batch to run as a K5G was B 3 on 12th May 1949.

Three stages in the metamorphosis of a small class are illustrated by B 2 in its original 1942 condition, B 1 photographed in 1947, and B 5 towards the end of its life in about 1952. The view of B 1 shows additional opening windows and revised headlamps, but the panelled emergency window and wartime sidelights are still in place. B 5 carries a glazed emergency exit, improved side lights and a slight livery variation introduced for 1948/9 overhauls of the class whereby the window sills on the lower deck are picked out in white rather than red. A post-war style destination display is also fitted and the vehicle, which has been converted to K6A specification, sports a nearside mudguard from a newer Bristol.
W J Haynes/D W K Jones/J H Aston

B 1-9 were destined to serve as K6As for a far shorter time than they had been K5Gs and withdrawal from service at Southall (as Hanwell was now re-named) commenced in June 1951 with Bs 8 and 9. Bs 1 and 7 were withdrawn in the autumn of 1951 and all the remainder, except B 5, followed suit during 1952. Very often, in the case of utility-bodied vehicles, withdrawal was dictated more by body condition than anything else, and because timber quality could vary considerably even within the same batch of bodies, it was by no means uncommon for some vehicles to last much better than their seemingly identical counterparts. B 5 must have been the best of this batch for it was the only one of the nine to last in service through to 1953, being finally withdrawn on 1st February of that year. This was not the end, however, for all of London's Bristols subsequently saw service with other operators as we shall see in a later chapter.

CHAPTER FOUR

THE GUY ARABS

The gradual running down and eventual cessation of new bus manufacturing in 1940 inevitably brought a growing clamour from operators for the government to organise some form of resumption, which meant making the requisite material supplies and factory capacity available. The Ministries of Supply and War Transport, working closely as they did with operators' representatives, were fully sympathetic to the urgent need for maintaining and even increasing vehicle availability to cope with public transport demand and arranged a temporary respite for hard pressed operators through the completion of some 415 unfrozen vehicles. Further relief was obtained by diverting for domestic use 93 buses and trolleybuses originally intended for export (of which London Transport received 43 trolleybuses). The government also hoped – largely in vain – that several hundred vehicles which had been requisitioned by the military at the start of the war might be given an early release to ease the position still further. Clearly a regular source of new buses had to be established with a major emphasis on double deckers because of their high carrying capacity. In July 1941, at a conference with manufacturing and operating representatives, the two Ministries announced that the construction of one thousand new double deckers would be authorised to take place in 1942 with chassis production divided equally between Leyland and Guy.

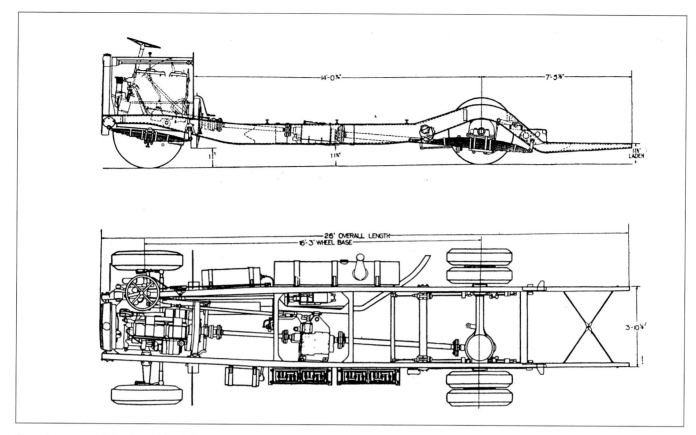

General arrangement drawings of the Arab, described at the time as the Guy "Emergency" double deck bus chassis, showing the basic dimensions of its low slung frame.

The operators' associations were very glad to receive assurance that even a limited number of new buses was to be made available but were less pleased by the news that Guy Motors Ltd was to produce 500 of them. To most operators Guy was an unknown quantity having built comparatively few double deckers in recent times and none at all since 1936. In fact the company had all but abandoned the civilian market in 1938, going over to defence production after having perfected a way of welding armour plate, and it was building all kinds of military vehicles from the small Ant up to six-wheeled searchlight chassis. The judgement of some operators may still have been clouded by memories of the ponderous FCX-type drop-frame six wheeler which had broken new ground in 1926 but whose popularity had quickly waned when more reliable and modern alternatives came on the market. Few had thought it worth while buying the Gardner-engined Arab of 1933-6.

No time was lost in despatching a letter informing Lord Leathers, the Minister of War Transport, that they 'viewed with alarm' the proposal that half the allocation should be of a new and untried type, and a deputation to both ministries requested that all 1000 should be built by Leyland. These approaches proved to no avail. The operators had failed to comprehend the great difficulties which the civil servants had had to overcome in securing production of any sort, and there could be no turning back. Worse news was to reach the operators early in November in the form of a rumour that Leyland may not now build any chassis at all. This was indeed the position

into which the Ministry of Supply had been forced although it did not notify its fellow ministry or the operators' associations officially of this fact until 19th November. It must have come as something of a surprise to Leyland themselves who had only just submitted plans for building high and lowbridge metal framed austerity bodies when they learnt that their production of wheeled vehicles of any sort was to cease completely by the second part of 1942. An urgent expansion of tank production programmes dictated that capacity to manufacture a huge number of additional tank engines and gearboxes should be urgently set up, and Leyland's facilities were required for this purpose. Henceforth all new double deckers would be Guys whether operators liked it or not.

Guy could not expand production beyond the level to which it had already committed itself and no other manufacturer was available to replace the Leyland element in the bus construction programme. The seriousness of the loss of these 500 Leylands could not be over-emphasised. Alternative strategies were required but only two serious options emerged. Bedford, who had contracted to build its 32-seater petrol engined OWB single decker had spare manufacturing capacity available and could be authorised to replace the 'lost' output in terms of vehicle numbers if not in total seating capacity. Alternatively articulated buses, with a power unit attached to a removable trailer, could be used for which purpose the Construction & Use regulations would be amended accordingly. This alternative was not viewed with enthusiasm despite small scale trials in Liverpool and Mansfield

whilst a third, tentative idea, to attempt the shipment of bus chassis from the USA, was quickly deemed impractical.

On 18th December 1941 the Ministry of War Transport notified the Regional Traffic Commissioners their quotas of new Guy Arabs for 1942 and the commissioners immediately circulated operators seeking details of their requirements so that licences to purchase could be issued. In each case the operator was allowed to indicate his preferred body builder, giving a choice of up to three in declining order of preference but without any guarantee that these wishes would ultimately be accommodated. Licences were granted on the basis of one for each new vehicle, and once received the operator had to place orders for chassis and body through the normal commercial process within one month, failing which the licence would be forfeited.

An exception to the general rule in the case of the London Passenger Transport Board, and also the Northern Ireland Road Transport Board, was that their allocations were made direct by the Ministry of War Transport and not through the local commissioners, but otherwise all procedures that applied elsewhere were followed here too. London Transport had already submitted in October 1941 its new vehicle requirements for 1942, stating that it wished all of them to be Leylands. In the event the twenty Leylands and Bristols were received from unfrozen stock (plus the 34 STL class AECs which are not dealt with in this volume) and on 28th February 1942 the Board's first 42 Guys were authorised.

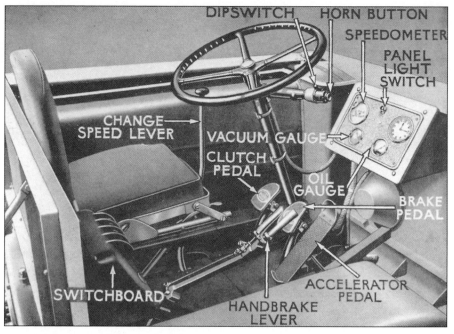

The Ministry of Supply allocated its own internal serial number to each new Guy chassis, continuing a process which it had started with the unfrozen vehicles, although these numbers did not match in sequence the chassis numbers allocated by Guy. The Guys were numbered by the Ministry in a G sequence, applying the same logic as London Transport who also designated its new vehicles as the G class. The same G numbers as allocated by the Ministry of Supply for production control were also used by the Ministry of War Transport for allocation purposes although behind the scenes a good deal of juggling often took place before licences were finally issued. Thus, whilst the Guys which ultimately became London Transport G 3-42 were destined for the Board from the start, the vehicles comprising Gs 1 and 2 had originally

been pencilled in for Newport Corporation but were diverted to London, possibly to gain earlier delivery, whilst two of the original London allocation were subsequently sent elsewhere. On 26th September 1942 a further 36 Guys were authorised followed by six more on 7th November, bringing the total expected in London to 84 although, as we shall see later, thirteen of them were subsequently diverted to other operators. If all 84 had been received the Board's new bus intake for 1942 would have consisted of only 137 units against the 360 which it had stated to be its minimum requirement, and even this figure was modest compared with the 527 new buses a year for 1940/1 originally called for in the Board's vehicle replacement plan of 1939.

As far as choice of bodywork went, London Transport's first preference was given as

being for Park Royal followed by Weymann and then Duple. The latter was a surprise choice given that the Board had in the past enjoyed no commercial dealings with Duple, and it can only be assumed that the decision was based on a combination of reputation and the company's convenient location at Hendon. With many operators nationwide requiring new buses and only a limited number of coachbuilders authorised to supply them, it was inevitable that many would receive bodies from suppliers which were not of their first choice, or even of their second or third Perhaps because of its size, London Transport was granted its choice to the extent that, of its first allocation of 42 Guys, 31 were bodied by Park Royal and 11 by Weymann, although even this was a modification of the original plan which had been for 29 Park Royal bodies

Top Left A rear view of an early Arab I chassis shows the driveline leading from the underslung worm type rear axle to the chassis-mounted gearbox, the double plate clutch and flywheel. The twin 12 volt batteries are contained on the nearside of the frame with the fuel tank, in this case of 28 gallon capacity, on the offside. Fuel feed was by pump mounted on the engine. Guy Motors

Top Right A cab diagram of the Arab I before modifications were made to the pedals, etc. to overcome drivers' complaints. Although an electric horn was fitted as standard, early Guy deliveries to London Transport were also provided with a bulb horn, a specification which was allowed to lapse later in the war. Guy Motors

Left The original wartime 5LW engined Arab design employed a flush mounted radiator, but subsequently all vehicles were built with the lengthened bonnet and outswept front wings of the style known as Arab Mark II irrespective of the power unit fitted. G 148 carries a Park Royal designed body assembled in Northumberland by Northern Coachbuilders. J H Aston and 13 Weymanns. As the war progressed Park Royal continued to be a major supplier to the Board and, although Weymann subsequently took something of a back seat as far as London was concerned, many Duple bodies entered the fleet though only one was on a Guy chassis. Later, London Transport found itself allocated large numbers of bodies by manufacturers not of its choice but, unlike some of its provincial counterparts, it did not complain but accepted the lack of standardisation which resulted as being inevitable. In pre-war days each contract had been closely supervised during the manufacturing stage for quality control but under wartime conditions no such safeguard was possible. It was acknowledged as inevitable that the materials from which new wartime bodies were built might be of inferior quality, especially the timber for the body frames which was mostly unseasoned. Standards of workmanship varied considerably between manufacturers but fortunately the suppliers with whom London Transport was linked maintained reasonable standards and no need arose to turn down any allocation of buses on these grounds which other operators occasionally found necessary. Derby Corporation, for instance, felt compelled to refuse a desperately needed allocation of new Guys when it was learnt that they were to be bodied by Pickering of Wishaw whose unhappy reputation elsewhere had already come to their notice.

At the Wolverhampton factory of Guy Motors Ltd the design for their new wartime double decker was completed early in September 1941. Rumour had it that Sydney Guy, the founder, chairman and managing director of the company, was offered current drawings by both Leyland and Bristol to help him speed up the design and manufacturing process but that he declined, preferring in his inimitable way to start from scratch and rely entirely upon in-house expertise. According to a contemporary press release Guy's design was based largely on the pre-war Arab incorporating improvements made in the years since it ceased production, but in fact there appeared to be comparatively little of the old Arab in the new model. A tremendous amount of work was carried out in a remarkably short time to transfer the new design from the drawing board to the production floor, and although the final production programme ran a little late, Guy's achievement in completing the first chassis on 31st March 1942 was noteworthy under the circumstances. A moving production track was installed, the first for any type of heavy duty chassis although Guy had itself used a similar device for its light military vehicles for about three years.

The wartime Arab did not outwardly resemble its pre-war predecessor, its main recognition feature, the cast iron radiator, being much narrower and looking far more businesslike than the earlier one. A major point of commonality, however, lay in the use of the Gardner engine in both five cylinder 5LW and six cylinder 6LW forms. The new chassis was, in fact, designed around the Gardner engine and no other form of motive power was used during the war by Guy. Wartime supply constraints dictated that the 5LW engine had to be fitted in all but a small minority of cases where the necessity for more power could be conclusively proven and, to a large extent, this was the undoing of the wartime Guy Arab. In normal circumstances the 5LW, with an RAC rating of 36.3hp and developing 85bhp at 1700 revs, may have been adequate for most purposes, but wartime vehicles were between 13.9% and 19.5% heavier than their pre-war counterparts, depending on the make of body, due to the enforced exclusion from chassis, engine and body construction of aluminium and electron as these were required for aircraft production. To make matters worse, standing passengers were now permitted and overloading was common, further affecting power to weight ratio and detracting from performance. Only about five per cent of wartime Arabs received 6LW engines and London Transport received none of these.

The Arab chassis frame was of fairly conventional design not unlike the Leyland TD7 in profile; both shared a common wheelbase of 16ft 3ins. At the front it was mounted on an axle built by Kirkstall Forge at Leeds incorporating Timken roller bearings in the front hubs. The Guy-designed rear axle, for which Kirkstall supplied the casing and David Brown the worm gear, was a fully-floating worm drive unit which could be easily recognised by its distinctive cone-shaped hubs. Brakes were of the internal expanding, two-shoe type with Lockheed hydraulic servo, and the steel disc wheels carried 10.50x20 tyres at the front and 900x20 at the rear. The large front tyres, which were specified to cope with wartime loadings, caused the turning circle to exceed the legal maximum of 60ft for which the government instructed Regional Transport Commissioners to grant special dispensation. The crash gearbox, with straight-toothed gears and sliding engagement of all ratios except top, was three point mounted on rubber cushions midway along the chassis, an unusual position for manual-type gearboxes although accepted practice for preselectors. A feature of this old-style unit was that the positions on the gear selection lever differed from the normal layout and this did not help to endear the vehicles to drivers. First gear was in the position normally occupied by third, third gear was in the conventional first gear position and so on; reverse could be found at the bottom far right hand side adjacent to second. The clutch was a double dry plate unit, a type fairly uncommon at the time, with a very large area to give long life, and open to facilitate adjustment and replacement. The fuel pump was supplied by CAV and a 24 volt electrical system was employed with equipment supplied by both Simms and CAV, the batteries being held in two cradles attached to the chassis nearside. No fan was provided for the engine which was

The early bodywork deterioration, which was to prove such a problem on most utility bodies, is already evident in the serious staining of the offside paintwork of Massey bodied G175 even though it is only a few months old. Operated by Barking garage, it is seen aside the half-timbered frontage of the Royal Forest Hotel at Chingford.
Alan B Cross

cooled through the grilled tube radiator by centrifugal pump with thermostatic control although provision was made to fit a fan if this was found necessary. Initially a 35 gallon fuel tank was fitted but this was soon superseded by a smaller 28 gallon unit and in London only the first ten vehicles had the larger tank.

Manufacture commenced with an experimental chassis numbered FD25450, upon which was mounted a standard Park Royal utility body. This bus remained in Guy's ownership, running on trade plates, and never actually entered passenger service. The chassis designation FD was an inheritance from pre-war Arabs, F standing for Forward Control and D denoting the next in sequence from the FC or Invincible model which the Arab replaced. The first production chassis numerically, FD24541, was supplied to Swindon Corporation and Guy's output was numbered sequentially thereafter. Numerically the first London chassis was FD25476 which was allocated fleet number G 2, but the first complete vehicle to be delivered to the Board from Park Royal was G 1 (chassis FD25478) which arrived at Chiswick on 26th August 1942. The first Weymann bodied vehicle to be taken into stock was G 32 on 18th November by which time a steady flow of new deliveries had reached the rate of about four a week. By the end of 1942 forty Guys were in stock which, because production had been slower to get off the ground than originally anticipated, marked a shortfall of 43 over the total promised for the year. G 1 was the first to be licensed for service, on 1st December, and it presumably began work on or shortly after that date. It was allocated to Tottenham garage where it had been joined by five others before the year was out. All 42 Guys of the first allocation had been received, though not necessarily licensed for service, by January 1943 and the next batch followed straight on consisting of one bodied by Duple (G 43), seven by Weymann (G 44-50) and 21 by Park Royal (G 51-71).

The wartime Arab could hardly be described as popular with drivers, at least in its 5LW version; the 6LW which some provincial operators were lucky enough to get was a different proposition entirely. The lack of pulling power was its main drawback and the vehicles often had to be driven as hard as possible to maintain schedule, and at maximum engine speed a pronounced vibration was often apparent. Clutch drag was a problem requiring clutch stops to be adjusted frequently, although many drivers were sufficiently experienced to manage without the clutch for much of the time. The back-to-front gear arrangement took some adjusting to, and the gearbox itself needed mastering and was understandably unpopular when, as was inevitable, London drivers compared it with the preselector. On the positive side, the Marles cam and double roller type steering was reasonably light to handle and, after some initial problems were ironed out, the brakes were positive and reliable. The passenger, unaware of the shortcomings experienced by the driver, was treated to a surprisingly smooth and comfortable ride, thanks in part to the three point engine mounting system incorporating oil resisting rubber blocks with steel springs in the front

two mountings to absorb low frequency oscillations. In this respect the Arabs were far superior to the similarly powered Bristol K5G. The Arab suspension consisting of conventional semi-elliptic springs with Luvax shock absorber did its job well and the gearbox was quiet. A particular feature of the Arab was the not unpleasant but pronounced whirring noise, amounting almost to a whistle, which emanated from the double plate clutch at each gear change and which made these some of the most audibly characterful double deckers ever to run in London.

London Transport's policy with new models had been to construct and operate a prototype before authorising production to commence in order to iron out the most obvious 'bugs', but even this usually failed to detect all the shortcomings which only full scale fleet operation would uncover. It was small wonder, then, that troubles soon manifested themselves on the wartime Arab which had gone from drawing board to production line without any testing whatever. An accumulation of problems was what the operators' associations had feared when objecting to the selection of Guy as the major bus chassis supplier, and in the early days it seemed that these fears would be borne out. Even before the first 71 London Guys entered service most if not all had made at least one journey back to Guy, either to Wolverhampton or to their London depot, for modifications and rectifications to be carried out. However, once in service, further problems very quickly became apparent. Some of the known modifications made as a result of these included a revised clutch shaft mechanism (affecting Gs 25–31 and 37 onwards), a redesigned second speed mainshaft and layshaft gear (Gs 49, 50, 66 and 68 onwards), new front brake mechanism (Gs 24–31 and 36 onwards), modified accelerator controls (Gs 24-31, 36-41 and 43 onwards), and 10.50x20 rear wheels and tyres (the same size as on the fronts) were fitted to all Arabs numbered G 44 and above except G 51. In order to improve road performance the original rear axle ratio of 6¼:1 was replaced by a lower ratio of 5.6:1 and this took effect in London on Gs 23-31 and 36 upwards although, in this instance, the remainder were subsequently brought into line. A major redesign originally intended to form a new standard but which ultimately proved unsatisfactory was made to the three point engine mounting system, its aim being to prevent the engine from moving fore and aft on acceleration and deceleration and to stop it from moving in a transverse direction when cornering or on torque reaction. This complex modification was soon abandoned in favour of a return to the original design but not before it had been installed on 28 vehicles destined for London (G 16-43); these required subsequent modification by the Board to achieve a satisfactory standard of reliability.

In London an operational fleet of 28 Guys had built up at Tottenham by February 1943 but all except a few were temporarily withdrawn on 1st March after experiencing brake and other troubles so that a programme of modifications could take place. Some were carried out, at Guy's expense, at Upton Park, Luton and Tring garages and also at Tottenham itself whilst others were dealt

with subsequently on a programmed basis. Operating experience had uncovered weak springs in the steering track rod which caused steering wobble, and air was found to be leaking into the Lockheed vacuum system. Another problem was the failure of the RP adjusters on the rear brakes. Clutches experienced an unduly short life which was diagnosed as being caused by a design fault in the spring loaded clutch stop whilst, later on, propeller shaft fractures began to happen. In common with other operators London Transport was impressed by the efficient way Guy's design staff at Wolverhampton and maintenance personnel at their Porteous Road, Paddington sales and service depot dealt with these problems. Guy had said right from the start that they would 'at all times be happy to receive any suggestions with a view to improving the breed if war-time conditions allow' and they stayed true to their word. So effective were they, in fact, at eliminating early teething troubles that the wartime Guy Arab subsequently earned for itself an enviable reputation as an ideal engineer's bus; economical and almost trouble free, simple to maintain and virtually indestructible.

Mechanical shortcomings apart, drivers' representatives through the Transport & General Workers Union found faults on the vehicles as drivers will often do, especially in the case of types which they do not particularly like. In this respect London's drivers led the field. The main objections, excluding some relating to the bodywork which varied according to the supplier, were that the angle of the organ type accelerator pedal was such as to cause operation of it to be unduly tiring and that the design of the footbrake and clutch pedals caused the foot to slip off. The problem with the two left hand pedals was not an original design shortcoming but occurred because the specified rubber covering had ceased to be available and was replaced by eight cross ribs which offered grip for the driver's feet but did not prevent them from slipping off sideways. London Transport's answers to these problems were to reposition the accelerator pedal and to weld lips on to the other two, the lip being on the offside of the brake pedal and the nearside of the clutch.

Even as initial production of the Arab was about to commence, some important modifications to its specification were under way. At a meeting at the Ministry of Supply on 7th July 1942 with members of the New Vehicles Sub-Committee, at which Sydney Guy's brother Ewart was also present, the Ministry proposed that the Arab's 24 volt electrical system should be replaced by 12 volt equipment. This modification was urged because battery materials were in very short supply, in addition to which a saving of 180lbs dead weight per bus could be achieved which would help to improve performance. After due consideration the operators agreed, but only so long as Gardner engines were fitted as these had a decompression facility to aid starting (although in London this fell into disuse as early as April 1946 and was subsequently removed from all vehicles). Because of the length and complexity of the material supply chain it was not possible to introduce this modification immediately; in fact it was only from the 501st chassis onwards that it was

When replacement engine crankcases were required in post-war years, aluminium alloy units were often fitted. This also applied to new gearbox and rear axle worm cases and, most noticeably, to radiator shells, the aim being to reduce vehicle weight and improve road performance. Park Royal bodied G 210 sports a new radiator as it pauses for a crew changeover at Palmers Green. Vanguard

included. The 501st chassis marked the start of a second contract with Guy, again for 500 vehicles, and it was on this second batch that another, more visible modification was introduced. The comparatively few Arabs of the first batch which had been fitted with Gardner 6LW engines had also been equipped with longer bonnets to house it, and they also had modified front mudguards which swept stylishly forward to end level with the radiator which now projected well beyond the driver's cab. For simplicity of construction it was decided that, with effect from the second batch, all new Arabs would have the longer bonnet and upswept wings irrespective of whether they were needed or not, and the result on the great majority of vehicles was a 5 inch empty space under the bonnet between the front of the 5LW engine and the radiator. The overall vehicle length in this form was 26ft 4½ins which well exceeded the legal maximum and required special dispensation under the Defence Regulations. In this form the model became unofficially known as the Mark II Arab, a designation which Guy themselves later adopted. By inference the earlier, shorter Guys became retrospectively Arab Is.

The Mark II Arab first came to London in July 1943 with the batch G 72-136. These 65 vehicles, all of which were Park Royal bodied, were allocated in batches of 25 (in February 1943), 4 (in May), 30 (September) and 6 (later in September). Along with 61 Daimlers they comprised London Transport's allowance of 126 new vehicles against 360 requested for 1943. The large discrepancy between what the Board requested and what it received partly reflected the Ministry's view that

London Transport's need for new vehicles was not as urgent as it was made out to be and certainly not as pressing as that of many provincial operators, and the fact that 291 of the Board's ST class were out on loan to other operators served to reinforce this view. However the Ministry acknowledged the need to maintain some sort of ongoing fleet renewal programme if total chaos was to be avoided when the war finally came to an end, and the allocation of 126 vehicles reflected this.

On the morning of Monday 8th March 1943 Sydney Guy proudly witnessed the 1000th wartime Arab rolling off the production line at a small ceremony. This had been no mean feat for a company which, though not large by the standards of other manufacturers, also managed to turn out many vehicles of other types for the armed forces. However all was not well. For as long as it had been the only type of chassis available operators generally accepted their allocation of Guys, albeit with resignation in many cases. However, as we shall see later, Daimler came back on to the bus manufacturing scene in 1943 and as a result a growing reluctance to take Guys became apparent. There were some provincial operators, and notably the Tilling group, who did their best to avoid taking either make; they preferred to adopt a policy of rebodying existing chassis or a general make-do-and-mend until the chassis builders of their choice came back into production. Guy were well aware of the general unpopularity of their product which stemmed almost entirely from the enforced use of the 5LW engine. Users of the 6LW version were mostly very satisfied and the Regional Transport Commissioners were never short of applicants for 6LW Arabs,

most of whom had to be disappointed. Conversely they seldom had enough requests to take up the full quota of 5LW Arabs which then had to be almost forced upon operators. Guy quite rightly saw a two-pronged solution to the problem. One was to obtain a much larger quota of 6LWs, but this was simply not possible. This excellent engine was also in heavy demand for war use, production could not be stepped up any higher than it was, and try as it might the Ministry of Supply could not obtain any more units for civilian use. The alternative was to build a lighter vehicle through jettisoning some of the heavy steel components in favour of light alloys. Guy were particularly incensed to learn that Daimler were managing to build buses some 25cwt lighter than themselves, having somehow managed to achieve an allocation of light alloy which Guy was not permitted. On 5th February 1944 Sydney Guy called at the Ministry of Supply to seek an explanation, stating frankly that he was worried about the company's post-war prospects if Daimler were to continue with their perceived unfair advantage. Examination of Sydney Guy's complaint revealed that in recent months there had indeed been a release of some secondary grade aluminium but lack of foundry capacity had prevented full exploitation of its availability. Daimler were fortunate in having their own foundry, hence their advantageous position in relation to Guy. However the Minister decided that, from about May 1944, he would permit Gardner to build engines with light alloy crankcases and other parts which would secure a weight reduction of about 350lbs per bus and should help to redress the balance.

With their 1943 allocation of new buses inevitably behind schedule London Transport declined to request a specific total for 1944 but notified a requirement of 409 to cover the period from 1st February 1944 through to the end of 1945. They asked that all should, if possible, have AEC engines, a request which if granted would have ruled out any further deliveries of Guys. The Board's requests for 1941-3 inclusive totalling 1080 vehicles had been met by the allocation of only 250, a shortfall of 77%, and there was little immediate reason to hope that the 1944/5 outcome would be much different. However in the background the situation was taking a rapid turn for the better. Daimler's annual production had soared ahead of Guy's, and it was

planned that from May 1944 onwards Bristol would also resume manufacturing, albeit only in a small way at first. Throughout the whole of 1944 London Transport was allocated only 33 new buses of which two were Guys, these being Gs 137 and 138 for which Weymann was authorised to build experimental metal framed bodies. At the very start of 1945 the situation changed rapidly. From a position of shortage there suddenly emerged a state of surplus whereby the Ministry of War Transport found itself unable to find takers for all the new vehicles on offer. The cause of this was not so much that manufacturing capacity had overtaken demand as that operators were holding back on notifying their requirements. With an end to hostilities now

at last in sight many hoped that they might obtain the chassis of their choice if they were patient. The Tilling group now declined to take anything except Bristols, whilst many in the BET and municipal sectors had held their plans in abeyance upon hearing from Leyland in November 1944 that they hoped to resume manufacture by about the end of September 1945. Shortly afterwards AEC stated that it, too, expected to be back in business very soon. Under this pressure the demand for 5LW Guys dried up almost completely. No fewer than 840 were due to be built in 1945 and the Ministry of War Transport was left with the clear dilemma that it would not be able to dispose of all of them. To make matters worse, few Daimlers were now wanted either. The Ministry hoped that a few Guys might be diverted to the colonies, and indeed some went to Kenya and Ceylon whilst a few more went to newly-liberated continental Europe, but the salvation lay to some extent in fulfilling London Transport's large requirement. As a result between January and June 1945 licences for all the remaining 376 out of the originally requested 409 were made available. Seventy-nine of these were Daimlers, Bristols and AECs but the great majority, 279, were Guys. They were allocated in batches as follows:

G 139-153 (Park Royal bodies)

G 154-218 (25 Park Royal, 20 Northern Counties, 20 Massey)

G 219-268 (39 Northern Counties, 11 Massey)

G 269-318 (43 Northern Counties, 7 Massey)

G 319-368 (39 Park Royal, 11 Massey)

G 369-398 (Weymann bodies)

G 399-435 (5 Park Royal, 32 Weymann)

These were delivered from the various coachbuilders between May 1945 and March 1946 and were typical of the final type of wartime Arab chassis which weighed some 10cwt less than their predecessors thanks to the increasing use of lighter components.

Even during wartime London Transport could not resist experimenting with and modifying vehicles, and in a class as large as the Guys eventually became it was inevitable that some experimentation would take place. Six Guys delivered in November and December 1943 (G 107, 109-111, 113, 114) were given experimental brake drum and wheel stud assemblies whilst Gs 108 and 112 also had front axle modifications based on an

By virtue of its sheer size, and also because of the variety of bodywork fitted, the G class was arguably by far the most interesting of the London wartime types. Three Arab IIs are in evidence in this typical scene at Dagenham. Gs 154 and 245 carry two styles of Northern Counties body whilst the more angular G 103 is a product of the Park Royal factory. Fuel consumption tests taken at about the time of this photograph showed that the Guys (along with the post-war Leyland PD1s of the STD class) had the best performance on urban work of any double deckers in the fleet at 10.5 mpg. F W Ivey

earlier experiment on G 49. Like most experimental London buses these were located at Hanwell for as long as the experiment lasted. The main source of experimentation lay, however, with the gearbox. The standard sliding mesh arrangement was not to London Transport's liking and in October 1944 five vehicles at Tottenham (Gs 7, 18, 19, 26 and 40) were fitted with constant mesh units. Guy were themselves considering at the time changing over to this more modern type of manual box and the units concerned may indeed have been supplied by Guy themselves. In January 1945 a slightly larger scale experiment found nine vehicles equipped with synchromesh boxes. The source of these is not known, and this type was never subsequently offered by Guy as an option. The nine (Gs 3, 4, 8, 10, 14, 17, 20, 32 and 54) ran at Tottenham in comparative trials against the standard sliding mesh and experimental constant mesh units.

In due course Guy introduced their own constant mesh box as standard fitment which, in the case of London Transport, was supplied on all chassis numbered from FD28077 upwards. Thirty four buses were delivered in this form (G 301-311, 340-357, 431-435) and, although it is only known for certain that one other (G 179) subsequently received a constant mesh box, more may have done so. The new box was reliable and positive but it introduced the complication that the gear selector positions were now the right way round instead of being reversed. This would have been fine had they been the only Guys in the fleet, but they were not and this provided a recipe for confusion. A slightly shorter gear stick with a red painted knob on top was supposed to indicate to the driver that the gear

positions were different, but the significance was not always immediately realised and was in any case difficult to discern after dark. Even a retrospective fitment to the majority of the Guy fleet of new gear lever knobs embossed with a diagram of the unconventional gear positions failed to eliminate the confusion entirely. The constant mesh box was accompanied by a new single plate clutch which was very light and had a very efficient spring loaded clutch stop. With their new style clutch and gear box these were definitely much easier vehicles to handle. It was possible to discern, just by sound, that something was different because, having discarded the old two-plate clutch, the gearchange whistle which had been so distinctive of Guys up to this point was now absent.

In common with buses of other makes purchased by London Transport during and just after the war it was not anticipated that the Guys would remain in the fleet for very long and a life of eight years was assumed for depreciation purposes. Their substandard construction and complete non-standardisation made them early candidates for withdrawal. However this did not prevent updating from taking place as opportunity arose, mainly through the replacement of original units by lighter weight ones. The most immediately obvious was the gradual introduction of radiators with aluminium shells which, though constructed to exactly the same design as their black-painted cast iron predecessors, succeeded in giving a modernised and less austerity look to those vehicles which had them. Possibly in the autumn of 1947, and certainly by March 1948 at the latest, the whole of the Guy fleet at

Alperton garage was modified by the addition of an electric heating coil to make starting from cold easier. Sixty vehicles were involved within various sub-types, and the modification to the electrical circuitry was considered sufficiently significant as to warrant reclassification under the internal coding system; however vehicles transferred into Alperton after this time were not modified in this way. Details of the vehicles that were dealt with are given under the description of each of the relevant subtypes in chapter 5.

During their predictably short London life the Guys played a valuable though mainly suburban role. For an all too brief hey-day they were notable for dominating the bus scene in the eastern suburbs such as Romford which they made peculiarly their own, but their presence was also strongly felt in other centres such as Enfield and Wembley. Their impact in central London was, however, small and an attempt to introduce them at Victoria garage quickly resulted in failure. In common with most utility buses the majority deteriorated rapidly because of the inherent weakness of their bodies which was a pity because they remained mechanically strong and healthy to the end with low maintenance and running costs to their credit. Effectively the writing was on the wall as early as mid-1947 when the first post-war RTs began to arrive, but in the end the widespread dislike of them by drivers led to a slightly earlier demise than might otherwise have been the case. For London Transport crews, traditionally cosseted by faster and more responsive vehicles and accustomed to the luxury of pre-selector gearboxes, the Guy Arabs meant hard work.

CHAPTER FIVE

THE GUYS DESCRIBED

1-31, 51-71 – PARK ROYAL

Park Royal was destined to be the largest supplier of utility bodies to London Transport, so it was perhaps fitting that the first few Guys to be delivered should have come from this manufacturer. The initial pair, which had not originally been intended for London Transport, arrived well in advance of the remainder with G 1 making its appearance at Chiswick on 26th August 1942 three weeks ahead of G 2 on 16th September. Once the Board's 'own' batch came on stream with the arrival of G 3 on 10th October delivery of the remaining 28 was fairly rapid, and at an average of just under three per week all had been received by 23rd December. None entered service immediately, for like the Leylands and Bristols before them, they had first to be painted and fitted with nearside indicator boxes, and the side lights had to be repositioned. This work was carried out in some cases at Chiswick Works and in others at the

former tram depot nearby which more recently has served as London United's Stamford Brook bus garage; at the time it was used as an overflow repair works and paint shop. G 1 was used for test purposes for a few weeks whilst the remainder, once prepared for service, were stored unlicensed at Tottenham and Putney Bridge. The Tottenham vehicles were for that garage's own eventual use but the Putney ones were intended for service at Victoria, a plan that was later deferred. The Victoria code letters GM were actually painted on the cabs of some whilst they were in store at Putney Bridge, and a few Guys even found their way to Victoria itself for storage in due course. As it happened, Victoria was destined to wait another 2½ years before running Guys of its own and its originally intended allocation found alternative employment at Hanwell in due course. G 1 was the first Guy to be

licensed for service, on 1st December 1942, but progress was slow and by the end of the year only Gs 2, 8, 13 and 14 had joined it. January and February found fifteen more in service, but at this point progress was halted for a while and most were delicensed for modifications to be carried out. Apart from a few which drifted back earlier, most were relicensed from 1st June onwards, and from 4th June Hanwell began receiving those which had not yet seen service and had been in store for anything up to ten months.

An official photograph taken before entering service shows G 13 in original condition complete with red livery which only a few of this batch carried in their early years. The word GUY on the radiator top tank was picked out in white only on the first few deliveries. On some vehicles the headlamps had chrome-plated rims and the surround to the radiator grille was picked out in white, but G 13 had neither feature. LT Museum

G 1-31 comprised part of the first batch of 42 Guys authorised in February 1942, and after a lapse of a few weeks they were followed by G 51-71 which were Park Royal's share of the balance of Guys allocated against London's 1942 requirements. Once again the final delivery did not entirely reflect the original allocation. Just as Gs 1 and 2 of the first batch had replaced two Weymann vehicles which were ultimately delivered elsewhere, so G 51, 56-62 were Park Royal replacements for vehicles with other bodies which were diverted away to allow the London batch to include as many Park Royal bodied vehicles as possible. G 51 arrived at Chiswick on 11th February 1943 and the rest followed more or less in numerical sequence up to the arrival of Gs 70 and 71 on 15th May. These were the last of this type of Arab to be delivered to London Transport, G 72 onwards being of the long bonneted model later known as the Arab II.

Although logically the first Guys should have received the chassis/body code 1G1, this was omitted for some unknown reason and the coding given to G 1-10 was 2G2, followed by 1/2G2 for the remainder, denoting that a smaller fuel tank was fitted. Although various other differences in specification were introduced within this batch, including a major change to the engine mounting arrangements on G 16-31, these were not reflected in any further new chassis sub-codes. At an unladen weight of 7tons 13cwt the Arabs were more than a ton heavier than the pre-war STL and it was inevitable that with this ten per cent weight handicap they would be slow performers. The spartanly-equipped Park Royal bodies were the same as those on the earlier Leyland and Bristol utilities, even to the inclusion of a slight 'V' in the front dome and the distinctive Park Royal lip below the driver's windscreen. The final nine (G 63-71) differed from the remainder in having a glazed upper deck emergency exit. This employed exactly the same type of horizontally hinged door frame which, instead of being panelled with a single steel sheet, incorporated a window with radiused outer corners and a central dividing strip. This marked the first of a number of relaxations permitted by the Ministry of Supply to the basic austerity body specification as the war progressed and materials availability altered. It was a popular move as the lack of a rear upper deck window not only gave a claustrophobic effect

but, more importantly, caused problems for conductors unable to see if intending passengers were approaching from behind.

The first four Guys to receive fleet livery were painted in the standard red and broken white with brown roof; these were Gs 1, 2, 8 and 13. From then onwards the painting programme coincided with the period between November 1942 and February 1943 when vehicles of all classes emerged from the works with brown replacing the customary red on the main panels, a temporary expedient brought about by a shortage of pigment for red paint. The shade of brown, officially called Indian Red, had been used for some years as the colour for bus wheels and was not the same as the bauxite shade used on roofs. In the case of the Park Royal Guys brown livery was applied to all remaining vehicles in the first batch of 31 and also to the first of the second batch, G 51, after which supplies of red paint became available once more.

Shortly before the war ended each vehicle was fitted with a conventional inset, illuminated rear registration plate in the bottom offside corner. A few months afterwards, and in most cases before the first overhaul cycle commenced in December 1945, they were modified again, this time by the installation of two additional half drop windows in the lower saloon and four upstairs. It is believed that, at the same time, the brown vehicles were repainted red. At their first overhaul the majority were given glazed emergency exits

which looked similar to those fitted when new to G 63 upwards except that the outer corners were not radiused, and some which escaped attention on this occasion were dealt with next time around, in 1949/50. G 31 is known to have retained its unglazed emergency door right to the end and there may have been one or two other survivors. In odd cases the hinged ventilator was removed from the nearside bulkhead window, but no concerted effort was made to do this as occurred on the Leylands and most of the Bristols.

In August 1950 London Transport introduced a new, simplified livery for its entire fleet in readiness for the time, not far off, when spray painting would become standard practice. From about the middle of August every vehicle which was given a new coat of paint, irrespective of type or age, received the new scheme which comprised an all-over base colour of either red or green relieved only by a single narrow cream band. The black mudguards and lifeguards were retained, relieving to a degree the potential air of overall drabness. On the previous occasion when a new livery had been introduced, in 1946, it

Above **Despite wartime problems of material procurement, London Transport soon obtained specially made enamel name plates to cover the Guy emblem on the radiator top. This post-war view of** G 53 **shows it with the radiator still bearing its white grille surround, but new headlamps and additional opening windows are now fitted.**
E G P Masterman

Something has managed to crunch the rear lower corner of G 57, just missing the in-built number plate added in 1945. One of the last vehicles to be delivered with an unglazed emergency window, it still carried this feature when photographed in September 1949. The fleet number on the rear dome indicates an Upton Park based vehicle and is for the purpose of vehicle recognition by re-fuelling staff at the garage. Alan B Cross

had only been applied to specific types of older vehicles such as the more recent STLs and to post-war deliveries; the utilities had been excluded and retained the old red and white scheme. The 1950 change of policy gave the opportunity for the appearance of the utilities to be updated. Although no Leylands or Bristols were ever in the new 'all red' colour scheme, and most of the earlier Guys received their last overhaul too early to do so, two whose bodies needed attention were subsequently repainted and, in 1951, G 13 became the oldest utility in the fleet ever to receive modern livery.

Although all the Park Royal Mark I Arabs were allocated originally to Tottenham and Hanwell, significant numbers of these early Guys spread to Alperton from August 1943 and Barking from February 1944. Those which were at Alperton in late 1947 and early 1948 were modified electrically and recoded 2/2G2, the twelve vehicles concerned being Gs 11, 15, 28, 56, 58, 61, 64, 67-71. The passage of time did not find this batch much in use elsewhere although Upton Park gained a few from December 1945 and seven passed through Hornchurch's hands between March 1949 and November 1951. A single vehicle, G 13, spent two months at Enfield in 1949 and, similarly, G 5 paid a brief visit to Seven Kings in 1950 although in this case only for a week. After it had been in service for a year G 30's body was destroyed by enemy action in June 1944 and the vehicle was later rebodied by Northern Coachbuilders. Withdrawal of the remainder commenced in November 1950 and no fewer than 22 out of the original 52 later became learners. The last survivors in passenger service were Gs 11 and 68 which were withdrawn at Alperton on 1st July 1952.

The oldest utility to receive the 1950 all-red livery was G 13 which was repainted early in 1951, only a few months before it was withdrawn. Although the Guys were renowned for their reliability, the fare chart leaning against the rear wall indicates that this one, which is a Hornchurch vehicle on loan to Barking, has broken down! F G Reynolds

Although incognito in manufacturer's grey paint, this newly-completed Weymann bodied Arab is intended for London Transport as evidenced by its outward-opening indicator box. The photograph was presumably taken at or near the Addlestone works just prior to delivery.

G 32-42, 44-50 – WEYMANN

Corresponding to the first two orders for Park Royal bodies were contracts with Weymann's Motor Bodies Ltd to supply batches of eleven and seven respectively. Until the arrival of these vehicles all London utilities had looked alike. Weymann's contribution to utility design, though generally similar in appearance to Park Royal's concept, illustrated through numerous small differences how each builder could stamp an individual identity on to a theoretically standard design. Though retaining all the major features, the Weymann body managed to look different from most angles, except perhaps at the rear where it most closely resembled the Park Royal product. Most noticeable was the frontal treatment where the harsh slope was softened by a less angled cab, giving a more gentle and attractive profile. Appearance was further enhanced by the absence of the fussy angled ledge below the windscreen which had been a feature of the Park Royal design. Weymann employed one-piece lower side panels, eliminating the secondary waist moulding which had been another fussy aspect of the Park Royal design. A distinguishing point on Weymann bodies, both in these and subsequent batches, was the height of the driver's offside window and door which reached right up to cant rail level, breaking the continuity of the white relief band. At the front end there was almost no inward taper, causing the body front to be slightly wider and resulting in a rather more roomy cab. As a result the inward opening ventilators above the front windows

stopped short of the outer edge of the vehicle, providing an instant recognition feature of an oncoming bus even when seen from some distance away. Internally there was little difference between the two manufacturer's products; on both the window pillars and other timbers were in a light varnished grain finish with white lower deck ceilings, brown painted lower panels, and brown leather-cloth-covered seats. Only in the use by Weymann of black grab handles on the seat backs instead of white were the two immediately distinguishable from one another.

The Weymann Guys were classified 1/2G3. The first, G 32, was received from Addlestone on 18th November 1942; three more came in the same month followed by five in December and the final two of the first batch in early January 1943. The second small order for seven was delivered between 24th February and 16th April 1943. Like the Park Royals, these were delivered without side indicators which were fitted when the vehicles were painted, the livery being brown in the case of G 32-42 and red on G 44-50.

Although theoretically similar to one another in specification, wartime utility bodies varied in price between manufacturers. Even when the materials used were basically identical, labour costs related to wages and productivity could cause variations in price as could the level of administrative costs and various factory overheads. Thus the Weymann bodies at £940 each were a little more expensive than the £917.8s.6d charged by

Park Royal. With the Guy chassis currently at £1297, the complete vehicle as supplied cost £2237. A higher price did not, of course, necessarily mean higher quality, and indeed it was necessary for all eighteen to go back to Addlestone between July 1945 and February 1946 to have the front bulkheads modified for greater strength. As in the case of the Park Royal vehicles, extra opening windows and an in-built rear registration plate were fitted in due course. Two of the batch, Gs 34 and 50, were at Alperton and were modified in the early post-war era to become 2/2G3. Several Weymann Guys were destined to retain their unglazed emergency exits throughout their lives and indeed the last one to be withdrawn, Alperton's G 45 on 1st July 1952, was in this condition to the end. Only one, G 32, was ever repainted into the 1950 all-red livery.

The life history of these vehicles naturally paralleled that of their Park Royal contemporaries. Arab Mark Is formed the entire Tottenham Guy fleet apart from occasional, short-lived allocations of Mark IIs, and Weymann-bodied Mark Is were also prominent at Hanwell, and subsequently Alperton and Upton Park. They played a minor role at Barking although only G 32 stayed there for any length of time (August 1946 to June 1951), whilst Hornchurch gained a sole example late in life when G 41 was rescued from trainer duties in January 1951 and stayed through until November. This was one of eight which were demoted to training duties at the end of their career.

G 39, in brown livery, demonstrates the slightly cleaner, mellower lines of the Weymann utility body. It originally entered service on 1st February 1943 but is seen just after being relicensed in June following modification, and is still in almost as-new condition except for a recently received knock on the front corner pillar, brought about perhaps by the horrendous difficulty of driving during blackout hours. The front wheel nut guards were not retained for long. S L Poole

Above Left A full frontal shot taken in July 1951 of G 41 shows the lack of inward taper which was a feature of this first batch of Weymann bodies. This vehicle has lost its bulkhead ventilator window and gained an aluminium radiator at various stages in its career. Alan T Smith

Above Right Interior view of G 34 taken in February 1953, after its withdrawal from service, showing the black painted grab rails on the seat backs which distinguished the Weymann bodies from those supplied by Park Royal. Weymann's style of upholstery differed from Park Royal's although both used a similar shade of brown leathercloth. John C Gillham

G 43 – DUPLE

G 43 was one of London Transport's oddities. The Guy fleet ultimately contained several unique vehicles of which G 43 was the first, and it was these that made it perhaps more interesting than the other utility classes. Allocated in November 1942 as part of the second quota of 42, it typified the wartime allocation system which mystified and infuriated so many provincial operators in being an illogical one-off which could in theory have been avoided. Duple Bodies & Motors Ltd of Hendon bodied their only Guy for London on the chassis of G 43 and it was delivered in primer on 25th January 1943. London Transport allocated the classification 1/2G4, fitted a side indicator box and applied a coat of brown and white paint at Chiswick before placing the vehicle into store at Putney Bridge along with several Park Royal and Weymann bodied vehicles. Like many of its contemporaries G 43 underwent a programme of mechanical modification prior to entering service at Hanwell on 1st July 1943 by which time it was more than five months old. When Hanwell received new Bristols in January 1946 G 43 moved eastwards along with many other Mark I Arabs to spend the remainder of its time at Upton Park. Soon after arriving there additional opening windows were fitted and red livery was applied.

When viewed from the front as it approached, G 43 was instantly recognisable. Early Duple utility bodies as supplied to several provincial operators were noted for their very wide upper deck centre pillar and G 43 was no exception. Like the Weymann Guys it had a higher than usual driver's door and side window, but the same applied in this case also to the windscreen itself and to the nearside cab window, a design which left no room for the white relief band to continue around the front portion of the bus. In its original brown livery the white window surround on the lower deck continued into a narrow strip below the windows which was a further distinguishing mark of this bus at the time. Yet another feature which distinguished G 43 when new was that it was alone at the time in having a glazed upper deck emergency window; however because it spent so long in store some of the newer Park Royal vehicles from G 63 upwards, which were similarly equipped, entered service before it.

The interior of G 43 was not unlike its contemporaries in having light varnished woodwork but it was unique in having red, moquette covered seats. G 43 was shown as having an unladen weight of 7ton 13cwt, exactly the same as the Park Royal and Weymann vehicles, but whether or not they really all weighed the same remains open to speculation. At £895 the Duple body was the cheapest ever obtained for any London utility, a fact which no doubt pleased London Transport who, even in wartime, were very cost conscious on matters like this.

G 43's distinctive shape was for several years an everyday scene on routes in the East End, but being based at Upton Park its existence remained purely suburban and it never ventured in service closer to central London than Limehouse. It was the first of the Guy family oddities to cease operation, being withdrawn along with all of Upton Park's other Arab Is on 8th November 1951 as the result of an influx of STLs.

Below **No photographs are known to exist of G 43 in its wartime condition but this snap showing the rear end illustrates the glazed emergency window carried from new, which has well radiused outer corners at its top edge. Judging by the freshly repainted panels at the rear, it may not have been long since the registration number was re-sited.** R W Burrell

Opposite, Left and Below
G 43 was always immediately distinguishable by the thick centre pillar at the front of the upper deck and the lack of a white relief band below the indicator box. Three photographs during its span of almost six years' service at Upton Park show that its appearance altered very little during this time apart from a minor livery modification during the middle period. It is seen on route 101 at Wanstead in 1947, at Dagenham on route 175 in 1949, and at almost the same spot again in 1951.
D W K Jones/Alan B Cross/F G Reynolds

THE LOW HEIGHT GUYS THAT MIGHT HAVE BEEN

When the Ministry of Supply contracted Guy to build 500 chassis back in 1941 it was the intention that 60% of the output would receive normal height bodies whilst the remainder would be fitted with the lowbridge style essential for so many provincial fleets. London Transport operated a small fleet of low height double deckers, and although it secured permission to build twenty such bodies at Chiswick to mount on STL chassis there remained an urgent need for more. It was accordingly arranged that an allocation of 36 Guys which was authorised in September 1942 would include fifteen low height vehicles. The Ministry of Supply's policy at the time was to order in advance batches of bodies from various coachbuilders consistent with the material supply position and their ability to construct them, the task of building normal height bodies being allocated to some and lowbridge bodies to others. For the fifteen low height bodies allocated to it, London Transport was scheduled to receive eleven from Strachans Successors Ltd of North Acton and four from the Northern Counties Motor & Engineering Co. Ltd of Wigan. Strachans, although a major London based coachbuilder, had not supplied any bus bodies for London operation since LGOC days and did not appear to be much favoured by the Board, whilst Northern Counties was a totally unknown quantity in the capital.

Having learnt of its allocation, London Transport approached the two body manufacturers to ascertain the height to which the buses would be built. The standard wartime specification, produced jointly by the Ministry and the operators' associations, was for a vehicle of 13ft 6ins unladen height whilst London Transport was seeking a maximum of 13ft 3ins. Strachans offered to build to a lower height, but this reduction would apparently have been achieved by eliminating one step from the staircase producing an unsatisfactory height on one or more of the remainder. Northern Counties, who despite wartime restrictions had permission to continue producing jig-built metal framed bodies, were unable to offer any height reduction. Dissatisfied by this, London Transport approached the Ministry to seek authority to build thirteen bodies of its own at Chiswick similar to the STL bodies which were actually going through the shops between August 1942 and June 1943, overlapping with the first Guys. If approved, their plan was to mount the new bodies on STL chassis and to transfer thirteen standard STL bodies to new Guy chassis. The difference of two between the fifteen Guys allocated and the thirteen bodies which the Board now wished to build represented a reduction in its requirement which resulted in two of the Strachans bodied allocation being transferred to Newcastle Corporation in whose fleet they duly entered service registered JTN 607 and 608. In exchange London Transport was allocated two additional Park Royal bodied highbridge Guys although the source from which these were notionally derived is not known. The Ministry of Supply did not take long to decide that it would not entertain London Transport's request to build thirteen more

bodies of its own; indeed it could not have done so even if the desire had been there as the supply of materials, which was very tight indeed, was already fully allocated. In due course London Transport negotiated to relinquish the thirteen remaining low height Guys provided that they could be reimbursed with an equal number of normal height buses on a later allocation.

The thirteen were reallocated on 15th December and entered service in 1943 with a whole variety of provincial operators. The Strachans bodied vehicles went to Potteries (JEH 472, 473), Aldershot & District (EHO 695), Red & White (EWO 484), A. Skill & Sons (GTV 427), Bradford Corporation (DKY 467), South Shields Corporation (CU 4549) and

Western National (HTA 887,888), the last two ultimately being built with Northern Counties bodies following a last minute reallocation. The Northern Counties vehicles which would have come to London were reallocated to four northern operators, Lancashire United (FTD 184), Western SMT (ASD 251), Glasgow Corporation (DGG 701) and St Helens Corporation (DJ 9089). All of these were amongst the final deliveries of Arab Mark Is as were London Transport's own vehicles in the series G 43-71 with which they were contemporaneous, and the vehicle which went to St Helens was, in fact, the first Mark II, heralding the start of Guy's second output of 500 new Arabs.

Bradford Corporation received its only Arab I in July 1943 thanks to the London Transport diverted order; it was the first low height vehicle to join the fleet for ten years. Withdrawn from passenger service in June 1951, it soldiered on as No. D50 in the Corporation's training fleet until 1958. The Strachans bodywork remained in remarkably original condition right through to the end without even the original meagre quota of opening windows being augmented.
John Fozard

The two Arabs reallocated to Newcastle Corporation entered service there in May 1943 as Nos. 247/8. The faded, patchwork effect on 247's paintwork appears to have arisen through the subsequent touching-up of the lower panels in a darker shade of grey than was originally used by Strachans. The clearly visible bulb horn acts as a clue that the chassis was built for London service. Both Newcastle vehicles were reconditioned just after the war but lasted in service only until 1950. Roy Marshall

G 72-136 – PARK ROYAL

Following fairly closely upon the heels of the last Arab Is, the first of what was destined to become a fleet of 364 Arab IIs began arriving at Chiswick in June 1943 led by G 75 on the 22nd. Four allocations by the Ministry of War Transport between February and September 1943 in batches of 25, 4, 30 and 6 respectively tallied together to make a total of 65 vehicles comprising the batch G 72-136. Included in the first allocation of 25 were thirteen replacements for the aborted lowbridge order. On this occasion there was no splitting of the contracts between bodybuilders; all were allocated to Park Royal although in order to achieve this unusually high degree of body standardisation some Park Royal bodies had to be transferred on paper to London Transport from other operators' allocations, known vehicles being displaced being a Pickering bodied Arab which ultimately went to Young's Bus Service at Paisley and a Weymann-bodied example which joined the fleet of the Sheffield Joint Omnibus Committee.

Externally the batch was immediately distinguishable from earlier Guys in the London fleet because of the longer bonnet and upswept wings although there was no change in the appearance of the Park Royal bodywork from the last nine of the previous batch. Nor was there any difference in their official unladen weight which remained, somewhat improbably, at 7tons 13cwt. Internally, however, it was a different story. Worsening supply problems had made the procurement of seating materials such as rubber and cloth increasingly difficult, and in January 1943 the Ministry of Supply was forced to

An unidentified Mark II Arab, photographed presumably at about the time of delivery, shows the original head and side lights, and also the grey livery which the final eighteen members of the class still carried when they entered service. *LT Museum*

G 72 was the lowest numbered Arab II although it was not the first of the type to be delivered or to enter service. All its working days were spent at Alperton. In this photograph, taken at Golders Green soon after it was licensed on 1st August 1943, G 72 already carries the new, smaller type of headlights which were presumably fitted at the same time as it was painted. It has also acquired an enamelled radiator badge. *LT Museum*

announce that, from the second quarter of the year, all new double deckers would be built with wooden slatted seats; henceforth the only upholstered seat would be the one provided for the driver. The announcement was not totally unexpected, wooden seats having been the standard fitment on Bedford OWBs since their introduction in the summer of 1942, but this represented their first regular use on double deckers since horse bus days. G 72 onwards duly arrived with wooden seats and caused quite a stir including a spate of letters to the press, though few were critical as most people realised from the difficulties in their everyday life how bad the material supply position had become. The slatted seats were not, in fact, as uncomfortable as might have been expected, and in this respect the fairly good riding qualities of the Guy Arab helped. Undoubtedly the absence of upholstery to act as a partial sound deadener meant that interior noise levels were higher, but on a positive note, the replacement of Park Royal's rather drab, dark brown leathercloth by light varnished wood gave an air of lightness which, in a perverse way, was beneficial on dark evenings in the blackout when lighting restrictions made the interiors of buses very gloomy.

The whole batch of 65 was initially classified 3G5 although no fewer than 35 were later given the Alperton electrical modification to become 3/3G5. These were Gs 72-80, 82-86, 88-92, 94-103, 105, 106, 109, 110, 113, and 136. Although all were theoretically identical there were in fact differences within the batch. A design modification eliminated the inward opening ventilator from the bulkhead nearside window and replaced it with a permanent air intake shielded by a rectangular cover located in the centre of the bulkhead above window level which distributed air taken in from louvres visible under the canopy. As far as can be ascertained this feature appeared on Gs 81, 83 and 85 onwards. It was claimed to eliminate draughts although at times it gave the impression of doing the opposite. From G 98 onwards an emergency exit window was fitted to the driver's cab above the bonnet and a prop was fitted for the bonnet top itself, all earlier buses being subsequently modified to match. Lack of time and capacity at Chiswick prevented the Board from installing a side destination box on the last eighteen vehicles (G 119-136), and there was also no time to paint them into standard livery so they were rushed into service at Barking on 1st May 1944 still in grey primer as delivered. However they did not remain grey for long, being repainted into fleet colours from October 1944 onwards. The last to be dealt with was G 131 which re-entered service in red and white on 13th January 1945. During the first half of 1945 some 43 vehicles were returned to Park Royal for their bulkheads to be strengthened.

London Transport's inability to find time to paint the final eighteen vehicles of the batch in fleet colours before entering service also left them without side indicator boxes, an omission which remained with them throughout their lives. G 135 looked smart when photographed in May 1950; six months later it was overhauled into all-red livery and lasted in service until the end of May 1952. Alan T Smith

Left and Below **Seven years separate these two rear end views. Although devoid of markings the vehicle in as-delivered condition was, in fact, G 74 taken on its day of delivery, 24th June 1943. In contrast G 106, filmed at London Bridge alongside STL 1813, shows the added side indicator box, half drops and rear registration plate, and also demonstrates the route number stencil holder which was added to the rear of all utilities in post-war days in lieu of a blind display. The division of the rear platform window into two was a very common modification on all types of double decker (except RTs) to make best use of glass availability.** LT Museum/Alan B Cross

As with all earlier batches of utilities, these 65 vehicles were later fitted with an illuminated rear registration plate and additional opening windows. At the first overhaul cycle, which occupied the twelve months between February 1947 and January 1948, they lost their wooden seat slats in favour of latex filled moquette cushions and squabs although the original frames were retained. Gs 75 and 94 were the first to appear in this form on 25th February 1947 and demonstrated a seat style which was to become familiar on both Guys and Daimlers as the old wooden units were replaced. The rebuilt seats employed London Transport's standard post-war moquette which was still quite novel at the time but soon became famous for its widespread use on many other classes including the whole RT family; they were edged in brown leathercloth and the seat backs were covered in green rex-ine. Though undoubtedly more comfortable than their predecessors, these seats looked utilitarian and not particularly attractive and they still lacked any form of grab rail or handle just as they had done in their slatted form.

When new a few of this batch were employed to build up the required number of Guys at Hanwell but the great majority were to be found at Alperton and Barking where they played a major role throughout. The only exceptions in the early days were a pair (G 80,81) allocated initially to Tottenham but only for a short while. With the exception of Victoria there were no Guy garages where this class was not present at one time or another although their impact at Upton Park was only small and their presence was only really felt at Enfield from as late as April 1951 onwards when some arrived as replacements for less healthy though newer Massey bodied vehicles. Most of this batch were given a heavy body overhaul at their second progression through Chiswick Works in 1950 which resulted in many receiving the latest all-red colours. One of their number, Barking's G 115, was in fact used as the prototype for this livery in respect of the utilities in June 1950 ahead of its general introduction in August. However not all received a second overhaul, and included within this category were two whose bodies were found to be so riddled with wood rot upon arrival in the works that they were immediately condemned, becoming the first Guys in the fleet to be withdrawn; these were Gs 113 and 73 whose early demise came in February and March 1950 respectively. The final members of this batch in public service were Gs 76, 83, 85, 96 and 109, all of which were withdrawn at Alperton on 1st July 1952.

G 137,138 – WEYMANN

After delivery of the last of the 3G5s a lapse of ten months occurred before the next Guy arrived on the scene, during which time London Transport became the owner of 34 new Daimler CWA6s. No further large influx of Guys was planned at this stage but two were allocated on 20th March 1944 which, although forming part of London Transport's main allocation, were also experimental. Gs 137 and 138 were scheduled to carry Weymann bodies, but ones very unlike those that had gone before. These were to be metal framed and were part of a small batch for which Weymann had gained special sanction to manufacture, and the fairly high retail price of £1075 each reflected their experimental nature and the extra work which went into constructing them. They were of a design described by the company as 'bearerless' which they had patented. The first of the type had been placed in service with Northern General on 1st June 1940 but the war had prevented further development; now Weymann wished to initiate a slightly larger scale trial with their post-war production programme in mind, and were pleased that two of the bodies would be operated in London.

The principle behind the bearerless body was that it would relieve the greater part of the extraneous deflections transmitted by the chassis in orthodox designs by eliminating all the intermediate cross bearers, securing the body to the chassis only at the front and rear bulkheads using four fixing points instead of the usual ten. Actually, because the Guy chassis incorporated the customary platform extension, the body was secured here too, but this was held to be of no concern as it did not affect the stability of the body, the rigidity of which was such that it could survive without a chassis extension to support it. The body sides were arranged as extremely stiff box girders terminating for all practical purposes at the front and rear bulkheads, and almost the whole weight of the body and of the upper saloon passengers was carried by these girders and thus transferred to the bulkhead attachments. These were especially sturdy to ensure that they were equal to the loads imposed. A Silentbloc bush was secured to the chassis frame at each fixing point to maintain the body side in a reasonable line whilst at the same time permitting unrestricted vertical movement to take place between the chassis frame and the body side. The Weymann theory, developed after trials at Addlestone, was that the conventional assumption that bus body sides sagged and needed holding up was incorrect and that reaction from the road spring shackles actually deflected the chassis itself, thus by reducing the points of contact body life should be extended. The most unusual feature was that the lower saloon floor framework was fixed to the chassis, becoming in effect an integral part of the chassis frame, with permanent connection to the body being made only at the bulkheads. Though not immediately apparent to the casual observer, close inspection would reveal that the floor and the body sides were deflecting differently when the bus was in motion.

Although the chassis were numbered consecutively and were delivered within two weeks of each other (21st September and 6th

Camera shyness appears to have afflicted the two metal framed Weymann Guys, as a result of which no photographs taken earlier than 1949 have been unearthed. This view of G 137 shows that the general profile of the Weymann utility style was retained, but window pans with radiused corners modernise the appearance, and the exaggerated curvature of the driver's cab windows is positively modernistic. Much corrosion has become evident at upper deck window level in the two years since the body was last overhauled. *Roy Marshall*

October respectively), the completed vehicles were received from Weymann's three months apart, reflecting the specialist nature of the body construction which was aside from their main production line. The bodies were a strange mixture of wartime and peacetime practice. The general outline now familiar on Weymann's austerity composite bodies was retained although with a slightly more pronounced inward taper at the front, as were the squared-off front corners and the 'lobster back' domes. However all the windows were mounted in pans with radiused lower corners and an exaggerated, modernistic curve was given to the top rear corner of the driver's cab door and the corresponding lower corner of his offside window, and also to the top corners of the rear platform window. The use of window pans was, of course, unavoidable on a metal body, and it was also necessary to provide cappings for all the internal window surrounds. The interior was, in fact, in dark varnished wood, but the two vehicles differed from each other in that G 137 had slatted wood seats whilst G 138 had moquette seats with repp-covered backs.

The nearside of the 'bearerless' body is demonstrated by G 138 in this August 1949 scene. The fact that no nearside indicator box was fitted is just discernible. *Alan B. Cross*

At the request of the operators' associations a relaxed austerity specification had been approved in January 1945 permitting cushioned seating in moquette or leathercloth to be used instead of wood, the fitment of up to ten opening side windows on each bus, the use of aluminium for roof panelling, and safety glass in all windows. The Ministry of Supply had already forecast on 15th December 1944 that it would accede to a request for a relaxed specification although lingering doubt survived over materials availability and there was concern that extra man hours would be required per body. Permission was also given for domed panels to replace the 'lobster back' arrangement when manufacturers were ready to do so. Some bodybuilders could now supply stretched panels so the shortage of skilled panel beaters was no longer such a problem. The only operators' request rejected by the Ministry was for linoleum to replace the rubberised material latterly used on lower saloon floors because supply was still inadequate, but its use was henceforth reinstated on upper deck floors and bulkheads.

G 137 was built ahead of the relaxation and originally had only two half drops on each deck whereas G 138 had a full complement. On both vehicles the windows were of the winding type which had already become familiar on utility Daimlers at Merton. They also had inbuilt rear registration plates from new and were delivered in standard red and white livery. At a weight of 7tons 15cwt G 137 was no lightweight, but G 138 tipped the scales even higher at 7tons 19cwt 1qr and was the heaviest – and presumably the most sluggish – utility bus ever to run in London. Like previous Arab Mk IIs they were given the chassis code 3G although they differed in carrying a new type of headlight which was considerably smaller than before and mounted closer to ground level. This was a new format by Guy to give an improved beam through the wartime mask, and subsequently London Transport – in common with a number of other operators – fitted their earlier Guys with the same type of small headlight. They also introduced a modified gearbox incorporating constant mesh on 3rd gear to which standard, again, all earlier vehicles were later modified. G 137's full classification was 3G6 (later 3/3G6 as this was an Alperton based vehicle) and G 138 was 3G6/1.

Both buses were allocated to Alperton when new, G 137 on 5th January 1945 and G 138 on 1st May. The older of the two spent its entire working life at Alperton, retaining its wooden seats until 31st December 1947 when it went into Chiswick for its first overhaul. However G 138 moved at the start of February 1946 to Upton Park where it then remained. When overhauled for the second time in October 1950 and February 1951 respectively both were found still to be in very sound structural condition. Several more years' life could, in theory, have been obtained from them but the general policy to dispose of Guys resulted in G 138 being withdrawn on 8th November 1951 (only nine months after its final overhaul) and G 137 on 1st July 1952.

G 30 – NORTHERN COACHBUILDERS

On 6th January 1945 yet another unusual member of London Transport's Guy family arrived at Chiswick. The circumstances here were certainly unique for G 30 was the only utility double decker anywhere in the country to receive a second new utility body as a result of enemy action. G 30 had been a standard 1/2G3 operating from Tottenham garage until 23rd June 1944 when its body was reduced to a state beyond repair by a flying bomb whilst it was proceeding on route 76 along York Road, Waterloo at 9.35 in the morning. Another Guy, G 65, was nearby at the time but fortunately only suffered broken windows. G 30's chassis was salvageable but the Board's engineers briefly considered breaking it down as a source of spare parts. However an approach to the Regional Transport Commissioner (with whom London Transport had to deal in respect of outside repair work even though their new bus allocation was made direct from the Ministry, by-passing the Commissioner) revealed that approval would be given for a new body to be constructed. Although it may have seemed obvious for G 30 to be rebodied by Park Royal or one of the other manufacturers accustomed to building on Guy chassis, the system did not work like that and it was almost inevitable that the new body would come from another source. The nation's bus bodybuilding capacity was effectively divided up into two distinct categories and they seldom overlapped. One group consisted of companies specialising in building on new chassis and the other comprised the remainder, who carried out the more difficult and time consuming task of providing new bodies for all manner of old chassis as well as repairing existing ones as far as possible. The only builder with a foot in both camps was Brush who, though mostly employed in bodying new chassis, also carried out some rebodying work. Manufacturers in the 'rebodying' category came under the aegis of the

Vehicle Maintenance Repair Division of the Ministry of Supply and one of them was Northern Coachbuilders Ltd, Newcastle-upon-Tyne. This company was working from a large converted airship hangar at Cramlington, a few miles from the city, and had developed its own basic style of utility body which it modified as necessary to suit each individual application. G 30's new body was ordered on 11th July 1944 and was despatched to Cramlington on 17th August to be built at a cost of £1050. This was rather more than most other new composite bodies but acceptable in view of the design and preparation work involved, G 30 being the only Guy Arab ever submitted to the company for rebodying.

Above **The distinctive lines of Northern Coachbuilders' standard wartime body are demonstrated by G 30 as it awaits departure from Edgware in December 1948. The NCB body, in both high and lowbridge styles, could be found amongst fleets in many parts of the country, but mostly in ones and twos and never in large batches.** Alan B Cross

Left **At the rear, the brown painted portion of G 30's roof sloped downwards to link the top of the emergency exit with the rainshield over the side windows. The dividing strip in the platform window is a post-war addition; the original was glazed in one piece.** Alan T Smith

Upon arrival back in London it could be seen that G 30's new body conformed closely to Northern Coachbuilders' standard, rather heavy looking style incorporating a more upright front than most other utilities and with a secondary waistband moulding around both decks. It was unique in that the upper deck projected a few inches to give an eyebrow effect over the windscreen. Northern Coachbuilders was the first to deliver a utility body to London Transport on which the front bulkhead windows did not dip towards their outer corners, and the cab windscreen was the only one on any London utility without a slope on its lower edge. The window behind the driver was divided horizontally in two, presumably so that the small upper section could be opened if required although in London service it remained fixed. A feature of NCB bodies was their emergency window, the two glazed portions of which were higher than they were wide. No side indicator was fitted and the vehicle was equipped with wooden seats although its half drop windows were of the modern, winding type. The interior had the customary light wood finish although in this case there were secondary cappings around the window pillars to hide the body frame whereas on all vehicles received up to now (except metal framed Gs 137 and 138) the exposed frame had been varnished. On the upper deck the whole of the roof framework was visible within the saloon, Northern Coachbuilders' standard practice being to panel over the top in preference to the alternative of leaving the main roof ribbing visible on the outside of the vehicle. This was the first London utility to have flat rather than rounded ceiling cove panels on the lower deck although others were soon to follow from Northern Counties and Massey. The unladen weight of G 30 was 7tons 10cwt and in its new guise it was classified as 1/2G7, modified later to Alperton specification as 2/2G7.

In its rebodied form G 30 led an uneventful life at Alperton. It began work there on 23rd January 1945 and finished when the garage lost its last Guys on 1st July 1952. Upholstered seats were fitted in March 1947 and the original red and white livery was retained through to the end.

Top and Centre **Two views in the upper saloon after the fitment of upholstered seats show the winding windows and the roof framework which was visible to passengers in its entirety. The rearmost windows on each side had an unusual downward slope to their top edge, and the use of individually constructed lamp holders in preference to a continuous trunking strip was another unusual feature.**
John C Gillham

Left **G 30's new body was the first utility in London to introduce flat-profiled ceiling cove panels and a straight lower edge to the front bulkhead windows. It was the only one with a horizontally-divided window behind the driver.**
John C Gillham

G 174-193, 258-268, 312-318, 358-368 – MASSEY

1945 started off as a quiet year for Guy deliveries, the only new one received in the first quarter being G 138, the second of the Weymann metal-bodied experimentals. However this tranquillity was broken on 17th April when Gs 176 and 178 arrived from a Wigan manufacturer who was a completely unknown factor in London but whose name, Massey Bros Ltd, was to become synonymous with bodywork of the utility style. These two Guys were the first of a huge influx of 297 Arabs allocated in batches between January and June 1945 which was to transform the bus scene in some parts of London over a period of a few months.

In the years leading up to the war Massey had been a well respected but localised body-builder, few of its products selling to operators far from the north west of England. Even in its position as one of the major suppliers of utility bodywork few had been allocated as far south as London, it being the Ministry's policy that, as far as possible, northern manufacturers would serve operators in the northern part of the country, southern manufacturers likewise in the south, whilst those in the Midlands would make up the balance when required. Now, however, there was no option but to link Massey with the London contracts in view of the large quantity of vehicles involved. Just before the war Massey had produced a very modern, rounded style of body and its utility offering was, in its way, just as bold. It seems that Massey's design staff, faced with implementing the austerity specification, decided to make a virtue of necessity by substituting the boldest of square lines for the previous curves. The resulting utility body, with its deep roof and square corners, managed to retain the essence of the gentle front and rear contours from pre-war years but squared off to provide a distinctive, rugged and harmonious design. Without doubt Massey's was by far the most distinctive and easily recognisable of all utility double deck bodies.

Unlike other manufacturers contributing to London Transport's 1945 programme of Guys, Massey was not yet in a position to implement the 'relaxed austerity' appearance using rounded domes, with the result that theirs were the last buses delivered to London Transport with 'lobster back' domes and a total 'utility' appearance. However as a concession to increased comfort they had upholstered seats and a full complement of opening windows. These buses were most unusual from a passenger point of view because, thanks to their unusually deep roofs, those sitting in the upper saloon had the sensation of being perched unusually high up. This was because the windows were placed lower than usual to accommodate the deep roof, with a consequential reduction in the depth of the upper deck side panels.

The first batch of Massey bodies, comprising a group of twenty (G 174-193) were all delivered by 23rd May at a price of £975 each. The first two in passenger service were G 174 at Alperton and G 175 at Barking, both on 1st May; when G 176 was licensed at Barking on the 4th it became the last new bus to enter service before the war in Europe ceased.

Top **Considered by some to represent the archetypal utility, Massey's contribution to the wartime scene had distinctive lines which were emphasised by the plain livery as demonstrated by G 267 when still only a few days old. The darker brown of the roof stretched from the second bay rearwards on some vehicles, including this one; on others it reached right to the front.**
R H G Simpson

Above **From the second batch onwards a side indicator box was fitted from new; this 1947 view of G 259 demonstrates the recently revised side blind style incorporating a route number which theoretically has replaced the route stencil holder mounted lower down, although in this case it is still in use. On the utilities these holders were subsequently repositioned in the back window.**
D W K Jones

Left **Photographs depicting the handful of Massey utilities which carried cream window frames as part of their original brown livery are rare. G 364 demonstrates that the brown of the roof also incorporated the rain shields, bringing it right down to upper deck window level.** R W Burrell

Manufacturers were now delivering bodies in a standard of paintwork fit for immediate service instead of grey, although because paint supplies were still unpredictable they by no means always conformed completely to operators' own liveries. Massey was unable to obtain supplies of red paint and used the plainest of alternatives, an all-over brown which, if anything, helped to enhance further the body's distinctive lines. The bulk of the body was painted in a milk chocolate shade, only the roof being in a darker finish. There was no side indicator box, but there were two quirky features exclusive to Massey which could not be missed. One was the little curved lip to the offside of the windscreen which permitted the lower interior of the driver's cab to be wider below the waistrail than above, and the other was the division of the platform rear window to permit the inclusion of frosted glass in the offside portion. This 'decency' window was a hangover from more genteel days and was meant to inhibit the ungentlemanly practice of viewing ladies' legs as they climbed the stairs. It was perhaps surprising that such an inheritance from an earlier time should have crept into and lasted right through the utility era; in fact it was continued by Massey well into the post-war years.

On 15th June 1945 Gs 258 and 259 of the second batch (G 258-268) arrived at Chiswick, and the third and fourth orders (G 313-318, 358-368) followed on without a break through to early September. These three batches, comprising 29 vehicles in all, differed from the original twenty in having a side indicator box mounted above a platform canopy which was itself higher than before. Once again they were in the all-brown colour scheme except for the final six, G 363-368, which had pale cream window reliefs.

The lower top platform edge and lack of nearside indicator box were features on the first batch of twenty bodies as illustrated by G 175. This was one of the few Masseys to receive the 1950 livery which, in consisting almost entirely of one colour, was almost a reversion to the original theme. Clear glass has replaced the frosted pane at G 175's November 1950 overhaul. Alan T Smith

Massey achieved the highest level of interior finish of any wartime manufacturer, and a glimpse forward in the lower saloon revealed a picture not far short of pre-war standards except for the lack of lining panels below the windows and the slightly spartan seats. The bodybuilder's gold lettered transfer can be seen at the top of the polished front bulkhead panel with a GUY transfer at window sill level above the flywheel cover. London Transport's unsympathetic repainting on overhaul succeeded in marring the effect totally, as witnessed by the lower saloon of careworn G 316 at the end of its life. J M Aldridge/J C Gillham

In established Massey tradition these vehicles showed a high standard of interior finish despite the spartan features imposed upon them. Mouldings covered all the pillar sections and all the visible woodwork was in a highly polished, dark reddish mahogany shade set off by chromium plated screws and cup washers. The seats were in red leathercloth, rather than the brown used by other manufacturers, and had white grab handles. On the lower deck at least, where the dark mouldings stood out against the white ceiling, the overall effect was striking and certainly almost as good as in pre-war days, though the upper deck was spoilt because all the roof timbers were visible. In this respect, as in the use of flat lower saloon coving panels, the Massey bodies echoed the style of the other north of England manufacturers, Northern Coachbuilders (on G 30) and Northern Counties.

The upper deck looking forward, where the bare roof sticks of the utility construction mar an otherwise presentable appearance. In operational use, the condensation which quickly formed on the single skinned roof lining quickly became discoloured brown by nicotine stains and by rust from screw heads. J M Aldridge

Although well constructed, the utility bodies were never to Massey Brothers' own satisfaction and the company was convinced that, because of the inferior materials which it was forced to use, its reputation could be marred. There was some justification in this fear, for the passage of time was to show that the timber employed in the Massey body frames was more prone to early deterioration than that used by many of their contemporaries. The London bodies were among the last of over 300 built during the war, all in the same typical Massey style, mostly on Guy chassis but to a lesser extent on Daimlers. Delivery to London was interspersed with a batch of ten for Kingston upon Hull Corporation and a couple for Newbury & District, but when Gs 366 and 368 were delivered from Wigan on 5th September 1945 they were the last of the line.

All new Guys from G 139 upwards were built to an improved specification with modified accelerator pedal gear, a new design of front axle with a modified Timken race assembly, a self-centring ability requiring less effort on the part of the driver, stronger clutch springs (with which G 1-138 were later modified) and a slightly higher floor level. The first ones actually delivered to London Transport comprised the initial Massey batch which introduced a revised chassis coding, the complete vehicle being coded 1/3G9 except for the sole example at Alperton, G 174, which later became 4/3G9. They tipped the scales officially at 7tons 9cwt and were the lightest Arabs yet received although even lighter ones were soon to follow. From November 1947 onwards they were taken one by one into Chiswick to be repainted into fleet livery, in some cases but not always as part of their scheduled first overhaul, and by mid-1948 all were in standard red and white. In November 1950 a second overhaul cycle commenced, but the work required in renewing body timbers was found to be unduly extensive and the programme was terminated after just four vehicles had been dealt with (G 175-177, 264). Many were withdrawn early to become driver training buses and the last, Gs 264 and 313 at

Enfield, were taken out of passenger service on 1st February 1952. The sole Duple-bodied Guy, G 43, had ceased operating earlier than this but the Massey contingent represented the first large sub-class to be withdrawn in its entirety.

The Massey Guys led a much more static life than other classes and were allocated officially only to five garages including Alperton's single specimen which was instantly recognisable as the only one of its type operating in west London. The remainder of the first batch (G 175-193) served their time at Barking before many became trainers. Victoria received all except G 258 of the second batch and also had G 312-314 of the third; these passed quickly to Enfield where they remained, representing the only time when an inter-garage transfer of Massey Guys for passenger service took place. The balance of the second and third batches and all of the fourth spent their lives at Hornchurch until several of these also took up training duties towards the end of their days. Surprisingly, although Massey-bodied Guys were always a common sight in east London, none was ever officially allocated to Upton Park, the most prolific operator of Guys, although they regularly passed close to its doors.

G 154-173, 219-257, 269-311 – NORTHERN COUNTIES

May 1945 saw the arrival of the first examples of two further new batches of Guys. Slightly ahead by a few days, on the 1st of the month, was G 154 from the Northern Counties Motor & Engineering Company Ltd which, like Massey, was a well established Lancashire manufacturer whose products had made little penetration into the southern half of the country in pre-war days. Over the course of the ensuing eleven months Northern Counties was to supply no fewer than 102 new bodies to London which, though they came from the same home town of Wigan, could not have been more different from the Massey products which they ran alongside. Northern Counties had been one of the pioneers of steel framed bodies, sometimes known as 'all-metal', the timber content within them being restricted principally to the front and rear bulkheads, which were steel reinforced, and to fillets for the securing of panels, etc. Because of their established production system Northern Counties were permitted to continue building metal framed bodies throughout the war, and their products were inherently far superior to those produced by Massey who had to rely on supplies of 'green' timber for body framing. As curvaceous as the Massey bodies were angular, they have often been described as handsome, and justifiably so.

The Northern Counties design employed the same steep degree of front end slope as Park Royal, but that was as far as the similarity went. The company had been quick off the mark in abandoning the total 'utility' appearance in favour of a relaxed austerity style by incorporating very rounded domes at front and rear and a full set of opening windows. Together with the radiused window pans to carry rubber-mounted 'Simplastic' glazing, which had been used throughout as an inherent part of the design structure, these features helped the Northern Counties body to take on a thoroughly peacetime appearance, and even more so once the upper saloon front ventilators were dispensed with as happened part way through the London production run. Inside the vehicles it was a different story. Single skin panelling was still the order of the day and the first batch of twenty (G 154-173) even had wooden seats, the very last to be delivered to London Transport. G 219 upwards were equipped with brown leathercloth-covered cushions and brown grab handles. All the wooden internal mouldings were also dark brown, and taking into account the fact that the windows were shallower than on all other utilities and thus gave in rather less light, the overall result was a rather sombre if solid appearance in stark contrast to the effect of bright airiness imparted by most of their contemporaries. The metal body construction naturally incurred additional weight, but at 7tons 13cwt the Northern Counties bodies were nevertheless lighter than the two metal bodies received from Weymann and one which was yet to come from Park Royal. London Transport classified the G 154-173 batch as 1/3G10 (of which Gs 155, 167 and 169 at Alperton were later 4/3G10), followed by G 219-257 and G 269-300 which had a modified

The first style of Northern Counties body carried upper deck front ventilators but no nearside indicator box. G 169 demonstrates these features and also the predominantly brown colour scheme applied to the earlier deliveries. It came as a surprise to find, upon boarding these handsome looking vehicles, that they had wooden seats. R W Burrell

Viewed from the rear, there was nothing in the curvaceous lines of the Northern Counties design to link it with the utility bodies coming from other manufacturers. G 222, photographed at Raynes Park soon after entering service, was numerically only the fourth Northern Counties vehicle to carry upholstered seats from new.
Alan B Cross

The single skinned ceiling in the upper saloon was particularly noticeable because the framework swept down into both domes. Perhaps because of the metal framework, the upper deck ceiling tended to drum more on Northern Counties bodies than on other utilities. A grab rail is missing from one of the seats on G 294, by no means an uncommon feature in later life. John C Gillham

rear bulkhead and were classified 1/3G10/1. The final eleven, G 301-311, were mounted on chassis with constant mesh gearbox and single plate clutch and became 2/3G10/1. In addition to the changeover to upholstered seats two other visible body modifications took place during the production run. The first saw the elimination of the upstairs front ventilators which occurred on G 222 and from G 226 upwards, whilst on vehicles numbered G 239 and above a nearside indicator box was provided above the platform. The Northern

Counties Guys were the first to incorporate a front destination aperture of the same 20inch depth as the standard side box instead of the 15inch version received hitherto, although the extra depth was never used and the lower section was masked out, originally in black and later in the main body colour, brown or red.

Like Massey, Northern Counties did not have ready access to supplies of London red paint and used brown as a substitute. The shade appeared to be slightly deeper than Massey's version, an effect heightened on

vehicles up to and including G 239 which were almost entirely brown with only a single pale cream relief band around the centre. From G 240 onwards the effect was lighter as these also had pale cream window surrounds except at the upstairs rear where the brown of the roof swept down attractively to embrace the dome and the emergency window. There were five exceptions which were delivered in London Transport's own red and white livery. These were G 173 (the last wooden seater) on which the brown roof swept down at the rear in the style subsequently introduced on G 240, and Gs 229, 238, 251 and 270 which were similar except that the brown of the roof stopped short of the rear dome which was painted red. Unusually on all vehicles, whether brown or red, the rear mudguards were painted in the main body colour and did not match the black ones at the front.

Above **G 285, photographed in September 1946 when almost a year old, shows the final development of the Northern Counties body including the side indicator box fitted to G 239 onwards, and the second style of brown livery making much greater use of cream relief.** D W K Jones

Left **On Northern Counties bodies the bulkhead windows were set at a higher level than the side ones. When new, the top bulkhead panel was polished, as on contemporary Massey bodies, but this was painted cream along with the adjacent side panels and ceiling at overhaul.** John C Gillham

For the first few months Northern Counties delivered on the basis of a regular fifteen buses each month, apart from a hiatus in September when insufficient chassis were available and only six were built. Towards the end, however, the rate dwindled significantly with none arriving between 28th December 1945 and 20th February 1946. The final delivery, G 311, came on 28th March. It is interesting to record that it was one of the last three Guy chassis to be supplied to London Transport under the wartime programme (Gs 310, 311 and 435 were all received on 16th February), and it only missed being the last completed Guy to be taken into stock by two days. Perhaps even more noteworthy was the fact that it was the last vehicle of all to be supplied for London service painted brown. This was also fated to be the last Northern Counties body purchased by London Transport or its successors for 41 years. During the course of the production run Northern Counties had also built a few identical bodies for the Corporations of Accrington and Edinburgh, and also for Youngs Bus Service of Paisley, Western SMT and Southdown. However by the end of the period other operators were already receiving bodies of an even more modern appearance with front domes blending into the corner pillars and outswept skirts but, presumably for standardisation purposes, the London Transport vehicles continued to be produced to the earlier style.

The batch of twenty with wooden seats retained them through to their first overhaul in 1948/9. The last of them to go for overhaul, Barking's G 168, finally ran with wooden seats on 16th February 1949 and was the very last London bus to do so, snatching the record from Merton's last wooden seated Daimler by just a few weeks. Because of the stronger structure of these vehicles the programme for their first overhaul cycle was still not imminent towards the end of 1947 when it was decided to set a repainting programme in train to put them into red livery. Unfortunately London Transport did not keep accurate records of the repainting dates from brown to red for any of its vehicles so it is not known for sure when the last brown ones disappeared. However Northern Counties-bodied Guys were certainly amongst the last brown ones to run in London with Gs 233 and 239 at Enfield and G 256 at Hornchurch still in their original colours well into the late summer of 1948. The style adopted for them when repainted was almost exactly the same as that carried from new by G 173 including the brown rear dome, the only difference being that the emergency window itself was picked out, rather fussily, in white. This scheme lasted only until the overhaul programme commenced in August 1948 when the livery was again modified by extending the white of the upper deck window frames around the back dome; on many vehicles the earlier scheme was carried only for a matter

of a few months, and in some cases weeks, before they received yet another coat of paint on overhaul. In 1951 about twenty received the modern all-red livery either on overhaul or as part of a small repainting programme.

The Northern Counties Guys were more ubiquitous than some other groups and only Seven Kings never had an allocation, but this garage came late on the Guy scene anyway. Admittedly Tottenham, which was noted principally for its fleet of Arab Mk Is, had only G 221 for three weeks in July 1945, whilst the class maintained merely a tenuous foothold in west London where the only examples to stay for any length of time were the three Alperton ones already mentioned and Gs 288 and 299 at Hanwell. Even Victoria collected 25 of them in 1945 as part of its short lived Arab fleet. At Enfield, Barking, Hornchurch and Upton Park they played a major part in the everyday scene throughout the Guy era.

As time passed a healthy respect grew for the strength and workmanship of the Northern Counties bodies, and though London Transport's engineers would have preferred to retain only this type through to the end of Guy operation a demand for them on the second hand market caused many to be sold ahead of less healthy specimens. At the close of Guy operation late in 1952 eight out of the final twelve at Upton Park were Northern Counties bodied; these were Gs 170, 252, 254, 257, 293, 297, 308 and 309 which were delicensed on 24th December.

The centrepiece in this scene at Golders Green is G 288, demonstrating the rear dome treatment of the second brown and cream livery. Like Massey, Northern Counties used a slightly darker shade of brown for the roof than was applied to the side panels. Coincidentally all three vehicles in this early post-war scene carry metal framed bodies, a type of construction then very much in the minority in the double deck fleet. On the left is a Park Royal bodied STL; on the right a Leyland bodied STD.
LT Museum

G 286 demonstrates the first, very short lived red livery as applied to many Northern Counties bodies which included a brown painted rear dome with the emergency window picked out in white. Most vehicles ran in this form for only a few months.
S L Poole

The standard red and white livery as applied at overhaul is shown on G 165 shortly after it was dealt with in April 1949, at which time it also gained upholstered seats. The continuation of the white window relief around the rear dome was not as well suited to the curved body lines as the earlier arrangement.
J H Aston

G 139-149, 151-153, 194-218 – PARK ROYAL/NORTHERN COACHBUILDERS

Park Royal was the appointed bodybuilder for the first fifteen Guys allocated to London Transport under the 1945 programme, to which fleet numbers G 139-153 were allocated, and they also gained a share of the second contract with 25 vehicles numbered G 194-218. The two orders were placed less than a month apart and for production purposes Park Royal treated them as if they were one. With special permission from the Ministry of Supply one body out of the first fifteen was a metal framed experimental unit built for evaluaton purposes with post-war production in mind; this became G 150 and is dealt with later in this chapter. The remainder were all based on Park Royal's standard utility body frame, but for the first time from this manufacturer they incorporated some relaxed austerity features. In truth these features, which consisted of additional opening windows and a rounded rear dome, did not amount to much in a visual sense as the overall utility shape was retained and so were the wartime-style front ventilators. Because the rear of the body remained austerely upright even the rounded, shallow rear dome barely made any impact. The family relationship between these and previous Park Royal utilities was very obvious although the new bodies were slightly neater in eliminating the secondary waist rail moulding to provide flush panelling on the lower deck.

As the time approached for the chassis to be delivered from Guy's it became clear that undue delay would occur in constructing the bodies unless steps were taken to clear a backlog of work which had accumulated at Park Royal. By arrangement with the Ministry of Supply it was agreed that some of the bodies could be built at Northern Coachbuilders' factory in Northumberland. The latter temporarily had spare capacity so the machined timber and other components from Park Royal's stock were duly transferred northwards. This was not the only time that construction of utility bodies was subcontracted; Duple resorted to the same remedy when overwhelmed by work on Bedford OWBs, but this was the only London order ever handled in this manner. Park Royal was, of course, still the main contractor and the completed bodies were always regarded by London Transport as having been built by them even though they carried a Northern Coachbuilders' transfer on the staircase rather than Park Royal's sedan chair motif.

Details of the exact commercial arrangements between the two manufacturers have not been confirmed but it appears that agreement was reached for a trial body to be built, depending upon the outcome of which a further fifteen were to be sanctioned. G 139 served as the test bed to iron out any problems which Northern Coachbuilders may have encountered through assembling a body different from their own, and it was delivered complete from Cramlington on 4th May 1945, three days after Northern Counties' first delivery. Both types entered London service for the first time on 1st June. The main production batch of fifteen came in a steady flow from 1st June and was complete by 5th July, the vehicles concerned being Gs 140-149, 151-

A black and white photograph cannot do justice to the striking brown and ochre livery which brought a colourful new dimension to the London bus scene when G 139 entered service on 1st June 1945. Although assembled by Northern Coachbuilders, the vehicle exhibits all of Park Royal's regular features including the sloping ledge below the driver's cab window, and bears little resemblance to the standard NCB body on G 30.

153, 194 and 195. Subsequently Northern Coachbuilders was asked to assemble a further ten (G 196-205) which were all delivered in the last two weeks of August. The bodies which they produced were totally indistinguishable from the standard Park Royal product except insofar as their upholstery was concerned. Although the seat frames themselves were of the type used (and probably supplied) by Park Royal, Northern Coachbuilders provided its own covering material which turned out to be an attractive orange/brown moquette, far more welcoming in appearance than Park Royal's usual dark brown leathercloth. Northern Coachbuilders also supplied their own paint, and here they excelled themselves by producing the most spectacular brown-based livery of any. The main mid-brown panels and reddish brown roof were relieved by window pillars in a rich ochre-type yellow, the resultant appearance closely resembling the attractive livery employed for many years by West Bridgford UDC. Only G 151-153 differed in that their relief was a much more sombre pale cream giving an appearance similar to that of many contemporary utility Daimlers. Park Royal specified a minor design change on the final ten bodies which resulted in the fitment of a deeper (20 inch) front destination display and the provision of a side indicator box above the platform entrance which the earlier bodies had been without.

Delivery on 31st August of G 205 meant

that Northern Coachbuilders had built its last motor bus body for London Transport. However its connection with the Board was not yet completely severed as twenty new trolleybus bodies were on the stocks to be supplied from December 1945 onwards. One more motor bus body would have been built if all had gone to plan in the form of a new utility style body mounted on the war damaged chassis of side engined single decker Q 217. Something went wrong, however, and Q 217's chassis returned to Chiswick from Cramlington together with a kit of newly machined body parts which were paid for but never assembled.

A short delay ensued before the arrival of G 206-218 built by Park Royal themselves, but when they finally came it was at the remarkable rate of one per day between 1st and 13th October. These were in standard London red livery and had leathercloth-trimmed seats, but in all other respects they were identical to G 196-205. Vehicles numbered between G 139 and 153 (except of course G 150) were originally coded 1/3G8 but this was soon modified to 4/3G8 in the case of four (Gs 142, 145, 148 and 153) which were at Alperton. The second batch was originally also coded 1/3G8 but their body classification was quickly revised to G8/1; this probably hid an inconsistency and it may well have been that only G 196 upwards, with the modified indicator arrangement, should have been recoded. With an unladen weight of 7tons 5cwt these were the lightest Guys ever to join the fleet.

The brown vehicles began to go to Chiswick to receive red livery, either on overhaul or repaint, towards the end of 1947. Most were dealt with within a few months but G 199 at Hornchurch was still sporting its vivid brown and yellow colours as late as September 1948. Just over half of the batch received all-red livery in 1951 even though some were withdrawn later in the same year. During their operating lives this batch of Guys was confined almost entirely to Alperton, Enfield and Hornchurch although Victoria received some of the Northern Coachbuilders contingent when new and there were also odd ones in the early days at Tottenham, Barking and Upton Park. History repeated itself when Tottenham and Barking received three and two respectively towards the end of the Guy era. Nine of the type lasted in service at Enfield until as late as September 1952, the last, G 198, being withdrawn on the 12th of that month.

The first and second batches of Northern Coachbuilders bodies differed from each other only in their route indicator equipment. This was presumably enhanced on later vehicles at London Transport's request although the extra depth of the front indicator box was never put to good use. Gs 145 and 205 were both photographed after receiving red livery; G 205 was the last of the Northern Coachbuilders contingent and, unlike G 145, still retained its original masked side lights. The 'genuine' Park Royal product is represented by G 215 which demonstrates that it is identical in external appearance to its Northumberland-built look-alike. F G Reynolds/D A Jones/Alan T Smith

Park Royal's relaxed austerity design included a rounded rear dome but otherwise made very little concession to the post-utility era. The plainness of this body design was emphasised, even more than before, when the drab 1950 livery was applied as in the case of NCB bodied G 141.
Alan T Smith

Moquette covered seats indicate that the saloon interiors illustrated here are of Northern Coachbuilders origin, the upper deck being of G 144 and the lower deck G 148. Except for the seats, there is almost no difference internally between these and later vehicles in the G 72-136 batch.
John C Gillham

G 369-430 – WEYMANN

Although they were delivered without a break, the vehicles in this 62-strong batch actually comprised two distinct orders for 30 and 32 respectively, construction of which was authorised in April and June 1945. Together with five from Park Royal, the second batch comprised London Transport's final allocation of utility Guys. All 62 were structurally identical but, as delivered, the first batch could be distinguished from the second through being in brown livery. Most had brown panels and roof with off white window frames although Gs 388 and 391 are reported to have been in all-over brown, but this has not been confirmed. G 399 onwards came in standard London Transport red and white.

The first arrival from Addlestone was G 369 on 31st August 1945; it entered service at Hornchurch on 15th September. More than two years had elapsed since Weymann's last major delivery to London, the only purchases in the intervening period having been experimentally bodied Gs 137 and 138. During the latter part of the war the company had concentrated mostly on building low height bodies and its return to the highbridge style introduced a new relaxed austerity design which was simple but reasonably attractive. The main recognition features of the 1942/3 period had been retained, including the softened front profile achieved by angling the windscreen less than the body line above it, and the high windows on the driver's offside. The rear was still as upright as before but only to the upper deck waistrail above which the entire rear dome was rounded. Unlike the earlier batches, the front of the body now had a normal inward taper, and opening ventilators were omitted from the upstairs front windows. A side indicator box was provided and the front box was now of the deeper type with the bottom 5ins masked in black.

Internally much of the previous Weymann styling was retained including the light varnished finish to the slender window pillars and other exposed woodwork, but the opening windows were now of the Beclawat winding type and the brown leathercloth seats were based on tubular frames with chromium plated top rails, the use of this type of seat frame having been officially permitted from March 1945 onwards. The interior was typically cheap and cheerful but also light and airy, the very opposite of the solid but much gloomier feel of the Northern Counties bodies which were being delivered at the same time.

These 62 buses represented the longest continuously-numbered batch of identical vehicles in the Guy fleet. Their construction, which was interspersed with identical bodies for Southdown, East Kent and Edinburgh Corporation, was completed with the receipt of G 430 on 5th December 1945. By now the semi-utility body style had already become obsolete and full scale construction of peacetime standard all-metal bodies was under way, bodies of this type having arrived from Addlestone since 26th November to fulfil the order for twenty AEC Regents (STL 2682-2701) which had also formed part of London Transport's 1945 allocation. In styling, standard of construction and quality of finish, the STL bodies were as different from those on the Guys as they could possibly be.

The 1945 batch of Weymann bodies had a crisp, uncluttered appearance both inside and out, and were quite handsome in a functional way. G 407 still showed signs of newness when photographed coping with bank holiday crowds at Chingford soon after the war.
S L Poole

The nearside of the Weymann semi-utility body is seen in this view of G 412 which was presumably on private hire duties when photographed. The practice of posting traffic notices and slogans on the nearside panelling, and circular advertisements on the window glass, did not last long into the post-war era. W J Haynes

Although the basic utility lines were still retained, Weymann managed to incorporate a modicum of modernity by rounding-off the upper rear portion of the body, in contrast to contemporary Park Royal practice.
The vehicle is G 400.
F G Reynolds

At 7tons 6cwt the unladen weight of G 369-430 was just one hundredweight heavier than the contemporary Park Royal bodied Guys to which the Weymanns bore the closest structural and visual resemblance. They received the coding 1/3G11 although three Alperton vehicles (Gs 370, 372, 376) later became 4/3G11. None ever received the 1950 all-red livery style. Being such a large class they were inevitably widely spread amongst Guy garages, all of which had an allocation except Victoria for whom they came too late.

However their use was by no means evenly distributed; Tottenham had only three for a three month spell in 1946 and for much of the Guy era only four were visible in west London, three at Alperton and one at Hanwell. Perhaps not as strongly constructed as some of the other Guy sub-classes, many suffered fairly early withdrawal and only 13 out of the 62 lasted beyond 1951. G 392 must have been better than the rest for it managed to soldier on at Upton Park until the operation of utility Guys finally ceased in December 1952.

G 150 – PARK ROYAL

G 150 was very visibly an odd man out. This vehicle carried Park Royal's experimental metal framed body which was built by permission of the Ministry of Supply as a trial run in advance of the company's planned post war production. Its chassis was taken into stock on 5th March 1945, but it then spent almost six months at Park Royal and the completed vehicle was not delivered to Chiswick until 1st September 1945. G 150 entered service at Alperton on the 10th; it remained there through to its withdrawal on 1st July 1952.

Park Royal had first introduced its own patented type of all-metal body towards the end of 1934. Its unusual pillar section was T-shaped with the flange of the T facing into the saloon; a channel section was added to the head of the T containing a wooden fillet on which to secure the exterior panels and mouldings. Because of the shape of the framework it was impossible to employ the customary wooden internal mouldings which even metal framed bodies (such as those built by Northern Counties and Weymann) normally had, there being no flat surface to fix them to. Park Royal overcame this by employing half round metal cappings which were normally covered in rexine, and in doing so became the first major bodybuilder to break away from the traditional polished wood interior trim. In London this style had already been employed on double deckers on a batch of 175 Park Royal bodied STLs and also on 50 trolleybuses, and it was again to be found on G 150. The advantage of Park Royal's patented body frame was said to be that, in the absence of any cavity, condensation was unlikely to occur. Additionally, in order to inhibit rust, Park Royal treated all joints with non-corrosive solution and painted the frame with carbolastic paint. Unfortunately, as London Transport was already finding to its cost and as Park Royal themselves were now aware, their pre-war metal bodies were by no means as corrosion proof as claimed and were, in fact, far more rust prone than the products of most of their competitors. It is presumed that one of the reasons for building G 150's body was to try out improvements to tackle the corrosion problem, and in its fifteen year existence (including its life after London) it certainly appeared much more corrosion resistant than earlier ones had done.

Top and Centre **Nearside rear views of G 150 taken just after completion in August 1945 but before the application of transfers, and still with its original paintwork in December 1948 after three years in service, show that the only minor modification made by London Transport was the fitment of an advertisement moulding along the mid-decks side panels. The 1948 view shows a very late example of the use of the old type of route-numberless side blind.** Park Royal/Alan B Cross

Right **The prominently radiused lower window corners and sliding ventilators were distinctive features of G 150's prototype body. The manufacture of ten more bodies of this sort was subsequently approved by the Ministry of Supply and these were supplied to provincial operators.** Alan B Cross

In general outline G 150 closely resembled the standard Park Royal wartime body in its slightly relaxed form and yet it managed to look entirely different at a glance from all the others. This was because of its prominently radiused bottom window corners and the fact that it carried sliding ventilators instead of the usual half drop windows, the only London utility to do so. The six upper deck and four lower deck sliders were the same in number as the half drops which would normally have been fitted, but as conventional metal rain shields were employed the opening apertures were partly covered and their effectiveness somewhat reduced. Internally much use was made of dark brown rexine to cover the window cappings and other mouldings whilst the seats were in matching brown leathercloth. The vehicle was delivered in standard red and white livery, which it retained throughout its time in London, and was classified firstly as 1/3G12 and later as 4/3G12. Being the last basic new type of body to be received on a Guy chassis, albeit only one day later than the first Weymann-built G11, this bus received the highest numbered body classification given to any of the wartime era Guys. At 7tons 15cwt G 150 weighed exactly half a ton more than its composite counterparts from the same factory, the slower performance and slightly worsened fuel consumption resulting from this being the price that had to be paid to obtain the longer life which the body offered.

G 319-357, 431-435 – PARK ROYAL

The final category of Guy came from the Park Royal factory between November 1945 and March 1946. Two batches, comprising 39 and 5 vehicles, represented respectively the major share of an April 1945 order for fifty for which Massey built the remaining eleven, and a June order for 37 of which Weymann built the lion's share of 32. Park Royal's deliveries were running well behind schedule and the first of the new vehicles, Gs 319 and 321, did not arrive at Chiswick until 17th November, more than two months after Massey had completed its part of the contract. It took until 3rd March 1946 for the last delivery in the first batch to arrive; the second group of five joined the fleet between 18th and 30th March. The final arrival, G 435, was also the highest numbered utility Guy and it came on the scene three weeks after the final wartime-style Duple bodied Daimler. It carried the very last of the 637 utility and semi-utility bodies supplied to London Transport by seven manufacturers. Disappointingly Park Royal made no attempt whatever to soften the body lines to give a more 'peace time' appearance and the vehicles were identical externally to those in the G 196-218 batch, keeping the almost bolt upright back and utility style front ventilators well after other manufacturers had dispensed with these features. The only improvements were internal; winding windows and tubular framed seats were now the order of the day.

These outmoded-looking vehicles came correctly painted in full London Transport red livery and carried the same weight of 7tons

5cwt as the previous Park Royal batch. Those numbered up to G 339 were classified as 1/3G8/2 whilst G 340 upwards were 2/3G8/2 to denote that they had the new single plate clutch and constant mesh gearbox. With the exception of three which were delivered to Barking (G 343-345) the entire class of 42 became almost inextricably linked with Upton Park. One of the Barking trio (G 345) later moved to Seven Kings, in whose small fleet it was the sole example with constant mesh box, and late in 1951 four of the lower numbered ones with the older type transmission moved across to end their days at Enfield. A constant mesh vehicle, G 353, also went to Enfield but only for a week in late January

1952 just before its withdrawal, this being the only occasion on which a vehicle of the 2/3G type was transferred away from east London. None of the small batch numbered in the four hundred series was ever allocated anywhere except Upton Park.

In 1951 twelve of the 21 non-constant mesh type received a second overhaul which found them in the new all-red livery, auguring well for them to last in service well into the closing stages of utility Guy operation. In fact three of the class – but strangely none of the more recently overhauled ones – survived to the last day of operation in December 1952; these were Gs 347, 350 and 432.

London's Guy Arabs were synonymous with the utility era, and it was perhaps fitting that the last to be delivered should be Park Royal bodied just as the first had been. G 431, one of the final batch of five, was photographed at East Ham in September 1949. Alan B Cross

Tubular framed seats and winding window mechanisms were the modern features which distinguished the final Park Royal batches from their forerunners. A view looking rearwards in the upper deck of G 335. Ken Blacker

CHAPTER SIX

THE DAIMLERS

When the demands of war caused the removal in November 1941 of Leyland from its planned position as one of the two wartime manufacturers of double deck bus chassis, the operating arm of the industry feared the worst. Only Guy was left to fulfil everyone's requirements, and as they were unable to increase production beyond the level already planned it seem inevitable that a catastrophic shortfall in double deck availability would be unavoidable. The Ministry of Supply encouraged operators to take the Bedford OWB instead to substitute in many of the roles where double deckers would normally be employed, but the difference in seating capacity between 32 and 56 was simply too great to make the Bedford an acceptable alternative except in a very few cases, with the result that only a small proportion of the total OWB output went to large companies or municipal operators. The Ministry had in fact suspected that this would be the case and worked very hard indeed to try to find a replacement for Leyland.

The solution lay with Transport Vehicles (Daimler) Ltd. Manufacturing capacity at Daimler's large Radford works had been completely knocked out during the Coventry blitz of November 1940, in the process destroying many partly completed bus chassis. The company had since set up dispersal factories and a building at Wolverhampton, quite close to Guy's works, was requisitioned from Courtaulds by the Ministry of Supply on Daimler's behalf for use in the production of tanks. The Ministry came to the conclusion that, if an increase in the supply of double deck bus chassis was essential, this would have to be the location where they would be constructed. Daimler's management assured the Ministry that, given a guaranteed supply of the necessary materials, they could organise a production line very quickly as all the drawings, design expertise and some of the tooling relating to the pre-war COG5 model had survived and modifications could easily be made to incorporate wartime specifications. The Ministry was not entirely convinced that resumption would be as quick or straightforward as Daimler had claimed but could see no alternative. They managed to secure an allocation of materials for an initial run of one hundred vehicles except for one seemingly insurmountable stumbling block; the country's entire engine production capacity was totally committed for the foreseeable

future and no suitable source of engines could be found. The only possible way out lay in diverting engines from another source, and in February 1942 the mandarins at the Ministry of Supply asked their counterparts at the Ministry of War Transport whether they would be willing to forgo the manufacture of one hundred Atkinson 12 ton lorries in order to release Gardner 5LW engines for fitting into an equivalent number of Daimler buses. The MoWT was reluctant, but early in March the Minister himself, Aubrey Clark, intervened and pronounced that the bus building programme held greater priority and should go ahead.

The sloping radiator of the CWA6, which caused the model to very slightly exceed the legal maximum length, is shown clearly on Duple bodied D 4. Lowbridge Daimler utilities quickly became an established feature in the provinces but London's fleet, which eventually totalled a mere ten such vehicles, remained something of a curiosity. S L Poole

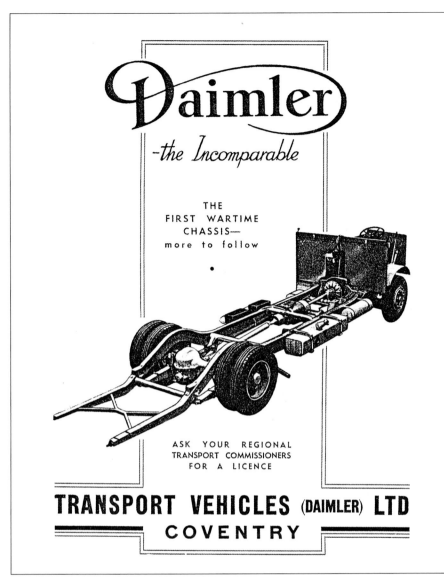

Daimler
–the Incomparable

THE
FIRST WARTIME
CHASSIS—
more to follow

•

ASK YOUR REGIONAL
TRANSPORT COMMISSIONERS
FOR A LICENCE

TRANSPORT VEHICLES (DAIMLER) LTD
COVENTRY

Production did not commence quite as quickly as expected. One initially unforeseen problem was that the only producers of heavy passenger chassis, Guy, Daimler and Sunbeam (for trolleybuses) were by coincidence all based in Wolverhampton and output was 'seriously menaced' – to use the Ministry of Supply's own term – by a shortage in the town of skilled labour which required the intervention of the Ministry of Labour to overcome. Once production started, a morale problem arose within the Daimler workforce who felt that their job was contributing much less to the war effort than the tank builders whom they worked alongside, and they needed special reassurance to overcome this. Daimler modified the COG5 as little as possible to produce the CWG5 (W standing for Wartime) and promised to build the first hundred chassis in twelve months with a stepping up of the production rate thereafter. In December 1942 the first one rolled off the production line.

The wartime Daimler conformed closely to its pre-war counterpart and even the substitution of cast iron for aluminium alloys only raised the chassis weight by 6cwt. The vacuum-hydraulic braking system was retained as was the worm-and-nut type steering gear, and the wheelbase stayed the same at 16ft 3⁵⁄₃₂ins. For a decade Daimler had standardised on a transmission system consisting of preselector gearbox coupled to a fluid flywheel and continued to do so throughout the war. There were presumably sound engineering reasons for this but nevertheless the continued production of epicyclic type gearboxes, which contained some 59 more moving parts than the simple crash box on the Guy, was surprising at a time when the utmost frugality in the use of manpower and materials was usually insisted upon. Daimler was no longer able to supply its own rear axle and a Kirkstall unit was substituted. The resultant vehicle was almost universally regarded as being rather more refined than the Guy Arab and it made a useful addition to the nation's stock of double deck buses at a time of desperate need. None of the first contract for one hundred Daimlers was allocated to London Transport; this was a deliberate decision by the Ministry of War Transport who considered that the Board had received all that could be justified in its allocation of Guys and that needs were greater elsewhere. However this omission was more than rectified in later production runs when wartime Daimlers became an everyday feature of the London bus scene.

From the 101st chassis onwards an alternative engine had to be sought as no more Gardners could be made available, and it was duly arranged that AEC would build the A173 version of its famous 7.7 engine for this purpose. Daimler gave the resultant chassis the model classification CWA6 and also fitted it with a new, one piece radiator distinguishing it visibly from the CWG5 and pre-war models. The painted cast iron shell· had a coarse, wire mesh grille and, as usual with Daimler, bore no maker's name, the fluted top tank presumably being considered an adequate recognition feature. Instead of being completely upright, as on the CWG5, the CWA6 radiator sloped slightly backwards; in fact the bottom projected forward of the earlier design resulting in the vehicle exceeding the regulation 26ft maximum length, and although the excess length amounted to rather less than one inch special permits had to be issued for the operation of these vehicles. The AEC engine had been fitted pre-war to a number of Daimlers built for Coventry Corporation, thus there were no problems over its installation in the CWA6. Unlike the Gardner engine on the Guy Arab (and indeed on the CWG5), it was not rubber mounted.

The Daimler utility double decker was by no means universally popular with operators on two scores; many were not happy with its transmission system which often required special training for both engineering and driving staff who were not used to it, and its price was considered far too high. At £1655 it was 47½% dearer than the pre-war Daimler and considerably more expensive than the Guy (currently £1395). Operators' and coachbuilders' representatives also queried why the Daimler could not have been built to achieve much greater standardisation with the Guy Arab to enable bodies and some other items to be interchangeable. Amongst the problems encountered, the Daimler had a lower chassis height but rose more at the front end, and it had approximately 1⅛ inch less body length available. The Ministry explained that the Daimler had adhered rigidly to pre-war dimensions so that existing jigs could be fully utilised, but nevertheless a full investigation was made to ascertain whether greater standardisation could be achieved. The conclusion was that this would be both difficult and uneconomic.

D 139, the third CWD6 to enter London service, shows the Daimler design of back axle by which these vehicles could be easily recognised. CWD6s were normally fitted with plain bonnet sides, but at a very early date, if not from new, London's had an inspection hole inserted, albeit in a different position from that on the AEC engined fleet. Lens of Sutton

London Transport viewed the opportunity to secure CWA6s with anticipation. Together with a nucleus of municipal operators it actually favoured a preselector-type transmission, whilst any opportunity to return to the AEC 7.7 engine upon which it had standardised in pre-war days was seen as welcome. The Board's first allocation of Daimler CWA6s, a mere six vehicles numbered D 1-6, was made on 18th October 1943. The first chassis was delivered on 15th February 1944 and the completed vehicles were received from the coachbuilders in April and May. These were low height vehicles bodied by Duple. Subsequent allocations under the Acquisition & Disposal of Vehicles Order brought the total up to 131 as follows:

January 1944: D 7-61, 28 Duple, 27 Brush
June 1944: D 62-73 Brush bodies (12)
November 1944: D 74-92 Duple bodies (19)
January 1945: D 93-127 Brush bodies (35)
June 1945: D 128-131 Massey bodies (4)

Delivery took place between July 1944 and November 1945 and the final batch, consisting of a further four lowbridge vehicles, was reallocated to Duple before construction commenced. Fortunately a serious early defect resulting in failure of the master cylinder on the braking system which plagued early utility Daimlers had been cured jointly by Daimler and Lockheed before London's first vehicles came on the scene. The new Daimler fleet was allocated entirely to Merton garage with which it became totally synonymous for the best part of a decade. Although far fewer in number than the Guys, the Daimlers became much better known because, to the casual observer, they were far more visible. The Guys led a largely suburban life and only Barking's route 23 penetrated the commercial and leisure hub of the West End by travelling the east-west axis of Oxford Street. Tottenham's route 76 skirted the centre to reach Victoria but otherwise made little impact. Merton's Daimlers, on the other hand, reached most of the main London 'sights' on routes 77/A but, more particularly, on the 88 which passed every point of note between Parliament Square and Marble Arch. The Daimlers were far more popular with their drivers than were the Guys. Although the AEC 7.7 engine derated as standard to 86bhp theoretically provided very little more power than the Gardner 5LW, it was a more responsive unit, added to which was the advantage of fast changes provided by the preselector gearbox. The gearchange selector lever itself was of Daimler's standard quadrant type mounted below the right of the steering wheel and totally unlike the AEC gearstick arrangement, so despite their many driving similarities the Daimlers were not exactly compatible with the STL fleet, hence their concentration at Merton. From the passenger's point of view the Daimlers were nothing special; the quality of ride was certainly no better and probably not quite as good as on the Guys, and whereas vibration was very noticeable on the 5LW when fully pushed, the 7.7 tended to thump at all speeds. The engine mountings were solid on the Daimler, unlike the Guy, and it may well also have been the case that wartime production methods or materials caused AEC's engines to be less refined than in pre-war days. Not surprisingly the CWA6s sounded fairly similar to STLs although with a discernibly different gearbox tone.

The final vehicle in the fourth batch, D 127, differed from all the others in being London Transport's first example of Daimler's new CWD6 model. This had an 8.6 litre engine built by Daimler themselves and also had a Daimler built rear axle, its flat hub being easily distinguishable from Kirkstall's more bulbous design. The radiator also differed in having vertical slats instead of a wire mesh grille, but this was a factor which any but a keen observer could easily miss. Daimler had been working on its CD6 engine since 1943 although the design concept dated from before the war, having culminated in some prototypes in 1939/40. The aim was to produce a smooth running, economical and compact engine occupying no more space than the Gardner 5LW. In common with the

So well known was the fluted radiator top that Daimler products, be they cars or larger vehicles, needed no accompanying name badge to identify them. However, London Transport's tradition was to fix its monogram to all vehicle radiators whenever possible and specially-made enamelled plates were riveted over the Daimler flutes. The version of the radiator carrying thin vertical slats instead of the wire mesh grille, first used only on CWD6s, had found its way on to AEC engined D 177 by August 1950. Alan B Cross

The D 132-181 batch comprised the only Daimlers delivered from Duple to carry side indicator boxes. More significantly, they were the last vehicles ever to be purchased by London Transport from this major London manufacturer. D 156, seen in original green and white livery, shows the positioning of the mid-decks Green Line motifs.

Gardner it retained the exhaust manifold on the driver's side of the engine, but it had a combined cylinder and crank case casting with removable dry liners and two separate cylinder heads. It introduced an unusual and ultimately unpopular feature in that the timing gears were placed at the back of the engine rather than at the front in the hope of producing more accurate fuel injection and smoother running. Fibre intermediate gears were installed in the timing case in a quest for greater quietness. The engine was capable of producing 100bhp at 1800rpm, the same governed rpm as the AEC 7.7 but 100rpm more than the Gardner. D 127 was noticeably livelier than other Daimlers. Its engine undoubtedly ran more smoothly and, though not particularly noisy, the vehicle had a distinctive and businesslike roar which was to become better known when further CWD6s joined the fleet.

In August 1945 London Transport agreed to take a further allocation of fifty Daimlers carrying Duple bodies; these became D 132-181. For the first time some members of the class operated from a garage other than Merton when 37 were painted green and sent to Romford for the post-war inauguration of double deck Green Line services on the main artery eastwards from Aldgate. The remaining thirteen went to Merton and all except one of these were similar to D 127 in being based on Daimler engined CWD6 chassis. London Transport had shown a degree of flexibility in accepting Daimler engines when it did not really want them. Some other operators, such as Manchester Corporation, flatly refused to do so, and as things turned out it would probably have been better if London Transport had taken a similar stand. Drivers favoured the Daimler engine for its nifty performance, except perhaps in the height of a hot summer when the closeness of the exhaust manifold to the cab side could render the cab uncomfortably hot, but it was much less favoured by Merton's engineers. The latter knew the 7.7 well, including its foibles such as high oil loss increasing with age and a tendency for the timing chain to slacken and sometimes to break, but overall it was an easy engine to keep in action. The Daimler soon produced irritating problems to such an extent that ten out of the thirteen were sent back to Daimler's agency in Willesden Lane in their second year

of operation for general rectification. A major drawback which was quickly discovered was that the position of the timing gear meant that the engine had to be removed whenever major repairs were necessary, and irritating problems such as cracks in the tops of cylinder liners further lengthened the time spent on repairs over and above that lost through unfamiliarity with the engine's unconventional features. Furthermore fuel consumption was significantly higher than promised. In 1950 London Transport decided to cut its losses and between March and September all thirteen vehicles were fitted with AEC engines which the engineers held in abundance due to the pace of the STL scrapping programme.

One more batch of Daimlers was yet to come to complete the D class. Exactly one hundred were included within London Transport's new bus allocation for the first half of 1946, the remaining double deckers being 65 Leyland PD1 (STD 112-176) and 166 RTs. On this occasion London Transport insisted that all one hundred should be AEC engined. Although chassis allocation still lay in the hands of the Ministry of War Transport, body procurement passed back into the hands of operators with effect from 1st January 1946. London Transport was unable to resume body construction at Chiswick where the works were fully stretched in catching up with the huge backlog of maintenance from the war years, so an order was placed with Park Royal for the bodies. The D 182-281 batch was delivered between April and November 1946 and was entirely allocated to Sutton garage. The bodies on these vehicles, though better finished than the utilities, were nevertheless closely based on the wartime body shell and were equally as susceptible to early deterioration. They were a cross between the utility on one hand and the full post-war standard on the other; a kind of half way mark. This final batch of Daimlers was never allocated anywhere but Sutton with the result that they normally got no closer to central London than Putney Bridge or Tooting. For this reason they never really gave the impression of being fully integrated into the main London fleet, remaining instead an isolated pocket of peculiar and distinctive vehicles found only in one compact area of suburban south London.

With the exception of the slightly unsatisfactory nature of the engines on the thirteen CWD6s the Daimlers suffered far fewer teething troubles than the Guys, as was only to be expected since the wartime Arab had been basically a new model whereas the Daimler CW series was merely an adaptation of an already successful design. Largely because of their greater acceptability to drivers, the Daimlers tended to remain longer in London service than the other utility classes. It was part of London Transport's strategic planning to retain them close to the end of the fleet renewal programme under which the RT family (plus a few low height RLHs) was due to oust everything else from the double deck fleet by 1954. To a certain extent rapidly deteriorating body condition dictated the pace of withdrawals, but it was a massive inflow of new RTs which brought about the final demise of the class in January 1954.

D 6 photographed very soon after entering service on 19th May 1944. Anti-splinter mesh has been fitted to the windows but is barely visible from this angle on the upper deck where it was only applied to the bottom halves of the windows, presumably for reasons of visibility. The high cab line, which readily distinguished Duple utility bodies from all others, is clearly demonstrated. No side advertisements were carried on this batch until after the war, and front ones were never fitted. C F Klapper

CHAPTER SEVEN

DAIMLERS IN DETAIL

D 1-6 – DUPLE

Nobody who has travelled on the upper deck of a wooden seated lowbridge Daimler utility will ever forget the sensation when all four occupants on one of the bench seats would slither sideways in unison on the slippery slats at each sharp turn; whenever the turn was a right hand one the outer passenger had to brace himself from sliding into the gangway. In London, at least, conductors generally loathed working on this type of vehicle but on routes such as Merton's 127 their use was unavoidable if double deck carrying capacity was to be harnessed. Until the arrival of new utilities the 127 was worked jointly by double and single deckers, but the granting of licences on 18th October 1943 for six new Daimlers to augment London Transport's hard pressed fleet of low height double deckers offered the opportunity of eliminating the remaining saloons from this route.

London Transport's earlier rejection of lowbridge Guys on the grounds that they would be higher than required had done nothing to solve the Board's desperate shortage of this specialised type of rolling stock. The subsequent availability of Daimler chassis offered a compromise solution; these were 1¼ins lower than the Guy so that, when bodied, they came a little closer in unladen height to London Transport's preferred 13ft 3ins. Duple was the nominated supplier of bodywork for the six CWA6s which were delivered between 24th April and 10th May 1944 and were totally identical to many supplied to operators nationwide, even to the extent of having an internally accessed front indicator box instead of the exterior opening screen previously insisted upon by London Transport. There was no side indicator box.

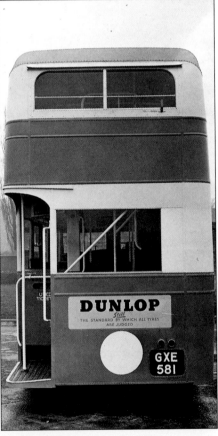

Before and after! A 1944 view of D 3 contrasts the original rear registration number arrangement with the modified version, as demonstrated by D 4, which was introduced when the vehicles were about a year old. The later view, taken in December 1947, also shows the revised livery treatment of the rear dome applied on first overhaul. W J Haynes/London Transport

Seating capacity in the standard utility body was 55, which was only one fewer than a conventional highbridge vehicle but rather more than many operators of this type had standardised upon in pre-war years. The upper saloon bench seats required very generous leg room to facilitate passenger movement, and this reduced the potential capacity to 27 comprising six benches each holding four passengers with the rear one, adjacent to the stairs, accommodating three. Downstairs two more passengers were squeezed in to compensate; this was achieved by adding an additional pair of transverse seats whilst at the same time reducing the wheel arch seat capacity from three to two, thereby achieving 28 seats in all. Internally D 1-6 complied completely with the standard for utility bodies in having single skinned side panels and roof and a general paucity of opening windows. Duple's interior finish was very like that of Park Royal and Weymann with a light grained effect created by varnishing the window pillars and various wooden mouldings. Rather surprisingly the whole of the front and rear bulkheads below cant rail level were covered in a patterned material called repp. This rather lavish feature contrasted greatly with the sheer austerity of the wooden seats and painted metal side panelling, and though the repp looked very attractive indeed when new and was theoretically hard wearing, in fact it took on a worn look fairly quickly through contact with knees and elbows and was not an entirely practical fitment for buses employed solely on hard urban work.

The six vehicles, which were classified as 1D1, weighed 7tons 6cwt which was 7cwt less than the latest batch of Guys, G 72-136, whose delivery had been completed just two months beforehand. They were painted into standard London red livery before entering service, a feature unique to this batch being that the narrow centre moulding separating the decks was picked out in black. Perhaps because of the very pronounced nature of the 'lobster back' arrangement as interpreted by Duple, which made it difficult to achieve a neat link between the brown roof panels and the white window band at the rear, the painters omitted the latter and extended the red of the upper deck panels upwards, embracing the emergency window and its surrounding panels and also taking in the lower of the two 'lobster back' folds.

At the first overhaul sequence, which occupied the period between July 1947 and April 1948, the wooden seats were replaced by moquette of the standard post-war pattern. Minor livery changes saw the elimination of the central black strip and continuation of the white upper deck window band around the back dome. Before this, rear illuminated registration plate holders had been fitted and the number of opening windows was increased to the accepted standard of two per side on the lower deck and three per side upstairs. On Ds 1 and 2 the additional half drops were of the pinch grip type resembling the originals, but the remainder found themselves with winding type windows in the lower saloon, retaining the pinch grip type on the upper deck only. D 2 further differed in that its lower saloon opening apertures were in the first and third bays instead of the second and fourth.

An upper deck view, looking forward, shows the original lamp covers fitted to comply with blackout requirements. Duple was unusual in picking-out the upper and end edges of the lighting panels with varnished wooden mouldings matching the rest of the interior woodwork. The long wooden benches were quite slippery, and it was by no means uncommon for passengers to slide sideways in unison when the vehicles cornered. LT Museum

The intrusion into the lower saloon of the sunken upper deck gangway resulted in very restricted headroom for passengers in the offside window seats and it was by no means an uncommon occurrence to hit one's head when standing up. The cloth lined front bulkhead contrasts starkly with the primitive wooden seats. LT Museum

The lowbridge buses at Merton were initially restricted by the Traffic Commissioner (with firm guidance from the Metropolitan Police) to route 127. After much persuasive effort, London Transport managed to get permission in about June 1948 to use those that were spare on Saturdays on special services such as Wimbledon Tennis and the Epsom Race service, but still only with the specific authority of the Commissioner. Presumably as a direct consequence of this, permission was obtained soon afterwards to run them on route 152 (like the 127, a purely suburban operation), which was then incorporated on the destination blinds. Between August 1950 and July 1951 all six received the all-red livery at their second overhaul and they ran in this rather drab style until December 1952 when new RLHs came along to replace them.

Right **The upstairs bench seats all accommodated four passengers except for the rearmost one which held three. This view shows D 6 in its post-January 1948 condition with its seating now covered in RT style moquette.** John C Gillham

Below **Slight livery and other variations marked out individual members of this small class in the period 1947-50 as shown in these four views, all taken at Morden station. On D 1 the white canopy band does not extend above the driver's cab window; D 2 shows its unique lower deck opening window layout underlined by white painted window ledges; D 3 carries the 'standard' livery arrangement; D 5 was the only one on which a nearside route number stencil was built into the bodywork. Seen on all four are the words LOW LOADER carried in white lettering on the push-out ventilator below the driver's windscreen.** Alan B Cross

D 7-34 – DUPLE

On 20th July 1944 D 7 was delivered to Chiswick; it was the first of 97 Duple bodied highbridge Daimlers destined to be delivered in three batches over a period of twenty months, with the second and third batches each showing design improvements over their predecessor as the wartime standards of body construction and equipment were gradually relaxed. The first batch consisted of 28 vehicles, D 7-34, representing just over half of a consignment of 55 for which licences were issued on 24th January 1944, the bodybuilder for the remainder being Brush. Delivery from Duple was completed on 8th October by the arrival of D 32 and all 28 were placed in service between 20th July and 24th October.

Both externally and in respect of their interior trim these were clear derivatives of the low height batch and at £895 the basic body price was the same although in this case it was reduced by £10 as they were delivered in primer and not in an undercoat-type finish. Chiswick's livery application was the same as on D 1-6 except that the centre strip was not picked out in black. A detail difference (apart of course from height) was that continuous rain shields were now fitted along each deck instead of a separate one above each opening window. A relaxation from the original wartime standard saw the incorporation of an illuminated rear registration plate from new, and another return to pre-war standards was marked by the provision of winding mechanism on the opening windows even though the quantity of such windows remained sparse. Sensibly the cloth covering on the front bulkhead was now restricted to the upper part with a more durable lino-covered section below. This batch of Daimlers tipped the scales at 7tons 7cwt and was given the London Transport code 1/1D2.

This was the first batch of utilities delivered to London Transport on which an in-built rear registration plate was fitted from new. The vehicle illustrated is D 23. *LT Museum*

The typical side profile of the Duple highbridge utility body is demonstrated by D 27 during a visit to Chiswick works in May 1946, including the exaggerated 'lobster back' dome arrangement favoured by this manufacturer. With the exception of the Northern Coachbuilders body on G 30, the Duple bodies were the only ones to carry a secondary moulding around the upper deck, which London Transport used as an upper edge for advertisements but never for livery purposes. *LT Museum*

However attractive in appearance the lining of almost the entire front bulkhead with cloth – as carried out on D 1-6 – may have been, it was hardly a practical arrangement, and the high level of wear likely to be encountered was acknowledged on the highbridge batch whose lower panels were covered in lino, which was considerably more kick resistant. In the lower saloon of D 27 can be seen the winding windows supplied for the first time on a batch of London utilities.
LT Museum

Six years separate these lower saloon views of Ds 27 and 30 taken in May 1946 and September 1951 respectively. Modifications which have been made during this period, apart from the obvious upholstering of the seats and the additional opening windows, include replacement of the cloth on the rear bulkheads by a painted finish and the provision of a standard London Transport style wooden floor using stout longitudinal slats in place of the original arrangement.
LT Museum/Alan B Cross

Soon after the war the process of installing additional opening windows started although not quite all of the vehicles had been dealt with before the first overhaul cycle commenced in January 1948. In most cases the extra half drops were of the same winding type as the originals but on Ds 21, 32 and 34 a full set of opening windows employing pinch-grip mechanism was installed. With the exception of D 7 which was dealt with slightly earlier, the whole of this batch was overhauled within a three month period which meant a rapid onslaught into the ranks of wooden seated Daimlers. The last wooden seated Duple example, D 32, ran on 31st March 1948. As with the low height batch, a livery modification at overhaul saw the continuation of the white upstairs window surrounds across the back of the vehicle in place of red. All 28 were subsequently overhauled into the 1950 all-red livery. Withdrawal of this batch commenced with D 27 on 14th October 1952 and was completed with the departure of D 24 on 2nd October 1953.

Post-war contrasts: D 13 illustrates the first post-war livery style, which in the case of this bus was carried for three years from April 1948 onwards, while D 19 demonstrates the final appearance which all this batch adopted between November 1950 and August 1951. S N J White/F G Reynolds

The war in Europe had less than two months still to run when D 50 entered service on 25th March 1945. The D 35-61 batch were the last utilities to be delivered with only two half-drop windows per deck and the first to carry the deeper style of destination screen. Brush chose to set the offside opening windows a bay further back than was customary at the time. J F Higham

D 35-61 – BRUSH

Despite its relative importance as a passenger vehicle builder over many years Brush Coachwork Ltd was never a major supplier to London Transport or its predecessors although a couple of batches of trolleybuses had been supplied in the mid-nineteen thirties which, as it turned out, were not particularly hard wearing examples of their type. Under the Ministry of Supply's allocation scheme Brush was unusual in building bodies for reconditioned as well as new chassis; it was also a major contributor of bus bodies for new Daimlers and it was therefore almost inevitable that Loughborough built bodies would find their way to London in due course. Judged by the standards of composite bodywork of the time they proved to be quite good. The first 27 were allocated fleet numbers D 35-61, following on from the 28 Duples, and were given the next classification in the body series to become type 1/1D3.

Brush's version of the utility body was, at first glance, not unlike Duple's as both shared the same basic outline, but there were in fact many differences to help distinguish one from the other. Viewed from the front, the ventilators surmounting the front opening windows were less wide on the Brush body and a deeper, masked indicator box was fitted. From

the side view the differences were marked by the ventilators inserted above the lower saloon windows and by the lack of continuous rain shields. On the offside the bottom edge of the driver's cab windows was on the same level as the main passenger windows and not raised as on the Duple version, and the slight ledge below the windscreen was another tell-tale Brush feature. The unmistakable recognition sign at the rear was the single window in the emergency exit which was unique on wartime bodies to Brush. At roof level Brush chose to encase the roof trusses with flat external panelling, leaving them visible on the interior, whereas Duple preferred the opposite treatment.

Internally the much favoured light wood finish was employed although Brush did not have supplies of cloth with which to line the bulkheads; opening windows were again of the winding type and the seats were of the current slatted wood variety. Brush managed to shave off 2cwt in weight to produce vehicles at 7tons 5cwt, but at £925 each body was a little more expensive than Duple who consistently managed to undercut all other manufacturers on price.

Although the order for 27 bodies was placed with Brush in February 1944, almost a year

was to elapse before the first pair (D 35, 36) were delivered on 26th January 1945. Brush had been fulfilling its orders less promptly than Duple and, presumably in recognition of this, Duple appears to have been given priority on chassis deliveries. The arrival of D 61 on 16th March 1945 marked the last of the wooden seated Daimlers although Guys were delivered in this form from Northern Counties until June. Upon arrival D 35-61 were painted into full livery before proceeding to Merton where they entered service between February and April 1945. On these vehicles the white upper deck relief was carried around the back of the vehicle from the start.

The usual modifications made soon after the war were the fitting of additional opening windows, which were of the winding type on all 27 bodies, and the upholstering of the seats at overhaul. Several of this batch ran with wooden seats throughout much of 1948 and a few lasted in this form into 1949, the last of all being D 61 which proceeded to Chiswick for overhauling on 1st February. Like their Duple counterparts this batch later received the all-red livery but they outlasted the Duples in service by a few weeks, the final one being D 52 which was withdrawn on 1st January 1954.

There was no mistaking a Brush utility when viewed from the rear thanks to the distinctive single emergency window, and the fitting of ventilators above each lower saloon side window, which was another unique Brush feature. D 52 was photographed at Kingston in May 1951. Alan T Smith

The initial batch of Brush Daimlers, as they appeared in their final days, is demonstrated by D 44 as it sets out from Wrythe Green for Raynes Park on 19th September 1953. It was withdrawn from service on 1st October. John C Gillham

D 62-73 – BRUSH

On 5th June 1944 the Ministry of War Transport made its third allocation of Daimlers to London Transport, consisting this time of a small group of twelve with Brush bodies. In reality they were built as one batch with the D 36-61 series, with the result that Ds 70 and 71 were delivered before the last six of the earlier order, arriving at Chiswick on 27th February and 1st March 1945 respectively. They were not, however, identical. Having been licensed for construction at a later date, Brush had been able to obtain materials for D 62-73 which permitted certain relaxed austerity features and as a result they had upholstered brown leather-cloth seating and additional opening windows. The windows, however, were of the more old fashioned pinch grip type and not the winding variety employed previously. D 62-73 were coded 1/1D3/1.

Delivered between February and April 1945, these were the last to arrive from any manufacturer painted grey. Most were duly put into fleet livery before entering service but four vehicles (Ds 64, 65, 68 and 69) were placed into service still in grey but with fleet names, etc. added. They ran in this form for a surprisingly long time and were not painted red until January and February 1947, the last grey one being D 64. Indeed they even received a local touch-up-and-varnish to prolong their grey existence. In December 1948 the last five of the batch to go through overhaul (Ds 67-69, 71 and 73) underwent a transformation when they were repainted in two tone green for Green Line service at Romford where they replaced STLs required

for conversion into SRTs. At the same time they were fitted with heaters and recoded 5/1D3/5. As recorded later in this book, they were subsequently returned to the central area where they ran for a while retaining their green livery before becoming red once more between May and July 1951. These repainted buses were the first of this small batch to receive the modern all-red style but the remainder followed a few months later when the second overhaul cycle commenced and this resulted in the ex-green ones receiving yet another coat of paint when they, too, were overhauled.

Internal transfers of any of Merton's Daimlers to other garages were rare and the few which took place were confined almost entirely to this small sub-class. In addition to the five reallocations for Green Line service three vehicles were officially reallocated to Sutton to operate alongside this garage's slightly later Daimlers; these were actual transfers and not to be confused with the various unofficial loans which took place from time to time. D 66 ran from Sutton between January and August 1949; D 72 was there for an earlier and longer period from December 1946 to April 1948, overlapped by D 73 between November 1947 and its transfer to Romford at the end of 1948. D 73 again made history when, on 8th January 1954, it became the very last member of Merton's once huge Daimler fleet to be withdrawn from passenger service. It was the last utility bus of all to serve Londoners, and with its passing went the squared off lines and the 'lobster back' domes which had so typified its era.

Above **The only external difference between D 62-73 and the previous Brush batch lay in the number of opening windows, and even this ceased to apply when the earlier vehicles were modified in 1947/8. D 69 was still substantially in original condition when photographed in Parliament Street near the end of the LPTB era except that the original black masking in the indicator box had been overpainted in red.**
S A Newman

Above Right **The application of a smart two tone green livery substantially enhanced the character of the five vehicles transferred to Green Line work in December 1948, and the fitting of saloon heaters brought a vestige of extra comfort to an otherwise very rudimentary design. D 68 basks in sunshine at Aldgate.** Alan T Smith

Right **After carrying the attractive Green Line colours, D 73 looks very commonplace when repainted in a coat of almost unbroken red. This was destined to be the last vehicle with utility 'lobster back' dome to run in passenger service.**
F G Reynolds

D 74-92 – DUPLE

Almost half a year elapsed following the allocation of Brush bodied D 62-73 before the next acquisition of new Daimlers was authorised on 8th November 1944. The authorisation consisted on this occasion of nineteen vehicles with Duple bodies which were allotted fleet numbers D 74-92 and introduced yet another new type code, 1/1D2/1. At this stage Duple were still fulfilling contracts very promptly, and as a result the new vehicles began to arrive from 7th March onwards and all nineteen were in stock before the last of the previous Brush batch was received.

As in the case of the most recent Brush contract, Duple were able to build to a relaxed specification which resulted in D 74-92 being delivered with a full set of half drop windows and upholstered seats. The latter had moquette covered cushions and squabs and cloth-covered backs, and were of a style unique to this batch with sturdy, prominent vertical supports to the back but no handgrips of any sort. For these improvements customers were charged approximately £54 extra per body bringing the total to £949 15s. 0d each. In all other respects D 74-92 were virtually identical to the previous Duple batch and were the last Daimlers delivered with the wartime style back dome. It was now the normal practice for coachbuilders to deliver vehicles fully painted and ready for service, but like several others Duple found supplies of London Transport red to be unobtainable and settled instead for a shade of brown very similar to that used by Weymann on its penultimate batch of Guys. Relief was provided by pale cream window frames on both decks.

A speedy repainting into standard red and white commenced towards the end of 1947 and was completed by the spring of 1948, and the appearance of the vehicles changed again when they received the modern 1950-style livery between February and November 1951. Like so many of the D class they spent a totally uneventful career at Merton from which the last two members of the batch to remain in public service, Ds 80 and 82, were withdrawn on 1st December 1953.

Top **The second Duple highbridge batch were the first Daimlers to enter London service in brown livery. D 81 was still in original condition when photographed at Clapham Common. Apart from the provision of additional opening windows from new, there was no external structural difference between this Duple batch and the last.**
D W K Jones

Centre and Right **The style of upholstered seats fitted from new, which was unique to this batch, is visible in these interior views looking forward inside D 88. The repp covering the back of the seats tended to get very worn and frayed through knees constantly rubbing against it, and was sometimes replaced by plain green rexine as shown in a few instances here. The circular 'Keep Britain Tidy' notices on the front bulkheads were a feature of London buses and trolleybuses throughout the nineteen-fifties.** Alan B Cross

D 93-127 – BRUSH

Brush was the recipient of the body contract for the next allocation of Daimlers for which orders were placed in January 1945. Consisting of 35 vehicles this batch was significantly larger than the two previous, rather meagre allocations and took the Daimler stock numbers beyond the one hundred mark to D 127, constituting a formidable fleet allocated entirely to a single garage. Delivery commenced with D 93 on 12th May 1945, less than a month separating this from the last of the previous Brush batch, and with the exception of D 127 which was a slightly late arrival, it was complete by 12th July.

D 94-127 inherited all the characteristic Brush features found on earlier deliveries from Loughborough but sharp edges were now eliminated from both front and rear domes marking a further step in the progress towards implementation of full post-war standards. Additional opening windows and upholstered seats had already arrived with the earlier D 62-75 batch, the brown leather-cloth seats with their matching grab handles producing a generally more gloomy effect than on contemporary Duple bodies with their ample use of cheerful moquette. D 93-115 were identical mechanically to previous Daimlers but D 116-126 differed in that their dynamo was belt driven from the gearbox to provide improved performance compared with the earlier arrangement which employed a shaft drive alongside the engine. This required an extra trap door in the lower saloon floor rendering the bodies non-inter-changeable without physical modification. D 93-115 were coded 1/1D3/2 and D 116-126 were 2/1D3/3, leaving D 127 in a category of its own as 2D3/4. Delivered on 20th August 1945 it was London Transport's first Daimler CWD6, introducing to the capital the new Daimler engine which had been gradually fil-tering through into service with provincial fleets since earlier in the year. In addition to the new type of engine D 127 also incorpo-rated an experimental type of fluid flywheel; these alterations resulted in the vehicle weighing 2cwt more than others in the last batch at 7tons 7cwt. D 127 was the first London Daimler, and the only one supplied by Brush, to feature a nearside indicator box above the platform. It was also destined to be the last bus ever built for London Transport by Brush although, coincidentally, three brand new Brush-bodied Daimlers ordered by Maidside Corporation were hired to run alongside London's own Daimler fleet (at Sutton garage) between April 1949 and September 1950 when their true owner was unable to pay the loan charges on them.

Top **The rounded rear dome which distinguished the final Brush delivery from earlier batches is barely visible from the front nearside angle at which D 95 was photographed. It is often impossible to tell from photographs that vehicles are in brown rather than red livery, but in this 1947 view at Morden D 95 was still brown.** Alan B Cross

Centre and Right **When upholstering its late wartime vehicles, Brush employed a very plain brown leathercloth which did not even have the grain effect to simulate the leather found on many Guy bodies. Like Northern Counties and Massey, Brush used flat rather than rounded coving panels in the lower saloon.** Alan B Cross/John C Gillham

As delivered D 93-127 were in very similar shades of brown and cream to the previous Duple batch, but a minor livery modification resulted in some of the later ones having cream instead of brown surrounds to the off-side of the driver's cab whilst the cream was extended an inch or so downwards all around the lower saloon. These vehicles were repainted into standard red and white during 1948 ahead of their first overhaul programme which was not due to commence until the following year. Over a ten month period between October 1951 and August 1952 all except D 122 gained the all-red livery. One vehicle of this batch, D 119, spent an official sojourn at Sutton between April and August 1949 as an overhaul replacement for that garage's own fleet of slightly newer Daimlers. D 127 received an AEC engine in May 1950 in place of its Daimler unit, in effect becoming a type CWA6D which was the classification given by the manufacturer to AEC-engined CWAs when fitted with a Daimler rear axle. Four members of this batch lasted in service right up to the last few days of Daimler operation in January 1954, the final one to be withdrawn being D 121 on 6th January.

Still in brown livery as late as May 1948, D 123 was one of the later vehicles in the batch delivered with the driver's side windows framed in cream, on which the horizontal strip under the lower saloon windows was also picked out in cream. Unlike earlier Brush vehicles, the window louvres on this batch formed a continuous strip.
Alan B Cross

Left D 103 demonstrates the combination of typical Brush utility rear end and rounded rear dome found only on this batch of 35 vehicles.
Alan T Smith

The unique D 127, still in brown livery, stands at Morden station while Alan Cross chats to its driver. The nearside indicator box was a distinguishing feature of this vehicle, as was the proliferation of inspection holes found in the bonnet side! Alan T Smith

Near the end of its days, D 127 carries its final livery but is no longer powered by a Daimler engine. However the flat rear hub still proclaims that it was once a CWD6. F G Reynolds

D 128-131 – DUPLE

London Transport's final allocation of Daimlers to fulfil its 1945 vehicle requirement was a further quartet of low height vehicles authorised in June 1945. These were obtained to bring the number of Daimlers available for route 127 to ten which was regarded as adequate to meet the maximum scheduled requirement of nine, releasing lowbridge STLs for use elsewhere (although odd ones subsequently returned from time to time to cover for overhauls, etc). By this time the demand throughout the country as a whole for new low height Daimlers had dropped almost to nothing, but to cover such requirements as may arise the Ministry of Supply designated Massey as the sole lowbridge body supplier on Daimler chassis for the second half of 1945. Accordingly D 128-131 were allocated Massey bodies, which would have been London's first lowbridge bodies from this source. Unhappy at introducing a second make of body into Merton's lowbridge fleet, the Board enquired of the Ministry whether it would reallocate the contract to Duple. Throughout the war the Ministry had strictly enforced the principle that it would not revise body allocations to meet operators' preferences, presumably to avoid the snowballing effect which could arise, but in this case it eased its own internal constraints and, in August, granted the Board's request. As things turned out, Massey built no lowbridge Daimler bodies in this period because, apart from London Transport's four, no operators required any such vehicles.

D 128-131 were CWA6s with the designation 2/1D1/1. They were delivered in the first ten days of November 1945, entering service later in the same month. Though bodied at Hendon, as were D 1-6, they could be immediately distinguished from the older batch by

the absence of opening ventilators from their front upper deck windows and by their rounded rear domes. They also carried a nearside indicator box, which was smaller in depth than those on other utilities, and they carried a full set of opening side windows. Tubular seat frames were introduced for the first time in Daimlers, the seats themselves being upholstered with a not particularly attractive moquette in shades of brownish orange with uneven patches of dark blue; the top and sides were edged in leathercloth and the seat backs were rexine covered. Duple managed on this occasion to obtain red paint so the vehicles were delivered in standard London Transport

livery. Whereas the great majority of Merton's Daimlers received two overhauls during their London lifespan, D 128-131 passed through Chiswick only once, missing out on an opportunity to gain the later all-red livery except in the case of D 130 which received a body repaint at an unknown date.

Seven years and one month after entering service D 128-131 found themselves redundant with the arrival of new RLHs. D 131 had the honour of being the last lowbridge Daimler of all to be licensed for service in London; it was withdrawn on 18th December 1952.

The omission of opening front ventilators gave an air of plainness to the second lowbridge batch but also made them immediately distinguishable from D 1-6. D 128 and D 129 demonstrate the near and offside of these vehicles respectively, the first in as-delivered livery and before the application of advertisements began in 1948, and the second after first overhaul when a slightly expanded area of off-white now included the narrow band below the windows.
F G Reynolds

The rounded rear dome is demonstrated by D 128 as is the side indicator box. The latter was identical in size to the front one but smaller than that fitted to full height utilities; no route number was displayed in it even after this had become standard practice in the rest of the fleet. Alan B Cross

Above Left **Although the seat cushions were trimmed in moquette the backs were covered in rexine rather than the cloth found on earlier Duple deliveries. The bulkheads were now in a plain brown rather than a patterned finish. This view looks forward on D 130.** John C Gillham

Above **A rearward facing view on D 128 shows the style of moquette used on this batch, combined with brown leather-cloth trimming covering edges where wear was most likely to occur. The single skinned interior lining can be clearly seen along the offside gangway.** John C Gillham

Left **From December 1948 onwards D 130 carried two livery styles, both of which distinguished it from its three partners in the batch. The first was similar to that shown on D 129 opposite except that it had an all-red cab area with no surmounting off-white band; this was followed by the 1950 style livery applied at an unknown date.** Alan T Smith

D 132-181 – DUPLE

The circumstances by which the next batch of Daimlers came into London Transport's ownership were unusual in that the vehicles concerned did not comprise part of any particular annual vehicle programme, the requirement for 1945 having already been totally fulfilled. With the war in Europe having drawn to a close, and with operators relishing the prospect of a return to freedom of choice over which makes of vehicle they would be able to purchase, the Ministry of Supply was placed in an enormous quandary. Many operators were holding back from accepting allocations of Guys and Daimlers whilst, on the other hand, over one thousand requests had been placed for Leylands and AEC double deckers, few of which could realistically be fulfilled. Bristol was also oversubscribed although to a lesser degree. At mid-July 1945 the Ministry was still awaiting applications for 120 Guys whose construction was imminent, 20 Albions which were to mark this company's peacetime return to double deck bus manufacturing, and – most seriously of all – no fewer than 250 Daimlers. It had now become clear to the civil servants that they would find it impossible to place all of these 390 vehicles under the normal procedure and they thought up three ways of tackling the problem. One was to bow to operators' persistent requests to build some as single deckers, marking an about turn in a policy which had rigidly prohibited the production of full size single deckers on the grounds that they represented an unsatisfactory use of scarce resources under restricted supply conditions. A second outlet was to export some, whilst a third option was to make a direct approach to large operators in the hope of inducing them to take some of the surplus. London Transport was asked in June 1945 if it would accept fifty or even one hundred and, although it at first refused, the Board agreed in early August to take fifty Duple bodied Daimlers. The Ministry duly showed its appreciation by acceding to the request that the body contract for the four lowbridge Daimlers, D 128-131, should be switched from Massey to Duple, quoting it as a 'special concession'. As for the provincial operators who declined an additional allocation of new buses when it was offered, some may well have lived to regret doing so when, only a little further into the post-war era, a serious shortage of new buses developed.

In a sense the unplanned provision of fifty additional double deckers was fortuitous. Resumption of Green Line operation was being actively planned to commence early in 1946 and would ultimately require a small fleet of double deckers to be based at the old Hillman garage in London Road, Romford to run the close headway services eastwards from Aldgate to Brentwood and Upminster which, until the war brought about their closure, had been worked by some of the newest STLs. The problem of finding suitable rolling stock could be solved if 37 of the forthcoming Daimlers were to come in Green Line livery, and Duple was duly instructed to paint them accordingly. Utilitarian-looking Daimlers may hardly have matched the semi-luxury image traditionally associated with Green Line, but then routes 721 and 722 (as they

Red D 140 and green D 172, both seen in their early days, demonstrate the features which visibly distinguished Daimler's CWD6 model from the much more common CWA6. The differences in rear hubs and bonnet apertures are clearly visible, but only those who are particularly observant would probably notice the subtle difference in radiators especially when, as in the case of D 140, a winter blind partly obscures the view. The D 132-181 batch comprised the only Daimlers delivered from Duple to carry side indicator boxes. More significantly, they were the last vehicles ever to be purchased by London Transport from this major London manufacturer.
S L Poole/J F Higham

The last of the series, D 181, demonstrates the improved, modernised appearance imparted to the standard Duple utility body shell simply by omitting the fussy front ventilators. The rounded rear dome and deeper destination box are further features distinguishing this from the D 74-92 batch. C F Klapper

became under the post-war numbering scheme) were hardly coach services in the normal sense but more akin to express bus operations. This would leave the balance of thirteen to join all the other Daimlers at Merton to constitute a fleet of 144 against a maximum scheduled requirement of 169 double deckers, leaving a small minority of STLs still in place there.

There was hardly a pause between delivery of the last of the low height batch, D 131, on 10th November 1945 and D 132 just four days later. Apart from the height difference the two were basically similar in appearance with all the usual Duple design features, but perhaps because its added height resulted in better proportions, the highbridge version was arguably the more attractive of the two. D 132 was a standard Daimler CWA6 and so were 37 of the remainder, but twelve of the batch were Daimler-engined CWD6s. The first Daimler-engined vehicle, D 138, was received on 30th November and the remainder came dotted haphazardly between CWA6 deliveries. The twelve CWD6s were D 138-140, 142, 150, 155, 160, 162, 163, 171, 180, 181. These twelve, along with D 132, were allocated to Merton whilst the rest were Green Line vehicles on which Lincoln Green replaced the standard Bus Red. The broken white window reliefs, brown roofs, and black mudguards were common to both, but the Green Line livery included five mid-deck bulls-eye motifs which precluded the use of advertisements. This was the first batch supplied by Duple to carry a 20 inch deep front destination aperture which the green vehicles used fully without masking, being the first utilities to do so.

The unladen weight of this batch, whether AEC or Daimler engined, was officially the same as previous highbridge Duples at 7tons 7cwt. Under London Transport's classification scheme the CWA6s were coded 2/1D2/2 and the CWD6s were 2D2/2. When the Green Line fleet was overhauled in 1948/9 the opportunity was taken to fit heaters whereupon the vehicles were reclassified 4/1D2/3. On 14th March 1950 D 138 lost its Daimler engine in favour of an AEC unit and the remainder gradually followed suit throughout the ensuing spring and summer. This was not carried out in any particular number sequence and was probably done as each vehicle became due for a major docking. The last to retain its Daimler engine was D 155 which was converted to AEC on 20th September.

After replacement by new RTs the Romford Daimlers joined their contemporaries at Merton between November 1950 and January 1951, where they continued to run in green livery for several months before being repainted in the now standard 'all red' colour scheme. The majority of Merton's original vehicles in this batch also adopted the new livery but four kept their original red and white to the end. Ds 171 and 180 were the last of the four and were withdrawn on 16th December 1952 by which time this livery was becoming a rarity over the fleet as a whole; however it was not yet totally extinguished amongst the utilities as a number of similarly bodied Bristols carried it through into 1953. This was the year of massive Daimler withdrawals but four of this batch lasted through into the first week of 1954, the last in service being D 147.

Photographed towards the end of its life in London, D 180 was one of the few Daimlers still retaining the old red and white livery. Now AEC engined, it carries the CWA6 bonnet side although in the case of this and two or three other conversions an extra, high mounted inspection hole has also made its appearance. F G Reynolds

Tubular framed seats may have injected a vague air of modernity to the Duple utility body, but the general decor and fittings fell far short of the standard of comfort and semi-luxury normally expected on Green Line services. When photographed, D 151 had been demoted to bus work, but apart from the installation of a few advertisements nothing visible has changed from coaching days.
John C Gillham

D 182-281 – PARK ROYAL

The final batch of Daimlers, delivered between April and November 1946, consisted of exactly one hundred vehicles, D 182-281, and were the last to be purchased from Daimler until the XF class Fleetlines came on the scene in 1965. Although these Park Royal bodied vehicles were visually almost to full post-war standards they are included in this history partly to complete the D-class story, but also because the chassis (but not the bodies) were allocated under the wartime arrangements which continued for a while into the post-war era. Beneath the skin they differed little from wartime bodies even to the use of unseasoned timber prone to rapid deterioration which, if anything, weathered even less well than the slightly earlier and much more utilitarian bodies produced by Duple and Brush.

Starting from 1st January 1946 the Ministry of War Transport ceased controlling the allocation of bus bodies, leaving it up to operators to procure them as best they could for the chassis which they were allocated. In the old days London Transport would have built the bulk of its new body requirements in its own works at Chiswick but this was now out of the question, so in about October 1945 the Board turned to its two preferred suppliers, Park Royal and Weymann, with the proposal that if they made capacity available to fulfil London's new bus orders all new contracts would, as far as possible, be put their way. Joint meetings were held and at one such meeting Park Royal agreed to body the one hundred Daimlers with the proviso that it could only do so if the bodies were of the wartime-derived, composite type and not to

post-war, metal framed standard. Because of capacity problems Weymann declined to contribute bodies towards this batch. There were now no constraints as to the materials which went into body construction, it being left to each builder to obtain what he could from a very limited supply. Some manufacturers were able to go almost immediately to full peace-time specification whereas others, such as Park Royal, changed piecemeal.

Apart from a fully rounded rear dome the new Daimlers followed very closely Park Royal's standard utility profile. However they incorporated many features which ensured that they could never be confused with the utilities, notably the provision of full, three piece indicator displays at front and rear and a totally different livery consisting of all-over red relieved by two narrow cream bands. This had been intended initially as the post-war standard colour scheme for newer vehicles and was applied between November 1945 and May 1946 to several hundred STLs, but it was replaced by a more pleasant scheme employing cream upstairs window frames and, apart from D 182-281 and three RTs, no other vehicles except STLs ever carried it. In fact the Daimlers continued to arrive from the factory in this colour scheme for several months after it had been officially abandoned. Windows were glazed in pans with radiused lower corners and half drop windows were fitted at the upper deck front in addition to the usual side apertures. Internally the difference was most dramatic. Gone was the utility style varnished wood, the window surrounds now being in the finish so beloved of London Transport in pre-war days, comprising brown up to the half way mark on the vertical

window mouldings with creamy-yellow above, capped by a pale green band separating these from the cream ceiling. Side panelling was brown and the seat backs were covered in green rexine. The chromium plated tubular framed seats were upholstered in London Transport's standard post-war moquette which was a modification of that introduced in 1940 on the RT2s and was still very novel at this stage. A noteworthy addition was a bell cord running the length of the lower saloon, the first time such a fitting had been specified by London Transport for its motor bus fleet. Until now they had been a feature only of the trolleybuses and had been ignored and even derided by the bus fraternity before this change of heart. According to the technical press at the time, bell cords were introduced because conductors were sometimes finding difficulty in reaching bell pushes when the full complement of twelve standing passengers allowed under wartime regulations was being carried.

Above **A side profile shot of D 194 taken just before entry into service in May 1946 shows that, at the front end at least, the straight slope of the standard Park Royal utility style is still retained. An attempt at modernity is apparent at the rear but its effect is partly nullified by the attachment of a prominent and untidy set of projecting destination screens.** LT Museum

D 194 shows the reversion to London Transport's decor styles of later pre-war years already familiar on large numbers of STLs and on the STD class. The tubular framed seats and white grab rails are not yet up to full London Transport standards but the moquette is of the standard post-war pattern and the lower saloon bell cord has made an appearance. The row of three advertisement panels on the front bulkhead was reduced to a single, central one at first overhaul.
LT Museum

When the new order was placed it was stipulated that all one hundred vehicles should be AEC-engined models of the CWA6 type even though Daimler had brought out its improved post-war CV range by this time. Technically they differed from the previous CWA6s only in having Clayton Dewandre instead of CAV exhausters to create the vacuum for the servo brake; this was acknowledged by a modified chassis code, the vehicles being classified 3/1D4. A single feature inherited from the CWD6 range was the vertical slat-type radiator shell but, in any case, these became intermixed with others as time went on. Some degree of standardisation was achieved by sticking with the CWA6 and simplicity of maintenance was further achieved by allocating the whole batch to Sutton garage which, under the engineering arrangements of the time, was subsidiary to Merton where all major docking was carried out. At the time they could not, in any case, operate from Merton for physical reasons. The Park Royal bodies were higher than anything bought previously which meant that, even though the Daimler chassis itself was lower than the Leyland, Guy and Bristol utilities, the overall height of this batch was the same at about 14ft 6ins. The vehicles could not safely use Merton's front entrance until it was raised some time later, and although they could pass under the back entrance for docking this was not normally used for operating purposes. By happy chance Sutton required 92 double deckers for scheduled service and throughout their London career D 182-281 were never allocated to any other garage. Even in their later days when doorway height had ceased to be a problem, loans to the parent shed were few and far between. In one way history had repeated itself. Here at Sutton was a unique batch of exactly one hundred buses, presenting a parallel situation to that at Hendon where the hundred strong STD class Leylands were such an established feature. However the Daimlers lacked the character and stamina of the Leylands and were destined never to become as well loved or as long lived.

The first chassis, that of D 182, went to Park Royal on 5th February 1946 but the completed vehicle was not delivered to Chiswick until 23rd April. Though the reason for it is not known, the whole of this batch spent much longer at the coachbuilder's than usual – commonly two months or more. D 182 entered service on 6th May 1946, and Sutton's Daimler conversion was completed on 18th November. Surprisingly, after 98 completely identical vehicles had arrived, the final two were visibly different from the remainder. For some unknown reason Park Royal manufactured Ds 278 and 280 with deeper rainshields than all the others, and as the upper deck ones were picked out in cream this feature rendered them instantly recognisable. In April 1948 D 215 appeared after accident repairs in an up-dated livery incorporating cream surrounds to the upper deck windows, and the remaining 99 were dealt with in a similar though not completely identical manner at their first overhaul from which they emerged over a thirteen month period between January 1949 and February 1950. Yet another livery change overtook 52 of the batch from December 1951 onwards when

The D 182-281 batch was the first to be delivered by Daimler with red painted radiators. D 212, seen on home territory at Morden, demonstrates the typical appearance of the Sutton Daimlers in their early years. It seems to tower over the low height vehicle standing behind. Alan B Cross

Although not quite the last of the batch numerically, D 280 was the final one to be delivered. In common with D 278, it carried the slightly deeper upper deck rainshields which distinguished these two members of the class from the remainder. Alan B Cross

D 215 was the first to receive cream upper deck window surrounds when it was repainted after accident damage. The livery application differed from the subsequent standard in that the rainshield was picked out in red rather than cream. At this stage D 215 still retained the now-disused nearside route number holder which was removed from all vehicles at first overhaul. Alan B Cross

The revised livery styling of 1949 suited the Sutton Daimlers particularly well. In appearance they were modern looking vehicles displaying few hints of their 'utility' ancestry, though beneath the flattering paintwork the body framework was decaying just as fast as on all the earlier Daimlers. D 208 was one of those which subsequently received all-red livery. Alan B Cross

they adopted the latest all-red style which was, in fact, almost a reversion to their original condition except that the cream band over the upstairs windows was now absent. The remainder were not dealt with because the overhaul programme was abandoned mid-stream in November 1952, leaving mainly the higher numbered vehicles to end their days in red and cream. These, naturally, were also the first to be selected for disposal, the final red and cream vehicles (Ds 272, 276, 277, 279, 281) being withdrawn on 16th February 1953. Thirteen of the overhauled ones lasted right through 1953 and two, Ds 226 and 250, were still present on the very last day of Daimler operation and were withdrawn on 8th January 1954.

The ungainly rear indicator display is shown on D 233, carrying original livery, and D 249 in the second styling. The full blind displays were never used, and for a while in 1948/9 a few vehicles even had their restricted rear display painted over in red. The Sutton Daimlers carried an advertisement on the offside rear corner but not on the nearside where there was insufficient space for this purpose. Alan T Smith/F G Reynolds

CHAPTER EIGHT

THE SECOND BRISTOL BATCH

At the end of September 1943 the double deck manufacturing plans for the first half of 1944 were revealed; these were for 200 Guys and 240 Daimlers. No mention of any other manufacturer was made at this stage but, behind the scenes, plans were well advanced for Bristol to resume production even though their works at Brislington were still effectively under the control of the Ministry of Aircraft Production. At a meeting at the Ministry of War Transport on 8th December 1943 it was revealed to operators' representatives that the Bristol Tramways & Carriage Co. Ltd was about to be given the go ahead to construct 250 chassis, the first of which should be available in May 1944 with about 150 to be completed during the year and the balance in 1945. This was the announcement that an important sector of the industry, namely the Tilling group, had been waiting for. Indeed they had been holding back for some time in the hope of new Bristols becoming available.

The sting in the tail, at least as far as the Tilling companies was concerned, was an announcement that the new chassis would be powered by AEC 7.7 litre engines. Having standardised before the war on the Bristol/Gardner combination, they did not now favour having AEC engines forced upon them, and through their spokesmen they began a strident campaign to get this decision reversed. The Ministry pointed out that the entire Gardner engine production for bus use was already fully allocated to Guy. Why, asked Tillings, cannot Guy fit AEC engines so that the Gardners can power Bristols? Finally it was arranged that an AEC engine would be loaned to Guy to ascertain the feasibility of this proposition but an examination disclosed problems necessitating redesign work on

the Arab chassis which would have been so substantial that the proposal was quietly dropped. Another minor falling out occurred, this time with the Ministry of War Transport, who learnt that the Tilling Association had tentatively planned for the entire Bristol output to be retained by its own companies and had to remind them that responsibility for allocating new vehicles lay with the Ministry, not operators. When they finally arrived on the scene the new Bristols were widely allocated although many did, indeed, go to Tilling companies.

The K6A, as the new wartime chassis was designated, was substantially similar to the K5G of which nine examples had been running successfully at Hanwell for a couple of years. Bristol was fortunate that the K6A came on stream just as a certain amount of aluminium was being released for civilian use and they were able to take advantage of this with a resultant saving in weight over other wartime chassis to the order of 10cwt. The AEC engine required modifications to its mountings so that it would pick up on a front bracket and a backplate on the Bristol chassis which were at a spacing provided for Gardner engines, and the controls and exhaust pipe positions were also modified; in this form the 7.7 engine was known by AEC as the A202.

The first two sanctions of new Bristols, numbered W1 and W2, comprised 150 and 100 chassis respectively but none of these came to London. London Transport's first and only allocation came with the W3 sanction when twenty vehicles with Duple bodies were authorised in June 1944. They were allocated fleet numbers B 10-29 to follow on from the K5Gs. Even before resumption of production, Bristol had made it known that at some stage in the

future a new radiator would be introduced to give a more modern appearance and to provide better nearside visibility, and its introduction coincided with the start of the W3 sanction. The twenty chassis were taken into stock by London Transport from 13th October 1945 onwards, but were not delivered to Chiswick as was normally the case. Instead they were stored at Bristol and proceeded direct from there to Duple with the exception of B 10 which arrived at Chiswick in chassis form on 25th October, presumably for inspection and evaluation. Consequently it was bodied out of sequence, B 11 being the first complete vehicle to arrive from Duple on 24th November 1945. The batch was completed with the arrival of B 28 on 31st December and, to those accustomed to the ubiquitous K type Bristols with their unnecessarily high and plain radiator, these new vehicles marked a sensational break from tradition. London's were the first to feature the sleek, low mounted PV2 radiator with its gentle curve inwards towards the bottom, a handsome design which was to become widely known over the next decade and a classic in its own time.

B 10-29 joined the nine K5Gs at Hanwell where the first two, Bs 11 and 13, entered service on 12th December 1945 with the remainder following in January 1946. They ran with the usual Bristol efficiency but were noticeably very unlike the K5Gs. The noisy, harsh ride so typical of the K5G was absent to a large degree, and even though the 7.7 engine was rigidly mounted the ride was considerably smoother and was accompanied by an unfamiliar combination of AEC engine and Bristol gearbox sounds. Nearside visibility apart, from the driver's angle there was a wealth of difference between the earlier

Bristol's new front end design made a deeper windscreen possible, and Duple modified its bodywork to suit by bringing the lower edge of the cab side windows down to the same level as those of the saloon. J F Higham

The upper deck of B 12 looking rearwards. Internally the Duple bodies on B 10-29 were the same as those on D 132-181 except for the distinctive red seat moquette. John C Gillham

The last Bristol double decker ever purchased by London Transport was B 29. Photographed towards the end of its London career, it now carries its nearside fleet number centrally on the ridge of the bonnet top and has acquired a slightly modified livery through the deepening of the white reliefs to include the window ledges. New side lights and a nearside front mudguard taken from one of the unfrozen batch complete the changes which have been made in the seven years since it was new. D W K Jones

Bristol batch and the new one, not least because, whereas the K5Gs needed to be driven hard simply to maintain good timekeeping, life was easier on the K6As. The usual Bristol bonus points of a positive gearbox and light steering were still applicable even though the steering had now reverted to an earlier Marles cam and roller type instead of Bristol's own worm and quadrant arrangement. The vehicles were coded 2B2 and weighed 7tons 4cwt unladen, 3cwt less than contemporary Duple bodied Daimlers. Apart from weighing less than the Daimlers they also cost less at £2512 per complete vehicle as against £2689, a not inconsiderable saving of nearly seven per cent.

The twenty new Bristols passed through Duple's Hendon body shops at the same time as the first few Daimlers in the D 132-181 batch and were identical in external appearance except in the vicinity of the windscreen which was deeper on the Bristol to accommodate the lower radiator. It might have been expected that the two types would have been identical internally, but in fact the Bristols made a completely different impact through being upholstered in a florid style of red moquette which was unique to this batch. Their lives in London were totally uneventful and during their public service career they never strayed away from Hanwell (later Southall) garage. Their appearance remained the same throughout as none ever lost the traditional red and white livery in favour of the 1950 all-red applied to many Guys and most of the Daimlers. Deterioration of the bodywork finally dictated the commencement of the withdrawal programme which began with B 10 in September 1951 and was completed when Bs 14, 17-19 and 29 gave way to new RTs on 10th April 1953.

London Transport never again owned any Bristol double deckers although many more came on temporary loan in 1948-50 when 190 brand new vehicles were diverted from their intended owners to relieve a serious vehicle shortage. These included both K5G and K6A models, all with standard Eastern Coach Works bodies of both high and lowbridge types. It is interesting to recall that, at the end of the war, London Transport would have purchased many more Bristols of its own if it had had its way. On 11th April 1945 the Board asked the Ministry of War Transport for no fewer than one hundred in preference to an anticipated allocation of Guys or Daimlers, but this and a subsequent less ambitious request for fifty were declined. Ministry officials privately conceded that they might let the Board have ten, which later grew to the twenty represented by B 10-29. Seven months later the Ministry, faced now with a possible glut of new chassis in 1946, changed its tune and offered 50 Bristols in addition to the 331 new double deckers already on order (D 182-281, STD 112-176 and 166 RTs). However the Board's position had also changed; it could scent an influx of new RTs on the not too distant horizon and was no longer prepared to acquire further non-standard vehicles. On the basis of the standardisation argument, and also invoking the strong attitude allegedly taken by road operating staff to a multiplicity of vehicle types, it declined the offer.

CHAPTER NINE

THE UTILITIES ENTER SERVICE

On 1st December 1941, STD 101 was taxed ready for the road. This was a time of comparative quiet in wartime London. The major enemy blitz of 1940/41 was over and air raids were only intermittent. In this lull before the arrival of the V bombs the first new double decker ever purchased by London Transport to a design other than its own was about to enter service with Victoria garage as its operational base. The reason for selecting Victoria is not known but an influencing factor must have been that, being a much newer building than most in the fleet, it possessed ample roof clearance to accommodate the 14ft 6ins height of the new vehicle. Subsequently, as the fleet of utilities rapidly expanded, height was to prove a severely limiting factor in deciding the garages to which they could be safely allocated.

The date on which STD 101 actually entered passenger service is not known for certain. Its first task was to run alongside STLs on route 22 (Putney Common–Homerton) where it evoked a certain amount of interest from newspaper journalists but only a muted response from the travelling public. It remained unique for a full six months before the next two Leyland utilities (STDs 102 and 103) were licensed on 1st May 1942 to join it. However the arrival of these two went virtually unnoticed because all eyes were now switched to the western suburbs where, on the very same day, the first four utility Bristols began work at Hanwell on route 97 (Greenford–Brentford). This first small allocation, consisting of Bs 1-3 and 6, was quickly augmented by the remaining five in the batch

which were all operational by 1st June. Route 97 required exactly nine vehicles for its Monday to Friday allocation and had obviously been selected for this reason. For the remainder of the war B 1-9 seldom if ever strayed from it although on Saturdays, when a larger allocation was required, and on other days when servicing or repair needs dictated, other vehicles from Hanwell's mixed fleet of STLs and LTs provided cover.

On 1st June 1942, when the final Bristols were licensed, STD 104 also entered service and the remaining Leylands came in dribs and drabs thereafter, culminating in the arrival of STDs 110 and 111 on 19th August. Soon afterwards, on 28th October, the fleet of Leylands on route 22 was further augmented by six of the pre-war batch which were temporarily not required at their home base of Hendon, and this small ex-Hendon contingent at Victoria gradually rose by January 1944 to its maximum of twelve. Victoria's STD allocation now greatly exceeded its scheduled output on route 22 so the balance was put to work as the minority weekday allocation on route 10 (Victoria–Abridge) augmenting Leyton's far larger contribution of LTs which were mostly of the oldest, open staircase variety.

Exactly a year had passed since the introduction of London's first utility bus when, on 1st December 1942, the first Guy Arab was licensed at Tottenham. The commissioning of G 1 was, in some ways, a much more momentous event than the arrival of the Leyland and Bristol utilities had been. Most importantly it represented the first example in the capital of a purpose-built austerity chassis rather than

the unfrozen types received previously. The supply of unfrozen chassis had clearly been a limited and short-term expedient and because of this it was obvious that the STD and B classes which derived from them would not for the time being increase in size. In the case of Guy things were altogether different and the promise of ongoing production led to the possibility that the small fleet initially intended for Tottenham would expand to a much larger Guy presence in due course. Even so, it is probable that no-one in authority at 55 Broadway envisaged at the time that as many as 435 Guy utilities would eventually be taken into stock, or that this largely unwanted model would play such an important role in London's bus transportation in the late wartime and early post-war years. But then, back in December 1942, no end to the war was even remotely in sight and nothing could be predicted for certain.

The tree-lined roads of Ealing have a genteel but almost deserted air in this 1942 scene as B 4 sets out for Brentford leaving a pair of STs laying over in its wake. New Bristol double deckers marked such a great deviation from normal London Transport purchasing practice that transport photographers were keen to record them for their sheer novelty value despite the acute shortage of film at the time. C F Klapper

With the arrival of the first Guy Arabs an even more unusual break from London tradition was achieved. The Bristol K5G may not have been a type favoured by London Transport but at least its capabilities were well recorded; the Arab was a step into the unknown. G 8, the third member of the class to enter service at Tottenham, was photographed at Lower Edmonton in January 1943 and was still awaiting the fitting of anti-splinter mesh.
S L Poole

Right The 'in town' end of route 76 in an uncannily quiet Victoria station where G 2 awaits departure for Edmonton when also brand new. Slight physical differences are apparent between this vehicle and G 8; the headlamps have no chrome-plated surrounds but the outer edge of the radiator grille is picked out in white and the GUY name is left unhighlighted. C F Klapper

As they emerged from the Chiswick paint shops new Guys were drafted into Tottenham in a fairly leisurely manner. G 1 was joined by G 13 on 8th December, G 8 on the 9th, G 14 on the 10th, Gs 2 and 32 on the 16th and so on, with the result that by the end of December six were in service, rising to 13 by the end of January 1943 and 29 on February 1st. Two notable events marked the first month's deliveries. G 14 was the first to run in wartime brown livery and G 32, with its Weymann-built body, marked the introduction of a utility style other than the now familiar one from Park Royal, giving a small foretaste of the multiplicity of wartime body shapes which later made the London bus scene so interesting and varied. The sphere of operation selected for Tottenham's new Guys was route 76, a busy but almost gradient free route whose main section lay between Victoria and Lower Edmonton. However the 76 differed from most central bus department services in being one of the few jointly worked with another, almost unrelated route, in this case the 34B. Basically the two had only about half a mile in common, between the Angel in Upper Edmonton and the town hall at Lower Edmonton, but certain peak hour journeys on route 76 were projected along the 34B northwards to Brimsdown to pick up the latter service there. The 34B was a weekdays peak operation linking Brimsdown with Walthamstow (Crooked Billet). Though, like Victoria's STDs, the Guys on route 76 operated into central London, the Gs took a lower profile routeing and the two classes used common ground for only a few hundred yards at the Bank.

The early mechanical problems which befell the new Guys brought about the abrupt delicensing of the majority on 1st March 1943 to enable modifications to be made. Earlier, their arrival at Tottenham had been accompanied by the despatch of LTs and STs for service at other garages; now STs were drafted back and the 76/34B were worked predominantly by this type until the Guys returned. Although a few were returned to service beforehand, most Guys were relicensed on 1st June and were accompanied by seven previously unused vehicles to complete the conversion at Tottenham. Three of these were in the standard red livery into which the more recent Arab deliveries were now being painted. On the very same day four Guys (Gs 61, 62, 64 and 66) made their debut at Hanwell, joining the small Bristol utility fleet there and expanding still further the unusually varied mixture of chassis types at this garage. Within a few days more had joined them, both Park Royal and Weymann, brown and red, with fleet numbers as low as G 5. July 1943 saw the arrival at Hanwell of yet more Guys notable amongst which was the only Duple bodied example, G 43, which started work on the first day of the month. The novelty of this was eclipsed by the licensing for service on the 10th of G 74. Not only was this the first Mark II Arab to run in London but, much more significantly, it was the first wooden seated utility to start work in the fleet.

The presence at Hanwell of a fleet of Guys made possible a comparison between two wartime classes for the first time, and in the popularity ratings – as seen from a driver's viewpoint – the Bristols won hands down even though both were powered by the same noisy and low powered 5LW engine. In wartime days Hanwell garage kept the two types strictly apart. The Guys were intended for route 18C (Wembley, Empire Pool–Hanwell garage) displacing LTs, and weekday route 83 (Golders Green–Hayes) plus its Sunday 83A variant (Golders Green–Kew Green) formerly worked by STLs. The 18C was a comparatively short-lived working for the Guys, being renumbered 92 on 18th June 1944 when a new mainly peak hour weekdays-only 92A (Wembley Trading Estate–Hanwell garage) was inaugurated.

Hanwell was not destined to stay a lone Guy outpost in west London for long. The garage at Alperton was a modern structure capable of housing over-high vehicles, and what is more it partnered Hanwell on routes 83/A making it an obvious choice for a Guy allocation. Route 18 (Wembley, Empire Pool–Edgware with journeys to the Aldenham works of London Aircraft Production) was also designated for Guy operation and in fact received them ahead of the 83 group. On 13th July 1943 Weymann bodied G 50 transferred in from Hanwell followed two days later by Park Royal Gs 68 and 69, and these three were probably used for driver familiarisation ahead of the main allocation of new and ex-Hanwell Guys which commenced on 1st August. Between 1st August 1943 and 22nd January 1944 Alperton received 31 new and 12 second hand Guys, all Park Royal bodied but including within the used contingent several more Mark I models. With one exception all the used vehicles transferred in were ex-

G 74 sets out from Golders Green for its run to Southall whilst, in the background, a 'Scooter' LT can just be seen arriving from Finsbury Park on route 210. The presence of Mark II Arabs means that the era of wooden seats has arrived. This vehicle was the first wooden seater to enter service, being based originally at Hanwell, but after four weeks it was transferred along with others to Alperton whose code letters it carries here. LT Museum

G 109 was one of a number of Arabs bearing experimental features which were allocated to Hanwell. It is seen at the home terminus of the 92A, a new route introduced in June 1944 which was Guy worked from the start. Photographed later in the same year, the vehicle has already received modified headlights and an enamel radiator badge proclaiming its London Transport ownership. J F Higham

Hanwell; the exception was G 80, one of a pair of Mark IIs delivered new to Tottenham on 1st August (the other being G 81) to cover the temporary absence of other vehicles. Like most other Mark IIs later received at Tottenham, they lasted there for only a short time. By early September 1943 Alperton had sufficient Guys to have replaced all of its STLs from route 18 and the end of the first spate of Guy arrivals in January 1944 left it with almost enough for the 83 although a few STs remained still officially allocated.

When Alperton's G 93 was transferred to Barking garage on 10th January 1944 to take up driver training duties it became clear where the final Guys in the current round of new deliveries were destined to go. No immediate influx followed, a mere six Guys arriving at Barking during February consisting of two new and four second hand specimens, three of the latter from Hanwell and the fourth from Tottenham. The ex-Hanwell vehicles had been displaced by new Arabs incorporating experimental features which dictated that they should be allocated there, and a fourth vehicle arrived at Barking on 1st March from the same source. This was the very same day that 21 new Guys were licensed, eighteen of which (G 119-136) were in all-over grey livery. The combination of Barking's location well out in the eastern suburbs together with its quite extensive network of local services marked it out as a very suitable choice for an allocation of Guy Arabs. It was all the more surprising, therefore, that the Guys were allocated not to its suburban operations but to route 23 (Becontree Heath–Marylebone), by far the busiest in Barking's roster traversing as it did the busy Commercial Road, the City and the heart of the West End. Here, more than on any other Barking route, the Guys with their slow performance were at their greatest disadvantage compared with the LT six-wheelers which they superseded. The 23 had no Sunday operation and as a result the new Guys remained inactive on this day. The delivery of G 136 marked the end of Guy purchases for the time being leaving many LTs scheduled to remain on route 23 throughout the remainder of 1944 and for most of 1945 also.

The pause in Guy deliveries after February 1944 was more than compensated by the arrival from April onwards of London Transport's fourth brand of utilities, the D class. Though just as spartan in their fittings as all the others, the Daimlers managed somehow to exude an air of greater sophistication which they quickly spread through the thoroughfares of south London. Prior to the arrival of the Daimlers, London's utilities had hardly made any mark south of the Thames, the only scheduled operations to do so being on routes 10 and 76 (which both crossed the river twice) and these did not stray far into the south London metropolis. London Transport's decision to base the Daimlers at Merton, which was eventually to receive no fewer than 144 of the type from new, was reminiscent of a similar programme a decade earlier when Merton received equally large quantities of STLs to modernise its stock within a comparatively short time. Now it was the turn of large numbers of STLs, and some STs too, to make way for the latest influx of new vehicles. The programme commenced quietly enough with six low-height vehicles, D 1-6, which were licensed between 6th May and 1st June 1944 specifically for route 127 (Morden–South Wimbledon), a circuitous operation taking 38 minutes to link two points only five minutes apart when travelling direct, with a low bridge at Worcester Park which precluded the use of normal height double deckers. This route had latterly been worked by a mixture of ST and STL low loaders and even after delivery of the Daimlers three STLs were scheduled to remain to complete the nine vehicle weekday allocation. Route 127 was never scheduled for Sunday operation (except for a short period between April and November 1947) which meant that D 1-6 stayed in the garage on this day.

The first really significant influx of Daimlers into Merton commenced with the arrival of normal height D 7 on 2nd August 1944 and continued up to October when delivery of the Duple-bodied batch D 7-34 was completed. The first Brush bodied Daimler,

Above **No apologies are offered for the very poor quality of this photograph which shows a line-up of Barking vehicles in Longbridge Road on 18th September 1944. Heading the queue is G 55 which has worked in on route 23C, a cross allocation from main route 23. One of only four Mark I Arabs then based at Barking, it had been transferred in from Hanwell in February. Behind are three of the Guys which ran in grey livery, and this is the only known photograph to record this feature. They were pressed into service so quickly that they did not even carry advertising material.** John C Gillham

Below **The May 1944 introduction of lowbridge Daimlers on route 127 was another of those rare wartime occasions which attracted transport photographers because of the sheer novelty of the new vehicles. At South Wimbledon terminus D 1 is seen laying over between journeys.** C F Klapper

D 35, resumed the programme on 10th February 1945 which then continued unabated up to 1st August by which time all vehicles up to D 126 were in service. The various design improvements permitted under the relaxed austerity regime saw the re-introduction of upholstered seats in March 1945 (although wooden seated examples were also received through to April). Peace-time levels of opening windows were achieved in March too, and rounded domes made their appearance in June. However the fact that supply difficulties still existed was illustrated by the arrival of brown-liveried vehicles from March onwards whilst between 14th April and 1st June four Daimlers (Ds 64, 65, 68 and 69) entered service in grey. The first Daimler-

engined vehicle, D 127, came on the Merton scene on 13th October followed in November by the second batch of lowbridge vehicles, D 128-131, which officially completed the conversion of route 127 to Daimlers although STLs and even STs still made their occasional appearance. Merton's programme was now almost complete, with only thirteen vehicles of the D 132-181 batch still to enter service between 1st December 1945 and 25th March 1946. Apart from D 132 itself the remainder were all further Daimler powered specimens, those with AEC engines having been set aside for Green Line work at Romford. Merton's fleet of 144 Daimlers made it by far the largest accumulation of utilities within a single garage anywhere in the country.

The utility classes were fortunate in surviving the rocket attacks on London largely unscathed. An exception was G 30, and these views show the extensive damage incurred during a fateful journey on route 76 on 23rd June 1944 after just a year in service. The chassis was salvaged and later rebodied by Northern Coachbuilders but the vehicle never again returned to Tottenham garage.
LT Museum

Conversion of Merton's extensive route network from STLs to Daimlers commenced by taking the busiest services first, starting with route 88 (Acton Green–St Helier with a Sunday projection to Belmont) to which Merton contributed 44 vehicles complemented by a small, north-end allocation supplied by Hammersmith with eight LTs. Next came route 77 (worked in two sections: Kings Cross–Tooting and Tooting–Wallington) which Merton shared with Chalk Farm (replaced by Victoria from 13th February 1946 onwards), and route 77A (Kings Cross–Raynes Park) on which Merton had a small eight bus minority allocation alongside Victoria's much larger share. Buses from the 88 schedule also covered weekday peak hour short workings between Rose Hill and North Cheam on Morden circular service 156, and further purely suburban operations in due course scheduled for Daimlers were routes 118 (Raynes Park–Clapham Common) followed by routes 152 (Mitcham–Hampton Court), 157 (Raynes Park–Wallington) and 32 (St Helier–Worcester Park peaks; South Wimbledon–Raynes Park off-peak). This left two major cross-London routes still officially in the hands of STLs except on Sundays; these were 49 (Shepherds Bush–Crystal Palace) and 137 (Archway–Crystal Palace). In practice, however, Merton made little attempt to follow the official split of Daimlers and STLs between routes, tending to regard the two types as interchangeable, so for example it was by no means unusual to find Daimlers on route 49 on weekdays. Over the ensuing years various official adjustments were made to the number and types of vehicles allocated to routes to accommodate service alterations, reallocations and vehicle overhaul programmes, but at ground level these remained largely academic. However one service which certainly lost its Daimlers at a very early date was the 137, whose weekday allocation was transferred from Merton to Camberwell and Chalk Farm on 13th February 1946, closely followed by the loss of the Sunday allocation to Victoria with effect from 17th March.

Top **On a hot summer day there are few windows in the Duple body of D 8 to throw open wide for ventilation, and an uncomfortably stuffy ride is assured. The 88 was the first of Merton's main routes to be thrown open to Daimler operation, but at the time no-one could have foreseen what heavy inroads vehicles of this type were destined to make into Merton's huge STL fleet.** J F Higham

Centre **As a fuel economy measure many buses were scheduled to lay over in central London between peaks. One of the designated waiting areas was Albert Embankment where a pair of new Brush bodied Daimlers take a break from route 77.** C F Klapper

Right **The first Daimler to enter service in brown livery was D 74 on 10th March 1945. It was one of the last to have its windows obscured by anti-splinter mesh as the use of this material was officially discontinued in April, and with the war in Europe now perceivably drawing to a close, the use of white mudguard markings also ceased soon afterwards. This view at Crystal Palace was possibly taken on a Sunday which was the only day of the week on which route 137 was officially Daimler operated.**

On 1st May 1945, a date when new Daimlers licensed for service spanned fleet numbers between D 63 and D 89, a major new Guy programme commenced which was to continue unabated throughout the remainder of 1945 and into the first few months of 1946. For several months things had been quiet on the Guy front, the only item of note being the licensing on 5th January 1945 of G 137 with experimental Weymann bearerless body, followed just over a fortnight later by the re-entry into service on the 23rd of G 30 with its new Northern Coachbuilders body. Both of these very interesting vehicles went to Alperton where they were destined to see their days out. The rate of intake of new Guys over the second half of 1945 was such that, for the first time in the case of utility vehicles, routes from more than one garage were scheduled for conversion simultaneously. For a start Alperton's route 79 (Colindale–Alperton with peak extensions to Northolt) was designated as suitable for Guys, and as this route did not operate on Sundays the vehicles were employed on this day of the week on route 72 (North Wembley–Esher), taking them into the county of Surrey for the first time. There remained, too, the outstanding matter of Barking's route 23 on which many LTs were still active even though Guys were in the majority. On 1st May Alperton received the second bearerless Guy, G 138, and also the first of a new and distinctive breed, Massey-bodied G 174. Barking also took in a Massey built vehicle on this date, G 175, followed by seven more over the next few days. These were most interesting times with new body shapes in various shades of brown appearing whenever further bodymakers came on stream. June 1st was no exception when Alperton received its first wooden seated all-metal Guy from Northern Counties (G 155) whilst Barking took delivery of the first of Northern Coachbuilders' very colourful output built to Park Royal design, G 139, in addition to Northern Counties G 154 and six more Masseys. Several more Northern Counties and Massey vehicles went to Barking up to and including 1st July, completing the current programme for this garage, whilst deliveries to Alperton persisted until 1st August consisting mainly of Northern Coachbuilders vehicles plus three more from Northern Counties. Alperton had now lost all its STLs to become an all-Guy garage apart from a small allocation of STs on the 187 (Hampstead Heath–South Harrow). This service never officially received a weekday Guy allocation although they appeared on Sundays during the winter of 1947/8 and again from the winter of 1948/9 onwards.

Top **From January 1944 Victoria's unfrozen STDs were a regular sight on route 10. In a typical scene, taken just after the war, STD 106 heads northbound across London Bridge with a Leyton-based LT on route 35 in hot pursuit.** S A Newman

Right **Barking was the first garage to receive a sizeable batch of new Massey bodied Guys which, from May 1945 onwards, introduced a new dimension to the London utility scene. G 184 sets out from the western end of route 23 on the long, flat run to Becontree Heath which will take it right through the heart of the West End and City.** S A Newman

Over in the east at Barking the unfinished business on route 23 remained, surprisingly, unfinished. The new Guys were employed instead on local routes 23B (Barking–Becontree, weekday peaks only), 23C (Barking–Creekmouth), 62 (Little Heath-Chadwell Heath), 145 (Chingford–Dagenham with peak hour projections to Dagenham Docks and Ford Works) and 175 (worked in two sections: Chase Cross–Poplar and Stapleford Abbots–Dagenham). The 23B and 23C had already seen reasonably regular Guy workings due to cross allocations with route 23, as was indeed also the case with route 148 (Leytonstone–Dagenham with projections to the docks and Ford Works), which was basically a Seven Kings operation with LTs and STs but with Barking vehicles scheduled to make a number of trips on weekdays. Route 145, which Barking shared with LTs from Upton Park and Seven Kings, and the 175 jointly worked with Upton Park and Hornchurch, were both of interest in that their operation was regularly augmented by "extras worked to local instructions", a very un-London-like arrangement which was eliminated from route 145 in a tidying-up operation on 30th April 1947 and on 12th November 1947 from the 175.

Next in line for Guys was Victoria where 45 were installed to completely convert this garage's share of routes 52 (Victoria–Mill Hill with projections to Borehamwood) and 77A. The latter was already worked by Merton's Daimlers and now became the first major cross-London service completely handed over to utilities and the only one on which Guys and Daimlers ever officially ran together. The 52 was not a complete stranger to utilities as the odd STD had appeared on it from time to time, and Victoria's flexibility of allocation meant that the Guys were not strictly confined to their designated routes and were certainly seen on the 22 and 137 on occasions. The influx of new Guys to Victoria overlapped with the completion of Alperton, beginning on 4th July 1945 and ending on 9th August, and led to the departure of RTs and Hendon-type STDs as well as the more mundane STLs. Victoria's Guy fleet contained representatives of the three variants currently being delivered; Massey, Northern Counties and Park Royal-style Northern Coachbuilders. Notable inclusions were the last three wooden seaters to enter service in London of which the very final one, G 173 on 9th July, was delivered from Northern Counties in full London Transport red livery and was one of only three red Guys at Victoria amongst a sea of brown ones.

Just after Victoria received its first Guys a strong clue was given as to the intended destinations for future deliveries when, on 7th July 1945, Gs 219 and 258 were despatched to Hornchurch to begin driver familiarisation duties whilst G 221 went similarly to Upton Park. Something must have caused a hiccup in the training process at Upton Park as G 221 was removed for service at Tottenham on 1st August, subsequently settling permanently at Hornchurch, but Hornchurch was sufficiently prepared for a regular allocation of new Guys to commence on 11th August. Only eight were received during August, but September saw an inflow of 43 new and three

Though not the first utilities to operate on route 52 – STDs having got there first – Victoria's Guys were the first to operate it in brown livery. The curved Northern Counties body lines of G 223 look thoroughly modern and far removed from the usual concept of austerity bodywork. G F Ashwell

used vehicles followed by twelve more new Guys and one almost new one in October. Inevitably, with so many vehicles involved, the whole gamut of current body styles was included within the Hornchurch fleet, in which the final Weymann batch made its debut starting with G 369 on 15th September just a few days before Massey's last-ever London bus, G 368, was licensed on the 21st. One by one the majority of Hornchurch's impressive array of services in the far eastern suburbs was converted to Guys. The first ones appeared on route 123 (South Hornchurch–Ongar), and although there was no fully clear cut sequence of conversion thereafter the order was roughly as follows: 247 Collier Row–Harold Wood; 86 Chadwell Heath–Brentwood; 103 Eastern Avenue–Rainham; 175 Chase Cross–Poplar; Stapleford Abbots –Dagenham; 66 Leytonstone–Hornchurch. Route 247 was unusual in being a joint

double/single deck operation, and the single deck T-worked section from Romford (Parkside) to Brentwood was, of course, unaffected by the arrival of Guys. Hornchurch had previously been scheduled to operate a mixture of vehicle types consisting mostly of STLs but with STs on the 247 and mostly LTs on the 175. The newly arrived Guys expelled STs first of all, followed by many STLs; LTs began departing on 20th September which would pinpoint the approximate starting date for conversion of route 175. Oddly, small pockets of the older classes were left; STLs for route 165 (Havering Park–Rainham) and the single bus weekday allocation on route 249 (Upminster–Corbets Tey), and LTs on route 86A (Limehouse–Upminster extended to Corbets Tey at weekends), although in practice appearances by Guys on all three were common and, indeed, the Sunday 86A allocation was officially Guy.

G 239 makes an interesting contrast on route 77A to Merton's Daimlers during its spell of little under three months at Victoria. This was the last of the Northern Counties vehicles delivered in the predominantly brown livery, subsequent ones having cream window surrounds. R H G Simpson

Varying shades of brown are on view in Hornchurch garage yard. G 258 has run in from route 175 and carries Massey's standard one colour livery; Northern Counties G 247 on route 123 is in brown and cream whilst, at the far end, G 204 – also on route 123 – displays the distinctive brown and ochre favoured by Northern Coachbuilders.
Alan T Smith

With the Guy programme at Hornchurch nearing its end and Upton Park apparently still not ready to accept its quota, another location was required to absorb the influx of new vehicles and Enfield garage was duly selected. The choice was a logical one as Enfield was within the same engineering group as Tottenham just as the east London Guy garages were linked, so too Hanwell and Alperton. The result was the opening up of yet another major sphere of Guy influence, this time in the northern suburbs to complement those already established in the east and west. New Weymann bodied G 377 and Park Royal G 207 were allocated to Enfield on 1st October for staff training, G 207 being the first 'real' Park Royal vehicle of the current programme to be licensed rather than a Northern Coachbuilders copy. However before the main influx started at Enfield a new stab was taken at completing the still outstanding commitment at Barking. Between 8th October and 15th November 22 new Guys were licensed to complete, at long last, the conversion of route 23, whilst night service 295 (Charing Cross–Becontree Heath) was now also usually Guy worked. In common with all other night routes its vehicle allocation came from a daytime service which, in this case was the 23 except on Sunday nights when route 87 officially supplied the three buses required. After this latest influx of Guys route 87 (Gidea Park–Rainham) remained the only Barking route officially retaining LTs although, in true Barking fashion, LTs could and did appear anywhere at any time. Even the 87 was Guy worked on Sundays when the LTs were scheduled for Barking's once a week allocation on route 9 which ran right through from Mortlake to Becontree Heath on this day only. Logically the Guys should have been allocated to route 9, being the Sunday replacement for the 23, but presumably there was something that prevented their use. Perhaps Mortlake garage was too low, or the bridge at Barnes Bridge station? Most of the new vehicles in Barking's final major Guy intake were of the Weymann type supplemented by four Northern Counties and a solitary Park Royal specimen.

Enfield was now ready to place its first Guys into service and did so on 10th October 1945, two days after Barking's final batch began to arrive. Between then and 1st November 32 new Park Royal, Weymann and Northern Counties bodied vehicles were received, but in numerical terms they were exceeded by 45 vehicles drafted in under the first major re-allocation of utilities ever to take place. The Guy fleet at Victoria had proved extremely unpopular with drivers who, already much displeased by the performance of the unfrozen STDs, were unprepared to tolerate the Guys whose slow acceleration and general lack of speed was the cause of much late running which was particularly apparent on route 77A when compared with Merton's rather sprightlier Daimlers. To add insult to injury the classes totally ousted from Victoria by the Guys, the RTs and pre-war STDs, were the best and fastest performing double deckers in the whole fleet. Suburban north London was judged to be a far better proposition and a two-way swap was organised, Enfield's STLs for Victoria's Guys, and this took place in two sessions with 26 vehicles changing hands on 22nd October followed by the remaining 19 on the 31st. Most of Enfield's extensive operation was therefore converted from STL (or, in the case of route 121, ST) to Guy within the short space of three weeks, the routes concerned being: 102 Golders Green–Chingford: Edmonton–Chingford Hatch; 107 Borehamwood–Ponders End (weekdays); 107A Borehamwood (Sundays)–Enfield Chase (weekdays)–Enfield Lock; 121 Ponders End–Chingford (weekdays, non-continuous service); 135 Forty Hill to Brimsdown.

Route 102 was particularly interesting in that, with its sphere of operation some way from its home garage, crew reliefs were scheduled to be taken at Palmers Green. When delays occurred resulting in a relief crew being unavailable, it was not possible to remove the delayed vehicle into Palmers Green garage whose roof height prohibited the passage of Guys until the whole structure was jacked up by a few inches in about 1948, and a shunting manoeuvre outside the premises had to take place instead. The 102 was also noteworthy in that it met up with the eastern Guy network at Chingford and the western one at Golders Green; it was the only thread which ever linked the two. From November 1945 onwards the only Enfield routes still STL worked were 128 (Lower Edmonton–Chase Farm) and 144B (Forty Hill–Alexandra Park), and the latter succumbed to Guys in the first week of 1946 when six nearly new vehicles were trans-

ferred in from Upton Park plus one from Barking. On route 128 a railway bridge in Church Street, Lower Edmonton was reckoned to be low enough to make the operation of Guys risky. However for one complete week in 1948 the 128 was handed over to Park Royal-type examples of the class, which had presumably been calculated to be slightly lower in height than the remainder, but this experiment was never repeated.

With Enfield now replete and Barking almost so, it was time to tackle Upton Park for whom a very substantial fleet of Guys was planned, and on 5th November 1945 Northern Counties G 292 and Weymann G 406 were licensed to permit driver training to resume. Service operation commenced on 17th November and a constant inflow of new Northern Counties, Weymann and Park Royal vehicles was experienced through to the end of the year. 1946 saw a slackening off as the pace of new vehicle deliveries slowed, gradually diminishing to a trickle by the time the last of all, Park Royal G 435, entered service on 10th April. After 1st January 1946 the only Guys remaining to be delivered were of the Northern Counties and Park Royal varieties and all were of the new constant mesh type with revised gearchange positions. In theory these should all have gone to Upton Park which was the only garage now scheduled to receive new Guys, but for a reason which is not immediately clear, six out of the 34 went instead to Barking who, during January, sent six of its newest Weymann Guys to Upton Park to compensate for the shortfall. Three of Upton Park's services, 86, 145 and 175, were obvious candidates for Guys as the other participating garages already supplied this type of vehicle; similarly the Sunday operation on 86A. The only new candidate was the extremely frequent route 101 (North Woolwich–Wanstead) on which up to 54 buses per hour were scheduled over the busiest Royal Albert Dock–East Ham town hall section. In addition a short lived Monday-Friday allocation on route 66, which lasted only from 13th February to 16th April 1946 inclusive, found Upton Park's Guys working alongside those of Hornchurch. The small five bus allocation on route 86 did not last long and was handed back to LTs when its Guys were transferred to Enfield for route 144B in March 1946, whilst certain other Upton Park services such as 15, 40 and 100 (a subsidiary of the 15) were never known to see a Guy in action. This segregation of types was probably more due to restrictions caused by the listings on various destination blind sets than by any physical reason. During the period November 1945 to April 1946 large numbers of LTs left Upton Park to work elsewhere, notably at Palmers Green whose entire STL fleet was removed as a consequence, and when the programme finally ended Upton Park had amassed a stock of 92 Arabs which, at that time, was the largest in any London Transport garage.

The 1945 intake of new Daimlers to Merton continued alongside the Guy deliveries, although a slowing down occurred after August with no Daimlers at all licensed in September and only a trickle each month thereafter through to the end in March 1946. The last six months of 1945 had witnessed a remarkable influx of new utilities with no fewer than 294 licensed for service comprised of 244 Guys, 48 Daimlers and 2 Bristols. Statistically the busiest month had been July with 62 (43 Guy and 19 Daimler). With the end of the programme in sight the closing month of 1945 heralded the arrival of London's last new utility model, the Bristol K6A of which twenty were on order. Unsurprisingly it was decided that these should join B 1-9 at Hanwell, their original sphere of operation being designated as routes 92/A where the twenty vehicles were sufficient to cover the seventeen bus maximum requirement. This was the first and last occasion in the programme on which one type of utility had directly replaced another, Guys being rendered surplus as a result. Bs 11 and 13 were licensed for service on 12th December 1945 and the remainder between 1st and 14th January 1946, sweeping aside many Guys which mostly went to increase the fleet of Arabs at Upton Park either directly or, in some cases, through a three-way exchange involving Alperton. By this means Upton Park received twelve Mark I Arabs including the unique Duple bodied G 43, plus a few later types within whose ranks was the newer of the two Weymann bearerless vehicles, G 138.

With the licensing of G 435 on 10th April 1946 the purchase of utility and semiutility double deckers drew to a close; within a span of 4 years and 4 months, 656 vehicles had been absorbed into ten garages (including the Green Line Daimlers at Romford mentioned elsewhere), setting off chain reactions which resulted in an even larger number of subsequent reallocations of older classes. However one substantial batch of vehicles bearing the characteristics of utility construction under a veneer of post-war decor was still awaited and the first of these, D 182, was licensed at Sutton garage on 6th May 1946. From then until D 280 entered service on 28th November the batch of exactly one hundred Park Royal bodied Daimlers (D 182-281) maintained a steady inflow, enabling much needed STLs to take up duty elsewhere to restore service levels and provide the leeway which was so badly needed to set up a major renovation and rebuilding programme for these very useful vehicles. One by one all of Sutton's double deck operations were taken over by new Daimlers beginning with route 93 and ending with route 151, the complete list being: 80 Tooting Broadway–Lower Kingswood; 80A Tooting Broadway–Walton on the Hill; 93 Putney Bridge Station–Epsom (plus summer Sundays Morden–Dorking; 115 Wallington–Croydon Airport (weekday Sutton allocation only); 151 North Cheam (peaks)–Morden–Hackbridge (weekdays only); 156 Morden circular via Sutton and Cheam; 164 Morden–Epsom; 164A Morden–Tattenham Corner.

Although theoretically supplied with sufficient Daimlers to cover all its scheduled operational and maintenance requirements, in practice Sutton still continued to call in older vehicles. The fact that the one hundred vehicles were only just adequate for Sutton's needs was demonstrated when a mere one bus increase on route 151 from 5th February 1947 necessitated the official allocation of an ST for this duty which lasted, on paper at least, until the following November.

Guys from different ends of London meet up at Chingford. G 399 on route 102 was one of the vehicles supplied new to Enfield in October 1945 and it was the first of that year's Weymann deliveries to carry red livery. Brown G 302 was slightly newer; it entered service at Barking in January 1946 and was one of the first with the new design of clutch and gearbox. Alan B Cross

Route 101 was by far Upton Park's most impressive Guy route in terms both of frequency and the number of vehicles required to operate it. On 4th November 1946 a diversion was in force because of repair work to a blitz damaged swing bridge on the road between East Ham and Woolwich. Park Royal bodied G 357 is seen making the two mile detour via the King George V Dock past the SS Waiwera and a War Department locomotive awaiting shipment to China. Hulton Deutsch

Sutton's Daimlers were a great novelty when they first took the road. In their livery and indicator layout there was a strong hint of STL but the Daimler radiator quickly dispelled any illusion of family ancestry. Looking shiny and new, D 220 marks the start of an era at Morden where these distinctive vehicles were to make such a mark for the next seven years. J F Higham

CHAPTER TEN

THE LATE FORTIES – SHORT LIVED STABILITY

The early years of the post-war period were difficult ones in many respects, and while strenuous efforts were made to tackle the physical legacies and lack of infrastructure maintenance imposed by more than five years of conflict, commodity shortages continued and hard times were experienced universally. Public transport was by no means immune, and for London Transport the years up to 1950 presented many difficulties. Its bus engineers were overburdened by a severe maintenance backlog made worse by the enforced abandonment for half a decade of any coherent vehicle replacement programme. A huge proportion of the fleet, including all the numerous LTs and STs within it as well as many of the STLs, was by peacetime standards obsolete and would in normal circumstances have been replaced long since. The capital's pre-war double deckers, most of which carried Chiswick built composite bodies, had not been designed for a long life, and whilst it was possible to keep them going mechanically by a policy of make

do and mend, deteriorating timbers in the bodywork were a constant problem. All too often the Ministry of Transport's vehicle examiners would descend upon a garage to issue PSV 71 'stop' certificates which effectively consigned the recipient vehicles to scrap. Although from June 1947 onwards the magnificent RT family came on the road in impressive numbers, it was not until 1950 that the tide finally turned in their favour, and until then the unwanted and largely unloved utilities played an important role in keeping the wheels turning. But even they were beginning to fall foul of the PSV 71 syndrome, despite their comparative youthfulness, as an inevitable result of their sub-standard construction using many inferior materials. However from 1950 onwards London Transport was less concerned by the sudden and unplanned loss of an odd vehicle here or there; its goal was complete standardisation and its timetable which meant disposing of all the utilities by 1954 was, in fact, achieved.

Events in the post-war era affected the four utility classes in different ways, but with the exception of the Guys the common thread was their relative stability. Whilst much of the London fleet seemed to be constantly on the move – especially the STs which were regarded as the maids of all work and could appear on almost any route at any time – the eleven utility STDs and the 29 Bristols stayed put at their original garages. The Daimlers also remained basically static until the mass influx of Romford vehicles into Merton took place when their Green Line careers were over, and only in the case of the Guys were inter-garage transfers regularly experienced.

Above **Shortage of suitable rolling stock made the augmentation of services difficult in the early post-war years. However route 32 was improved by giving on all-day service to St Helier from November 1947. D16 is seen in Morden Road heading for Raynes Park.** Alan B Cross

Victoria's utility STDs were joined in due course by post-war versions of the same class; attractive and sturdy Leyland bodied PD1s which bore little in common with the utilities except their class designation and a general dislike of them by operating staff because of their slow gear change and poor pulling power. After the pre-war STDs temporarily at Victoria returned to Hendon (the last having departed in July 1945) the utilities were all concentrated back on route 22, in theory at least, and not until October 1946 when the post-war class arrived did an STD allocation resume on route 10. However the unpopularity of both types was recognised by a re-allocation of 30th April 1947 which, at the request of staff, spread the misery by allocating the 30 vehicles then scheduled for service amongst all routes in the garage. An equitable arrangement was devised whereby the number of STDs per route was apportioned in accordance with the total vehicle requirement. Thus on Mondays to Fridays the allocations were: route 77A – 8 STDs, route 137 – 7, route 22 – 4, route 52 – 4, route 77 – 4, route 10 – 3. No Sunday work was allocated to the STDs at this time; indeed throughout their career at Victoria Sunday work by STDs was, at best, spasmodic. The utilities were treated by the garage allocation staff as interchangeable with the post-war batch and could thus be found on any service, although operation on route 22 ceased when Victoria handed its workings over to Battersea in a reorganisation on 12th November 1947. Route 10 also fell by the wayside when new SRTs were allocated to it in May 1949 and, despite the problems which befell these vehicles and route 10's subsequent temporary reversion to STLs, the Leylands did not return to it. In a similar vein route 52 was lost to the STDs when new RTs arrived in October 1949.

At Hanwell the Bristols led an even more restricted existence than Victoria's Leylands, and although they later appeared on a scheduled basis on routes 83/A and at weekends on route 55 (Hayes–Chiswick), they are never known to have appeared on routes 105 or 120/A. Even on route 55 the operation was restricted to the first batch (B 1-9) whose overall height of approximately 14ft 3ins made them acceptable under the railway bridge in Acton Lane whereas the later and slightly taller Duple bodied vehicles were not. Route 97, traditionally the home of B 1-9, was considerably augmented in a number of stages from its original nine-bus Monday-Friday requirement to a maximum of sixteen by 4th December 1946. From the outset a larger Saturday vehicle requirement had meant the regular appearance of LTs alongside the Bristols, but from September 1945 these were scheduled on Mondays-Fridays too, their role being taken over by STLs during 1946. In May 1948 the Saturday operation of route 97 was officially converted to Guys on a swap arrangement with route 83 which received the Bristols instead. Sundays-only route 83A also became an official Bristol allocation at the same time but this only lasted until August 1949 when new RTWs arrived. On 13th April 1949 an all-B Monday-Friday presence was once again achieved on route 97 when eight post-war STDs, transferred from route 55, displaced an equivalent number of

Bristols from routes 92/A. For the 92/A this proved to be only a short term arrangement for, in October 1949, the now reduced Bristol presence ceased altogether, never to resume, their place being taken by STLs and also, at weekends, by RTWs. It had been decided to transfer the eleven Guys, which was all of the class still remaining at Hanwell, to other garages and as a result the Bs were moved across to route 83 as replacements, the last Guys departing on 12th October.

Through being allocated solely to one very specific corner of south London the Daimler fleet (or at least the majority section of it operated by the Central Bus department) gave an air of stability, even insularity, despite its substantial size. In fact very little happened of any significant impact. Despite the large number of Daimlers at Merton, there were by no means enough to cover all workings and many STLs remained, officially allocated on

weekdays only to routes 49 and (from March 1946) 118, but in fact they could and did appear on all services. STL numbers were strengthened further in December 1948 when five Daimlers were transferred to Green Line work, but even before this change minority STL allocations had officially come into force on routes 77 and 88, although in a counter move Ds were allocated back to route 118 on Mondays-Fridays from October 1949. Sutton, too, depended from time to time on other classes, either borrowed or officially allocated on a short term basis. Until 1949 STs were not uncommon; indeed a four bus Monday-Friday increase on route 93 on 14th December 1949 led to the last new allocation for these now obsolete petrol engined machines only a month before their final demise. After departure of the STs, members of the STL class regained a permanent presence at Sutton and worked alongside the Daimlers.

In May 1947 Sutton's Daimlers were joined on route 93 by Merton's utilities. Here D 93 is sandwiched at Morden between newer Daimlers and an STL, its brown and white colour scheme contrasting with the predominantly red livery carried by the other three. Alan B Cross

Although theoretically Sutton's fleet of one hundred Daimlers was sufficient to cover all requirements, this was not in fact the case. From April 1947 through to January 1948 former Thomas Tilling open staircase ST 996 helped out on a low mileage basis and is seen alongside D 213 at the Queen Victoria, North Cheam. Alan B Cross

A small number of service and allocation changes affected the Daimlers in the years 1946-9. Merton-type Daimlers began working alongside the Sutton variety on route 93 on summer Sundays and bank holidays from 4th May 1947, taking them on a seasonal extension as far south as Dorking, a practice which was resumed each summer thereafter. An all year round Merton presence on the 93 was established on Saturdays commencing 15th November 1947, on which date Merton ceased to divert buses from route 88 to provide Saturday journeys on route 156, serving it only on Mondays-Fridays henceforth. The heavy summer bank holiday demand for transport to and from Chessington Zoo sometimes found Merton working the Kingston to Leatherhead section of route 65, a service in which it did not normally participate, but this was always on a supplementary schedule which theoretically could be cancelled by local arrangement if deemed necessary due to weather conditions or other factors. On Merton's route 32, St Helier was served full time instead of peak hours only from 12th November 1947 but the Saturday operation was withdrawn after 9th April 1949. From 2nd January 1949 Sutton's route 151, hitherto a weekdays-only operation, became daily in one of the few major schedule changes to affect Sutton for several years.

The first major event to have an impact on the Guys once they had all been in service for a while was the summer programme which came into effect in May 1946. In a minus vein, Upton Park's weekday workings on route 145 (they did not participate on Sundays) were officially converted back to LT operation to enable the displaced vehicles to build up Guy stocks at other garages, although in practice Guys still managed to appear on a fairly regular though unofficial basis. However the main feature of the 1946 summer programme was the peacetime reintroduction of weekend and bank holiday extensions to places of leisure interest, and quite by chance the Guys played an unusually prominent role in this respect. On Saturday afternoons and Sundays Barking's route 62 was extended from Becontree Heath to Chigwell Row, Hornchurch's 247 likewise reached Chigwell Row from Collier Row, and Enfield's 102 was projected beyond Chingford to High Beach. On Sundays Upton Park's Guys on route 101 ran beyond Wanstead to Lambourne End whilst at Alperton new seasonal Sunday route 72A (North Wembley–Chessington Zoo) was Guy worked. First operated on Saturday and Sunday 25th/26th May, these extensions into the countryside became an annual seasonal ritual, generally ending for the winter in about mid-October. However Alperton only worked the 72A up to and including the 1948 season after which petrol STLs from Middle Row took over, whilst after two years at Chigwell Row, Hornchurch's route 247 was projected even further to Lambourne End from the summer of 1948 onwards. With the introduction of the winter programme of October 1946 Barking's Guys were removed from route 23C on Sundays in favour of LTs and likewise Hanwell substituted STLs for Guys on the Sunday 83A.

The year 1947 saw several changes to Guy operations. From 1st January Barking

Left The widespread schedule alterations of November 1947 brought Merton's Daimlers to route 5A on Saturdays. The Clapham Common terminus at Old Town finds D 180 standing alongside Holloway's ST 424 and Merton's STL 2007. The date is 13th February 1949, and changes in the fleet were rapid at this time. The STL has just received the last repaint of its career to see it through its final eighteen months; ST 424 is destined to be withdrawn for scrap in four days' time, and D 180 will have gone for its first overhaul and will have lost its Daimler engine before the year's end.
Alan B Cross

Centre left Another November 1947 schedule change found Tottenham garage working route 102 on Saturdays. Although this route was itself no stranger to Guys it had never before been host to the Mark I variety as Enfield's fleet consisted entirely of the later model. G 1 stands beside the Golders Green Hippodrome which for many years marked the western terminus of route 102. V C Jones

Bottom left Kew Green was a Sundays-only destination for Guys up to the summer of 1949 when RTWs took over on route 83A, although Hanwell's share of the route did not stay Guy worked to the end, Bristols becoming the norm from May 1948 onwards. Hanwell's G 114 and Alperton's G 372 while away the time between journeys. J H Aston

Right Alperton's Sunday allocation on route 72 brought Guys roaring through Daimler territory down into Surrey, but they always looked very out of place in locations such as Hook and Esher. Utilities in new-found red livery were very much a feature of 1948, and G 169, one of four Northern Counties Guys delivered new to Alperton, displays its new paintwork and now also sports a set of upholstered seats for the first time. A M Wright

Below right Car traffic on the Kingston By-Pass was sparse in the early post-war years. G 101 heads for Chessington Zoo with a light load during the second year of the seasonal 72A operation. Alan B Cross

followed Upton Park's earlier example by officially removing Guys from route 145 on weekdays. This was done partly to offset an increase in requirements on route 62, but a shortage of Guys had already led to frequent substitution by LTs and STs and the change basically acknowledged the prevailing situation. Thereafter Barking's supply of Guys to the 145 fluctuated. They remained a constant feature of Sundays until the route was taken over by RTLs in 1949 and made a return appearance on Saturdays from November 1947 onwards, but on Mondays-Fridays their appearances were spasmodic. From the summer programme of 30th April 1947 Enfield's routes 121 and 135 became daily operations, the 121 having meanwhile become a full time service no longer linked to factory times. On 17th September 1947 another Barking service lost its full time Guy allocation when the basic 23C weekday operation became LT worked, although Guys still made regular appearances on cross-linkings from route 23. The displaced vehicles went to Hornchurch to depose LTs from route 86A and the single STL which operated weekdays on route 249. One small pocket of STLs still remained at Hornchurch on route 165 and these were moved out in a gradual process between 5th December 1947 and 21st January 1948 when more ex-Barking Guys were transferred in.

The winter programme of 1947, deferred from October until 12th November because of delay over union agreement, introduced a reduced working week for bus crews requiring new schedules everywhere and involving, as a result, some substantial reallocations of routes between garages. The Guy-operated services escaped from the reallocation process almost unscathed except in north London where, in compensation for losing half of its work on route 102 to Palmers Green, Enfield gained a first-time foothold on route 144A (Alexandra Park–Enfield, Halfway House) in addition to a large increase on the 144B. For rostering reasons Enfield lost its Saturday presence on route 102 entirely, but this did not herald a complete loss of Guys on this day. Tottenham replaced Enfield on Saturdays using initially a mixture of open staircase LTs, STs and Guys, the latter introducing the Mark I variety to the 102 in place of the later type vehicles used exclusively by Enfield. Tottenham's Saturday allocation on the 102 underwent several official variations of vehicle types thereafter, but in practice Guys quickly became the mainstay until RTLs were available in October 1949, remaining even then in reduced numbers until about July 1950. Minor November alterations in east London saw the conversion of Upton Park's route 86 workings to Gs on Saturdays and the complete loss by Barking of its 175 workings on this day, whilst in the southern area Merton gained a Saturday foothold on route 5A (Clapham Common–South Wimbledon with a peak hour extension to North Cheam).

Although initially deemed to be covered by STLs, in fact Daimlers frequently appeared and in October 1948 they took over officially. On 16th April 1949 the 5A ceased to run on Saturdays and was replaced by the former Sundays-only route 5 (Clapham Common –Raynes Park). For Saturday operation the service was initially extended to Worcester Park although this extension ran only up to 22nd October, being withdrawn with the start of the winter programme.

From October 1947 onwards and throughout 1948 hired coaches made an invaluable contribution to peak hour services at a time when the shortage of serviceable double deckers was at its most serious. In this Dagenham scene on 23rd July 1948 Guys and hired coaches appear in equal numbers with a solitary ST on route 148 to uneven the balance. The only Guy whose identity can be discerned is Hornchurch's Weymann bodied G 413; the coaches range from a diminutive Dennis Ace via a Gilford and a Dennis Lancet to the almost new Guy Arab III bringing up the rear.

The shortest route worked by utilities was the 249 which ran three times every hour with an end-to-end journey time of just seven minutes. This one-bus shuttle working was taken over by Guys in September 1947, and in this view Weymann bodied G 382 prepares to set out from Upminster.
Alan B Cross

Few changes affected the Guy fleet in 1948 and all those that did so were related to the summer and winter programmes of 5th May and 20th October respectively. Notable on the former date was the introduction of utilities to a second night route, in this case Tottenham's 290 (Edmonton, Park Road – Pimlico). This marked a change of linkage for rolling stock purposes from day route 73 and its LTs to the 76/34B. The latest Barking-based service to see a return of LTs for its basic allocation was the 23B in May but this was followed by a reversion back to Guys in October, although – as in the similar case of the 23C earlier – a Guy presence had continued throughout because of the journeys cross-linked with route 23.

Right **On 17th April 1948 D 126 heads for Tooting still displaying its original brown paintwork. At the start of the year brown liveried utilities were quite commonplace with about 240 remaining, but such was the pace of repainting that by April they were becoming noticeably rarer.**
Alan B Cross

Above **The last month in which vehicles ran in brown livery was almost certainly September 1948. On the 11th of that month Northern Counties G 256 stands at the Rainham terminus of route 103, still in its original paintwork which has now gone very flat with rust marks pinpointing the screwheads on the cream area above the lower deck windows.**
Alan B Cross

Above right and Right **Between September 1947 and January 1948 Hornchurch's minority workings by double deck types other than Guys were eliminated through the transferring in of utilities from Barking. G 256 (now in red livery in contrast to the previous photograph) is seen on route 165, formerly the home of Hornchurch's last STLs, whilst similar Northern Counties bodied G 251 sets out from Upminster on the 86A previously worked by LTs. Both vehicles carry the revised destination blind layout first introduced in mid-1948.** Alan T Smith/F G Reynolds

Alone amongst Alperton's routes, the 187 never received a weekday Guy allocation although from the winter of 1947/8 onwards the type worked it spasmodically on Sundays until the arrival of new RTWs in August 1949. Northern Coachbuilders bodied G 142 heads for Hampstead Heath on a hot day.
F G Reynolds

In 1949 Sutton garage encountered the major snag that its one hundred Daimlers all became due for overhaul within a few months of each other. To accommodate the demanding overhaul programme a variety of vehicles were transferred in or borrowed. Keeping D 231 company in Sutton garage in July 1949 were two vehicles in the 'borrowed' category, six wheeler LT 395 on loan from Plumstead and STL 808 borrowed from Croydon. Alan T Smith

In the early part of 1949 the large Guy fleet was stretched so fully to its capacity that a scheduled increase of three buses in the Monday-Friday requirement on routes 76 and 34B, effective from 14th February, could only be met by an allocation of STs and it was not until January 1950 that additional Guys were drafted into Tottenham. Over the years Tottenham's Guy fleet remained remarkably stable with no transfers in and only one out between December 1946 and January 1950, although vehicles of this class were often borrowed from nearby Enfield and occasionally from elsewhere as occasion demanded. With the summer programme of 1949, introduced on 13th April, Barking's night route 295 was officially converted from G to RTL, three new vehicles being allocated to join the Guy stock on the 23 from which the night operation was drawn. Also at Barking, three regular workings were introduced to route 148 on Mondays-Fridays in addition to the odd journeys worked off route 23's allocation. These new workings were allocated to RTLs (in line with the main Seven Kings allocation on this route) but the Guys from route 23 still continued to put in a regular appearance. The same programme saw the introduction of a Sunday service on Alperton's Guy-worked

July 6th 1949 was the opening date of the spectacular, award-winning Central Line station at Newbury Park with its 30ft high, copper-covered reinforced concrete barrel vault roof. For just over two years it was served by Hornchurch based Guys such as Massey G 315 until they were displaced from route 66 by SRTs in October 1951. L T Museum

route 79 and as a result Middle Row took over the Sunday work on 72/A. During the 1949 summer, up to mid-August, Upton Park had a Sunday allocation on route 145 for the first and only time, which it covered with Guys until Seven Kings resumed using newer vehicles. On 20th July 1949 route 79 was extended to Northolt Aerodrome but the three additional Guys required were not available so STs were employed until 12th October when Hanwell finally lost its Guy fleet enabling deficiencies at Alperton and elsewhere to be made good. Similarly an increase in Barking's scheduled output on route 175 from two to eleven vehicles (ignoring the cross-workings from other routes) on 29th June had to be met with LTs and STs because Guys were unavailable. In this instance two Guys were drafted in from Hanwell in October but it was not until the following month that a full Guy allocation became possible as a result of Enfield receiving new RTLs. Barking's shortage of Guys became evident during the summer when its official allocation on route 145 reverted totally to LTs until August when new RTLs took over. Upton Park's Saturday Guy allocation on the 145 ceased at about the same time under an influx of RTs, and Guy utilities had gone from the 145 for ever.

Guys drifted slowly away from route 145 and none were to be found on it after 1949. The cause of the brown streaks running down the front rainshield on Barking's Massey bodied G 176 can be diagnosed as screws rusting in the rotting woodwork which lies behind. C Carter

On 26th October 1949 a new Guy operated route 86B (Romford, New Mill Inn–Harold Hill, Myrtle Road) was inaugurated using two vehicles which had already been transferred into Hornchurch from Hanwell in anticipation of its commencement. At about the same time the last utility-worked night route, Tottenham's 290, was taken over by RTLs after less than eighteen months of Guy operation, as was the whole of the Sunday service on route 76. Up to now no Monday-Friday allocation on any route had been converted from Guy direct to new RT-family vehicles, but this omission was rectified on 9th November when Enfield's share of route 144A received a small fleet of eight new RTWs. On this occasion the displaced Arabs were transferred to Barking to reintroduce a Guy allocation to route 23C in lieu of LTs, but this was only a short term measure as modernisation of the 23C was imminent. This route, along with the 62, was in prospect for new RTLs in December, as was Enfield's 144B, and this meant that alternative work would have to be found for the displaced Guys. At Barking it was a simple matter of transferring them to route 175 to ease out this garage's remaining obsolete vehicles but the fourteen due to be made surplus at Enfield presented more of a problem. One option would have been to move them to Alperton where route 18, though nominally still worked entirely by Guys, had been increasingly taken over by STs which were now fast approaching their last days in London service. It would appear, however, that a decision had already been taken not to build Alperton's Guy fleet back to strength. Just before Christmas STLs began to arrive after a lapse of some years and by about April 1950 these had taken over route 18 completely.

October 1949 changes at Hanwell saw the end of Guy operation and the official removal of Bristols from the 92/A. B 14 cruises along Wembley High Road on route 92A past one of the 'Joe' Lyons tea shops which were once everyday landmarks on the London scene. *Roy Marshall*

New route 86B made its mark on the Romford bus scene in October 1949 but was destined to be swallowed up before long by a revamped 247A. Romford Market Place is setting in April 1950 for this view of G 244. *Alan T Smith*

Above **The arrival of a small allocation of Guys at Seven Kings in December 1949 did not go down too well with the drivers there. Most were of the later Weymann bodied variety ex Enfield as typified by G 396 at Brentwood on route 86. Direct from overhaul came Park Royal G 345 which is seen at Stratford Broadway on the cinderella Sunday service 25.** S N J White/Alan T Smith

Left **Guys galore! A view of Barking garage yard taken just before new RTLs began to arrive in late 1949 for routes 23C and 62 shows a line-up of fourteen vehicles, many with their radiators covered to assist the morning start-up. Typical of the body mix of the time, eight are by Northern Counties, three Park Royal, two Massey and one Weymann. Some are too far from the camera to identify individually but the nine closest are, from right to left, G 303, 171, 158, 162, 300, 424, 302, 85 and 188.** D A Jones

Below left **A sign of changing times at Forty Hill. The crew of Enfield's G 228 are preoccupied by its broken life guard, but much more significant is brand new RTL 472 representing the new generation which has just ousted Guys and other older vehicles from route 144B.** D A Jones

Instead it was decided to set up a new operating base for Guys, at Seven Kings. Earlier this garage had been physically unable to accept these vehicles, but doorway heightening had now made access possible. Seven Kings still had a small fleet of LTs which were running, alongside similar vehicles from Upton Park, on route 86A, and alongside Hornchurch Guys on this route and also on the 86 itself. Like the petrol-engined STs, this class was now on its last legs and the Executive wished to replace the few remaining vehicles as speedily as possible. New buses of the RT family could not be made available for the 86/A so Guys were selected as the best alternative. On 1st December Enfield's G 400 was sent to Seven Kings for crew training and on 14th G 345 was received direct from overhaul to speed up the process. Guy operation commenced on 22nd December and at the year's end six were in service with more arrivals imminent. Seven Kings did not participate in the Sunday operation on route 86A, and the 86 was worked by RTLs on Sundays. However the Guys were not idle on this day of the week, being scheduled to replace RTLs on a curious four-bus afternoon and evening service 25 (Stratford Broadway–Little Heath); this was renumbered 25A on 3rd May 1950.

In the days before the motor car became king, the staging of major race meetings at Epsom Downs was a signal for the operation of special bus services which provided the only means by which many could get to and from the course. Garages from all over the fleet contributed vehicles; these could be seen departing from their home bases early in the morning with their special destination displays already in situ, and arriving back mid-evening well after the day's racing was over. An incredible mixture of vehicles took part ranging from the oldest in the fleet (which were usually in the majority) to some of the newest. Here, as nowhere else, was an opportunity for utilities of various makes, and from a variety of garages, to be seen running together.

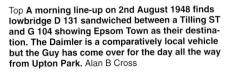

Top **A morning line-up on 2nd August 1948 finds lowbridge D 131 sandwiched between a Tilling ST and G 104 showing Epsom Town as their destination. The Daimler is a comparatively local vehicle but the Guy has come over for the day all the way from Upton Park.** Alan B Cross

Centre **A contingent of three Guys from Barking has found its way from Morden station to Epsom race course. The centre vehicle of the three cannot be identified, but the leader is Park Royal bodied G 329 whilst Northern Counties G 156 brings up the rear.** Lens of Sutton

From an enthusiast's point of view the Epsom racecourse service was fascinating because it could often attract some of the fleet's oddities away from their usual spheres of operation. Such was the case here, where the unique Duple bodied G 43 is immediately recognisable as it pounds along with an RT in hot pursuit and a couple of STLs trailing behind. G F Ashwell

The passage of time brought the inevitable increase in private car ownership and the demand for special Epsom race day services dwindled such that the need to call in buses from the far corners of the fleet faded away. In its last year of service D 6 stands in gloomy weather ahead of a Saunders bodied RT, the marked difference in height between the two being particularly apparent in this view.

CHAPTER ELEVEN

DAIMLERS IN GREEN LIVERY

When what remained of the Green Line network was withdrawn for the duration of the war on 29th September 1942 in order to conserve supplies of fuel and rubber, no-one could have known that more than three years would elapse before it would be possible to start the operation up again. Certainly no-one would have guessed that the two most frequent services on the network, which had latterly been run by the newest STLs, would recommence using rolling stock quite as austere as utility Daimlers, but this is what happened in the case of Romford-based Green Line routes 721 and 722.

When London Transport agreed in August 1945 to purchase fifty Duple bodied Daimlers the possibility of using a high proportion of them to restore Green Line operation to the Romford Road services east of Aldgate was very much in mind. Twelve of the batch were Daimler engined and not considered suitable, but the remainder were AEC powered CWA6s of which all except one were earmarked to be painted in Green Line livery for allocation to the London Road, Romford garage which had now been released from its wartime use. The 37 Green Line Daimlers were D 133-137, 141, 143-149, 151-154, 156-159, 161, 164-170, 172-179. Delivered from November 1945 onwards, they were stored at Grays, Epping and Northfleet garages and also at Romford itself

Top **Brentwood in March 1946, and D 137 is about to depart on its tightly timed run through Romford and Stratford to Aldgate. At this stage utilities in green livery are still very much a novelty, and the absence of advertisements gives a mild air of 'class' befitting their Green Line status. Use is made of the full depth of the front indicator box and, for the first time, a route number is displayed in the side box.** S L Poole

Above **D 176 was one of the later vehicles in the batch licensed in readiness for the start of route 722 on 3rd April 1946. Seen in the Minories bus and coach station at Aldgate, it now carries the black on amber blinds which replaced the original ones in May 1946.** S A Newman

ready for the day when they would be called into service. In due course twenty-two were licensed on 1st March 1946 in readiness to cover the twenty scheduled workings on route 721 which began its post-war existence on March 6th. The 721, which had been known in pre-war days as route Y1 and from 4th December 1940 until its temporary suspension as the 55, linked Aldgate with Romford and Brentwood and was by far the most frequent of all Green Line services, capable of rising to a three minute headway between Aldgate and Romford in rush hours. Its partner service 722 (Aldgate to Corbets Tey via Hornchurch and Upminster – formerly the Y2 and then 58) resumed on 3rd April 1946 with the balance of the Daimlers being licensed on 25th March (the first day of the licensing quarter) in readiness for this. These two services called for some quite high speed running along roads which, in the early post-war years, included many stretches still surfaced in granite setts, and many a thrilling, bouncy ride could be had on Romford's Daimlers. The only element of semi-luxury on the 721/2 at this time was provided by RT 97 which was fitted out for experimental Pay As You Board operation and ran alongside the Daimlers between April and July 1946, looking as handsome in its Green Line livery as the Daimlers were spartan.

For their first few weeks of operation the 721 and 722 vehicles carried traditional destination blinds with white lettering on a black background, but in May 1946 this was superseded by black on amber which was to be the Green Line standard henceforth. Just about this time, on 29th May, a third Green Line service started which was also to become synonymous with Romford garage, route 726 (Marylebone to Whipsnade Zoo). This seasonal, limited stop service was entrusted at first to Watford (Leavesden Road) garage who worked it with 10T10s, but by July Romford had got its foot in the door and from the 1947 season onwards worked the 726 in its entirety. The mode of operation was for vehicles to work up to Aldgate in service and to then run light across central London to pick up their scheduled 726 departure from Marylebone, the 'dead' running being a consequence of the closure of the central area zone to coaches under the Amulree rules established in the early nineteen thirties. Romford was scheduled to run STLs although none were specifically allocated until August when five were received to cover this work. The incoming STLs were of the 15STL16 type, the last pre-war deliveries and the best of their class; the same type, in fact, that Romford had operated up to 1942. These five STLs stayed at Romford even during the

winter months when the 726 did not operate, augmenting the Daimlers, and were themselves augmented by more of the same type in 1948/9 to cover Daimler overhauls. Romford's staff apparently regarded the Daimlers and STLs as interchangeable, and although the utilities were not officially allocated to work the 726 until 1949 they actually appeared on it long before this. For the 1948 season onwards the London terminus was revised to Allsop Place, Baker Street but otherwise the service worked unchanged throughout the Daimler era when a long line-up of utilities laying over at Whipsnade Zoo on a summer bank holiday was a sight to behold.

Above **Aldgate again, this time with a Green Line 10T10 coach in the background instead of a trolleybus. The paper sticker proclaiming LONDON TRANSPORT EXECUTIVE as the legal owner indicates that the photograph was probably taken shortly after nationalisation on 1st January 1948. A minor livery variation on D 145 is that the window ledges on both decks are painted green instead of the usual white.**
J H Aston

Towards the end of 1948 the need arose to find replacements for Romford's STLs whose chassis were required for conversion into the planned SRT class. Five of Merton's Daimlers were earmarked; all were Brush bodied vehicles (Ds 67-69, 71, 73) which happened to be going through overhaul at the time and were ready for service at Romford between 15th and 24th December 1948. From October 1948 onwards Romford's own Daimlers began to emerge from their first overhaul (which in some cases was also their last) and in doing so introduced a revised colour scheme. Gone was the brown roof, which was now painted green as were the mudguards and life rails. The window relief, formerly broken white, was now a rich shade of cream (although this tended to fade somewhat with the passage of time). When the Brush Daimlers joined the Romford fleet they introduced yet another livery variation, this time a much more attractive two tone green version of the standard Green Line livery as applied to single deckers. This must have met with approval for it was also extended to all the standard Romford vehicles earmarked for overhaul from 16th December onwards. As a result fifteen of the Duple batch ended up in green and cream with the remaining twenty-two in full Green Line style. On the latter the pale green on the lower deck was continued right around the driver's cab area whilst the Lincoln green of the roof swept down at the rear to meet the centre panels in a styling reminiscent of the Northern Counties Guys when they were new.

Operating base for the Romford Green Line routes was the spacious ex-Hillman garage in London Road. Being attended to over the pits are three Daimlers and a TF underfloor engined Leyland coach which has come up from Grays for routine docking. The Daimler on the left, D 168, has received a radiator badge which is a green version of the standard blue ones ordered for the Merton and Sutton Daimlers. D 145 stands on the right but the centre one is unidentified. LT Museum

In August 1949 fully laden D 135 corners fast at Golders Green on its inbound run from Whipsnade Zoo to Baker Street. Although not easy to discern in a black and white photograph, the vehicle carries the 1948 green and cream livery; the green mudguards give the game away. Alan B Cross

The smart two-tone green colour scheme introduced to the Romford fleet on the five Brush bodied vehicles transferred in from Merton is well illustrated in this view of D 69. Prince Marshall

The two ultimate Green Line liveries can be compared in this Aldgate scene taken towards the end of the Daimler era. Green and cream D 141 is on the left, all-green D 149 on the right. The presence of two 721s on the stand at the same time indicates the high frequency of this service compared to more traditional Green Line operations. Romford's Daimlers covered, on average, 55,000 miles per year compared with a maximum of 49,000 for the average service bus. D A Jones

Although accepted by the Country Bus & Coach department as a stop-gap measure, the Daimlers lasted a surprisingly long time at Romford, but in November 1949 it was decided that some of the 1950 allocation of new RTs should be earmarked to replace the "spartan and hard-riding Daimlers... good as they may be structurally and mechanically". When it came – a month later than originally anticipated – the takeover by the RT was impressively rapid and there were mass withdrawals of Daimlers on 4th and 8th August 1950. Some were stored temporarily at Grays and many others were delicensed but remained in Romford garage where there was plenty of spare space. In October almost all were gathered together at the old AEC works in Ferry Lane, Walthamstow, awaiting their fate. However not quite all of the green Daimlers were immediately withdrawn upon the influx of RTs, six vehicles being kept on until October to provide rolling stock for the Whipsnade service if required. Then, to the surprise of many, Ds 149, 151, 153, 161, 174 and 179 made a surprise reappearance at Romford on 1st December for the Christmas and New Year period, but when they finally moved out on 21st January 1951 their departure really did mean the end of the Daimler era on Green Line.

When withdrawal of the Green Line Daimlers was originally mooted there was a hope that Central Buses would take them into its fleet at Merton, and discussions to this effect took place in January and February 1950. The two departments were, however, in dispute over the number of new RTs being allocated for country bus work, and perhaps because of this Central Buses refused to take the Daimlers. By April it had been resolved that they should be absorbed into other garages within the Country Bus Department, displacing 42 STLs which would be painted red and transferred to the central area. However this proposition met with considerable resistance at local level, not least because of the problems of introducing a 'new' type at various garages along with the

Above **On 9th December 1950 D 170 makes a brave and unusual sight on route 5 in its two tone green colours. A London Transport fleet name has now been applied and the Green Line bullseyes have been removed.** Alan B Cross

It was inevitably only a matter of time before Merton's green Daimlers were earmarked to display advertising material. D 177 sports a full set of posters as it stands at Oxford Circus whilst working on route 88. F G Reynolds

training and other costs involved. Eventually expediency dictated a complete about-turn in policy to the extent that, at the time of the mass withdrawals in August 1950, the operational career in London of the Green Line Daimlers was now deemed to be over. The official line now was that the Daimlers were in poor structural condition, having accumulated high mileages at above average speeds over bad road surfaces, and that they should be disposed of. Authority was sought by the Chief Mechanical Engineer to sell all 42 even though most were not yet five years old and their combined book value was still considerable. However fate was to decree a change of plan leading to a substantial lease of life.

When they heard that the Daimlers were to be put up for sale, the staff at Merton – unaware that their departmental bosses had refused to accept them a few months earlier – asked if they could have them in place of STLs which, in their contention, were generally in poorer condition. The Executive duly conceded to let them try out six experimentally and on 16th November the designated vehicles (D 172, 173, 175-178) were collected from Ferry Lane to begin work at Merton six days later. They were found to be by no means in the exhausted state which had been latterly claimed and as a result an official change of

policy quickly took place so that, from 1st December onwards, the remainder began to trickle into Merton a few at a time. The final arrivals, towards the end of January, were the six which had been temporarily reinstated at Romford over Christmas and the New Year. On arrival the Green Line insignia were replaced by standard LONDON TRANSPORT lettering, and much of the vehicles' former glory was lost when they were disfigured by the subsequent posting of advertisements.

They were used indiscriminately on all of Merton's services where they provided an unusual splash of colour and, apart from D 133 which was repainted red in February, the remainder all spent in excess of six months at Merton in green livery. Eventually an intensive repainting programme commenced at the end of May, the last green Daimler of all being D 175 which emerged from Chiswick in its new coat of red paint on 31st August 1951.

Above and right **The last Daimler to carry green livery was D 175, seen here endeavouring to absorb a large queue in what is presumably the evening rush hour at Morden station. On 31st August 1951 the same vehicle heads through Chiswick back to Merton in its new coat of red paint.** Alan B Cross/Alan T Smith

CHAPTER TWELVE

THE CLOSING YEARS

Guys actively participated in sweeping away the final vestiges of the LT and ST era during the first few days of 1950. Seven Kings received several more, mostly Weymann bodied examples ex-Enfield, to bring its stock up to the required level of thirteen by 11th January. A notable exception to the former Enfield stock was G 5, latterly Hornchurch based, which arrived direct from overhaul on the 4th, but it was passed on to Tottenham exactly a week later and no other early-type Arabs were ever again allocated to Seven Kings. The very last of the splendid LT six wheeled double deckers ended their days at Upton Park, without commemoration, on 11th January and Guys took over their duties on the 86A the next day. In order to make the Guys available Upton Park had received an allocation of STLs whose normal sphere of operation was designated as route 101 where they made an interesting break from the usual mass diet of Guys. The time had now arrived for Guys to assist in ousting some of the very last petrol-engined STs which were scattered around various garages including Tottenham whose route 67 was the last to be officially scheduled with a complete allocation of this type of vehicle (though some were also to be found on the 76 and 34B). Although the 67 went over to STLs, Guys were acquired for the other two services in the form of ex-Enfield G 216-8; these were the only Arabs of the Mark II type ever to stay for any length of time at Tottenham, where they remained until new vehicles took over in March 1951.

The new decade began with all the utility classes continuing to fulfil a major role in the provision of London's public transport, but change was already in the air. The Executive's first post-war priority of replacing all the remaining petrol engined double deckers and the LTs had now been achieved, and the direct replacement of Guys by new vehicles of the RT family at the end of 1949 set a pattern which was destined to continue. The post-war rolling stock replacement programme envisaged the utilities remaining in service until 1953, but factors were arising which militated against this. Of major concern was the rapidly deteriorating condition of the bodywork on many, a problem highlighted by the enforced withdrawal in March 1950 of Gs 73 and 113 when they were found to be completely beyond economic repair. An equally intractable problem was the hostility of the driving staff towards two of the utility classes, the STDs and Gs, which their union representatives lost no opportunity to voice at their regular meetings with management. The most vociferous complaints were against the Leylands, and a management assertion in April 1950 that they were substantially the same as the one hundred Titans at Hendon and would remain in service until 1953, subject to body condition, only inflamed the situation. In fact, although the implication was not generally realised at the time, the phrase 'subject to body condition' marked a subtle change in official policy. The enforced withdrawal of the two Guys in March had caused the Executive to acknowledge what its engineers already knew, namely that the bodies on most of the utilities were deteriorating rapidly and that many could only remain serviceable until 1953 subject to considerable financial outlay. The Executive was forced to acknowledge that replacement on the basis of body condition rather than age was the best course to take even if this meant keeping STLs in service longer than originally planned.

Of the Guy garages, the staff at Hornchurch remained the most outspoken in demanding new vehicles in place of the utilities, but they received no consolation in being told that their double deck fleet consisting one hundred per cent of Guys could be considered as modern since only three out of the 82 then in stock pre-dated 1945. Barking garage jumped on the bandwagon of complaints in April 1950 by requesting new buses for route 23 where the Guys shared considerable portions of road with RT-types, only to be told that with 46 RTLs and 24 RTWs the garage already had its fair share of modern vehicles and could not expect more yet awhile. No doubt anxious to appease its more vociferous members, the Transport & General Workers Union even suggested that the utilities might be sent to replace trams in south London thereby releasing the RTs and RTLs being stockpiled for this purpose, only to be told in no uncertain terms that this could not be contemplated.

By 1950 the fleet was already beginning to show signs of the almost total standardisation which was to prevail during the later part of the decade. At Victoria in the spring of 1950 G 8 on route 76 contrasts, like a cuckoo in the nest, with the RT family vehicles which predominate. The modern vehicles are, from left to right, RT 1557, RT 1240, SRT 28, RT 2388 and RT 1597. Ken Blacker collection

Meanwhile the Guy presence in east London was at its height, and their importance was further enhanced by the introduction on 3rd May 1950 of new route 174 (Dagenham–Romford, Parkside) as a daily four-bus operation worked from Barking garage. A little before this, on 5th April, Hornchurch's hybrid route 247 had been converted entirely to double deckers (apart from one afternoon peak journey worked off route 250) for which four Northern Counties Guys were transferred from Barking where they had been rendered surplus by the arrival of new RTWs for route 23B. Further developments took place on 11th October 1950 when route 174 was extended beyond Romford to the Harold Hill estate replacing the 86B after only a year's existence and introducing a Hornchurch allocation alongside Barking's on the 174. Harold Hill estate was expanding sufficiently rapidly to justify the introduction of new route 247A (Collier Row–Harold Hill, Gooshays Drive) on 6th December 1950. This was also Hornchurch worked and inherited the single deck journey formerly on route 247. The latter was significantly reduced in frequency at its Collier Row end although the total vehicle requirement on the two services called for a two bus increase in Hornchurch's Guy establishment which now reached its maximum of 92 including engineering spares.

New route 174 was opened between Dagenham and Romford in May 1950 but it was not long before it was extended, in October, to Harold Hill in place of the 86B. G 171, a Barking vehicle, stands at the Dagenham terminus while its crew take a break. F G Reynolds

London's tram network had enjoyed a ten year reprieve because of the war but the scrapping programme was due to recommence in October 1950. However even as late as 1950 itself new conduit track was being laid down in York Road, Waterloo where Tottenham's G 5 passes by en route for Victoria on 20th April. John H Meredith

A strange Daimler in the camp! LKJ 779 is one of three Brush bodied CVG6s at Sutton garage on hire from Maidstone Corporation, and its ginger and cream livery makes a colourful contrast to the standard London red of D 239 in this February 1950 view at Morden. Alan T Smith

On 8th July 1950 D 4 squeezes under the railway bridge at Worcester Park which was the reason for low height buses on route 127. The vehicle still carries traditional red and white paintwork but not for much longer. A second overhaul cycle is about to commence which will see the end of the old style livery on D 1-6 before the year's end. John C Gillham

Starting in 1950 buses emerging from overhaul often did so without front advertisements, much enhancing their appearance. Alperton's G 61 is on a Sunday working of route 18. STLs have already begun to trickle in, and by April the Guy era on route 18 will be over. F W Ivey

For most of 1950 little occurred which had any impact on the other utility classes although the Bristols found themselves based at Southall following an official name change in July to avoid confusion with Hanwell trolleybus depot. Victoria received new RTs for route 137 in August which meant that henceforth their STDs were confined solely to the 77/A. On the Daimler front the allocation book for April 1950 showed Daimlers allocated to route 49 on weekdays for the first time, but their appearances were nothing new and this was merely a paper exercise. Far more significant was the drafting into Merton of green Daimlers rendered surplus at Romford, which commenced on 22nd November and continued into January 1951. Some arrived just in time to appear on Merton's Saturday coverage of route 5 which ceased after operation on 6th January.

Guys first reached Brentwood on 5th April 1950 as replacements for TD type single deckers. Passengers sat unusually high in relation to the windows on Massey bodies, a fact emphasised on heavily laden G 258 at Gidea Park. Alan B Cross

Below On 6th December 1950 route 247A was introduced; it was the last new service to feature the use of Guys. In this Romford scene Northern Counties G 247 loads up whilst identical G 291, an Upton Park vehicle, is about to swing past on the 175. Alan T Smith

By 1950 the long, busy route 65 was run by nothing but RT types, a rare exception being on some bank holidays when Merton provided Daimlers for short workings from Kingston to Chessington and Leatherhead. In a busy scene at Kingston garage three distinct eras in London bus history are represented by ancient 'Scooter' LT single deckers, a modern RT and D 53. D A Jones

Although they barely resembled each other in any way, Victoria garage treated its two STD batches as interchangeable for operational purposes. Both types are seen at Archway with STD 106 standing ahead of post-war STD 118 on route 137 from which they were banished after the arrival of new RTs in August 1950. Alan B Cross

On 13th October 1950 route 102 lost its Guys overnight in favour of STLs, leaving the Guy presence at Golders Green in the hands of route 83 which was itself destined to start receiving STLs three months later. Next to Enfield's G 263 stands Holloway based RT 1698 on route 58 which, though one of London's less well patronised services, had already received new vehicles. J H Aston

The first public acknowledgement that Guy withdrawals would commence earlier than 1953 came about in November 1950 in an unexpected way. After their service demise in January eighteen STs had been kept in use as driver training buses, but the rolling stock department was experiencing great difficulty in keeping them serviceable and in fuelling them, and came up with the idea of using Guy Arabs instead as these also had crash gearboxes and seemed ideal for the purpose. Subsequently it was decided that STLs with condemned bodies allocated to the training fleet might as well also be replaced by Guys. The feasibility of this had been tested since 18th October when Barking's G 179 was placed on training duties after its Massey body ceased to be fit for passenger carrying. The withdrawal of Guys from Tottenham was immediately authorised as these were, by and large, the oldest in the fleet and a replacement programme was quickly put in hand. The scheduled coversion of route 67 from STL to RTL was imminent and it was decided to follow directly on from this with the 76 and 34B. Withdrawal of the Guys from these two routes commenced on 28th November, the first replacement vehicles being STLs dislodged from the 67 which were used as temporary cover until sufficient new RTLs were available to do the job properly. More than thirty of Tottenham's Guys became trainers although in several instances a quick return to passenger service occurred, principally at Barking, allowing Massey bodied vehicles which were in worse condition to take their place. In March 1951 a few of the last Weymann batch also became trainers. In their new capacity the Guys were allocated for maintenance purposes to a variety of garages in the fleet many of which had never before handled this type of vehicle, no doubt causing quite a headache to mechanics, fitters and storekeepers completely inexperienced in their upkeep.

Tottenham's last utility departed on 25th March, but by now another route had also lost its Arabs. The driving staff at nearby Enfield had long harboured a sense of injustice that Palmers Green's share of route 102 should be worked by STLs whereas they were 'stuck' with Guys, and not totally without reason. It was a busy route and a hill start in Alexandra Park Road, for example, was not something that the average driver would relish in a five cylinder Guy carrying a full load. For the first time a formal representation for the removal of Arabs proved successful and a straight swap was ordered for 13th December 1950 whereby Upton Park relinquished its minority STL allocation on route 101 and received fifteen Guys from Enfield instead. With 107 Gs on its books, Upton Park attained the largest fleet of Guy utilities ever to be held by any garage. By now the Executive's resolve to resist calls for the early withdrawal of Guys was clearly weakening, and on 28th November approval was given for 165 of them to be taken out of service during 1951, two years ahead of schedule, and for an equivalent number of STLs to be retained. This would still have left more than two hundred Guys in passenger service, but the fate of these was finally sealed in a most unexpected way. The country was in the throes of a re-

armament drive which had the effect of lengthening the ordering period for spare parts to as much as two years, and it was therefore necessary to be sure that the vehicles for which the spares were being ordered would still be around in two years' time. Such was the unpopularity of the Guys that there could be no guarantee that this would be the case, so on 3rd April 1951 the decision was taken to replace all of them ahead of STLs. Both types were considered uneconomic to repair but the cancellation of orders for Guy spare parts plus some savings in the overhaul programme made this a cheaper and more sensible option. A very substantial fleet of recently overhauled STLs was being stockpiled to augment transport facilities for the massive and prestigious Festival of Britain planned for 1951; they would become surplus in the autumn when the Festival closed and were the vehicles earmarked to set the Guy replacement programme in motion.

Above and Below **Within a short space of time the training bus fleet was seemingly flooded out by an influx of ex-Tottenham Guys of which Park Royal G 66 was one. Some, such as this one, were later restored to passenger service when vehicles identified as being in worse structural condition, such as Massey G 359, were drafted in to take their place. The Guy learners often carried garage allocation plates totally alien to this class of vehicle such as SP (Sidcup) on G 359.**
S N J White/John C Gillham

After the frenzied activity of the years 1947-9 during which a massive intake of RT types had swept away a huge section of the pre-war fleet in a spectacular fashion, a major lull was now evident in the bus replacement programme. The focus had shifted to scrapping the capital's remaining trams, all of which were housed at south London depots with the exception of a small allocation retained at Highgate for the Kingsway Subway routes. Stage one of the conversion programme had taken place in October 1950; this and the ensuing stages called for large numbers of new buses as tram replacements with the result that very few new RTs could be spared for other purposes, effectively halting the bus modernisation programme until mid-1952. Meanwhile a few Guys played a small and unexpected role in the tram conversion programme itself. Stage 2, which took effect from the night of 6th/7th January 1951, saw the removal of trams from Brixton depot (better known as Telford Avenue) and its Brixton Hill annexe. Total reconstruction of the main premises to form the new Brixton bus garage was not completed in time, and in order not to delay the implementation date a yard was rented behind the Streatham Hill Theatre to form an overflow operating base. This was equipped with temporary changing and rest rooms for staff and even a mobile fuel tank, all of which were based on redundant Guy buses. The staff rooms comprised Park Royal G 92 and Massey Gs 180 and 259 which were fitted with temporary saloon doors, whilst the fuel tanker employed the chassis of G 99 from which all the original bodywork except the cab had been removed. All four were driven on to the site on 5th January and remained in use until the 25th, after which they were removed to Chiswick for storage prior to proceeding to Penhall Road to be scrapped. A little later on, two other Massey bodied Arabs were also used as staff changing rooms although in a rather different context; these were Gs 174 and 192 which were used from May through to August 1951 in connection with a mobile X-ray programme during which time they were officially based at Cricklewood garage.

Although the main Guy withdrawal programme was not expected to commence until the late summer of 1951, casualties fell by the wayside during most months because of body condition, of which those used temporarily at Brixton were typical examples. Some were diagnosed by the engineering staff and taken out of service, but others were forced off the road through the unwelcome receipt of a PSV 71 certificate. At Barking, for example, six Guys were lost as a result of Ministry checks between November 1950 and August 1951 (Gs 127, 130, 32, 35, 95 and 124 – in that order), and it was necessary to deplete Alperton's already diminishing Guy fleet to provide replacements. However the most unexpected withdrawals to take place early in 1951 did not involve Guys at all, but Victoria's STDs. The driving staff there had reached the end of their tether with these most unsuitable machines and gave the ultimatum that, if a deadline was not set for their removal, they would refuse to drive them. The Executive presumably considered this battle not worth fighting and on 5th February 1951 six STDs,

representing just over half the batch, were taken out of service. The remainder were withdrawn on a more piecemeal basis, and the final official day of operation for the last two was 30th April although it is not known if they actually ran on this date. On 1st May STDs 108 and 111 joined the other nine in temporary storage at Potters Bar. London's first utility class had officially ended its public service role, although subsequent careers as staff buses, and later as trainers, meant that most of the eleven TD7s remained actively employed for another three years or more.

STDs 105 and 103 prepare to bid farewell to Victoria garage where they have spent their entire service lives. Included within the first tranche of withdrawals on 5th February 1951, they are heading for storage at Potters Bar and an as yet undecided future. D W K Jones

STD 111 managed to hang on a little longer, being one of the last two TD7s to be withdrawn on 1st May. In the twilight of its public service career it has just crossed Lambeth Bridge on its way to Tooting. F G Reynolds

In May 1951 it was the turn of Southall's staff to moan about their utilities. The catalyst for their complaint had been the arrival of STLs on Alperton's share of routes 83/A from about March onwards, a process which continued steadily as the Guys were whisked away to fill gaps elsewhere and which was completed in June. Southall's drivers were unhappy that their crash gearbox Bristols compared unfavourably with preselector STLs and claimed that, on the grounds of poor condition, the Bristols should be replaced. Their plea was rejected on the basis that the Bristols were mechanically sound and had enjoyed a good reputation until Alperton's STLs had come along; they would remain, subject as always to body condition, until 1953. No sooner had the staff's complaint been rejected than some credence was attached to it by the fact that Bs 8 and 9 had to be taken out of service in June because their bodies were no longer fit for use; however 25 out of the original 29 remained in service into 1952.

At about the same time official union representation was again made for the early replacement of Guys at Hornchurch, which still had no new RT-type vehicles of any sort, and also from Barking's route 23. This time the response was favourable; STLs would be placed temporarily on route 175 followed by the 23, with Hornchurch to be given priority for new buses at the end of the year. Perhaps emboldened by this response, the union made a further request in July 1951 for the early demise of Enfield's Guys, suggesting that pre-war STDs might be transferred in from Hendon as replacements. Even though they had crash gearboxes the union acknowledged that these pre-war Leylands were still in very good condition and should remain in service until the end of the replacement programme in 1954, but felt that it was only fair that Hendon's staff should receive some modern vehicles to run alongside Cricklewood's RTs on route 13. This suggestion, too, was duly accepted, and it was agreed that STDs should be sent to Enfield in due course to serve on routes 121 and 135 and also to replace single deckers on routes 205, 242 and 243 provided that the Waltham Cross railway bridge had been strengthened by then. Enfield's other remaining sphere of Guy operation, the 107/A, was designated at the same time to be the future recipient of STLs once the 175 and 23, and then the 86 group (which was now largely RT at weekends) had been dealt with.

Little in the way of service changes occurred during 1951 to impact upon the utilities although a fresh sphere of operation for Merton's Daimlers came with the introduction of new seasonal Sunday and bank holiday service 152A (Mitcham–Chessington Zoo) with the start of the summer programme on the first weekend in May. This same summer programme saw the Guys on the comparatively new route 247A reach Chigwell Row on a weekend basis in place of the former Lambourne End summer extension of route 247 which was not repeated after the 1950 season. On 27th June new Daimler territory was opened up when route 152 was extended beyond Hampton Court to Feltham in place of route 201, bringing double deckers through Bushy Park daily for the first time.

The only Massey bodied Guy ever allocated to a west London garage was G 174 which spent its short six year career at Alperton. After its demise in April 1951 following the arrival of STLs on route 83, it served for a short while as a mobile changing room in connection with London Transport medical department's X-Ray service. S N J White

An April 1951 scene on the Kingston By-Pass finds D 162 looking deserted except by its crew. These were early days on new seasonal route 152A and the photograph was probably taken in the early part of the day when the vehicle was heading against the main Chessington-bound traffic flow. Alan B Cross

Route 152 found its way westwards to Feltham in June 1951, a month after D 49 received its last overhaul and gained the new standard livery. Utilities were then appearing in this rather unimaginative colour scheme at a rapid rate. G W Morant

Doomsday for the utilities came on 1st July 1951 when the first mass withdrawal of Guys took place starting a process which was destined to continue beyond the originally planned 165 withdrawals for 1951, unabated until the utilities of all classes had gone from the fleet. On this day 27 Guys were withdrawn from service at Hornchurch, eight at Barking and seven at Upton Park, all from route 175 which received STLs surplus to Festival of Britain requirements. Of the 42 vehicles displaced only one was retained for service elsewhere; for the remainder this marked the end of the road. A number of Guys still remained on the 175 working from Barking and Upton Park garages but only for one further month, for on 1st August STLs displaced from Hackney by new RTs were drafted in to complete the task. The next blitz came on 1st October. Most Festival of Britain services had now ceased, releasing sufficient STLs for route 23, and this also meant the end of Guy journeys off-worked from this on to routes 23B, 23C, 62 and 148 as well as the remaining weekend Guy workings on route 87. It was also the end of Guy operation into central London. The pressure continued unabated and further Festival STLs went to Hornchurch, Seven Kings and Upton Park on 1st November for the 86/A, marking the end of Seven Kings's short spell as a Guy operator. On 1st December the spotlight once again fell on Hornchurch where the new RTLs promised earlier in the year for route 175 began to arrive, allowing STLs to be progressively transferred to routes 123, 165, 174, 247/A and 249. This process was completed in January 1952 after which only a small number of Guys remained at Hornchurch for route 103. Likewise only a few remained at Barking for its share of the 174. Within less than half a year the bus scene in the far east of London had changed almost beyond recognition as Guy numbers were decimated; in particular the streets of Romford, which had once echoed loudly to the unmistakable tones of these characterful machines, now saw them only as a very small and precarious minority which was destined not to last very much longer.

The Guy replacement programme for 1952 was carried out at a less frantic pace than in the previous year but in just as determined a fashion. New RTLs which were now being drafted into Barking for route 23 marked the end of Guys at this garage on 1st February when the displaced STLs were moved across to the 174. On the same date a major swing in location found Enfield's Guy population diminished by no fewer than 36 units when STDs at last arrived to take their place. The original plan to convert routes 121 and 135 with these vehicles had to be abandoned and they went instead to the much larger 107/A; this was because the Waltham Cross area single-deck services which were to have absorbed the balance of STDs still could not do so and conversion of the 107 group was the only way to employ all the available Leylands. In fact the STDs had been replaced at Hendon by new RTLs on 1st January and spent a month in store before arriving at their new home. Included amongst the withdrawn Enfield contingent were the last two Massey bodied Guys in the passenger fleet; this was the first time a major sub-class had been totally eliminated.

A huge influx of STLs hit route 175 with force on 1st July 1951, marking the start of massive Guy withdrawals from east London services. At the start of its last summer of operation, Weymann G 138 – carrying experimental 'bearerless' body – covers an Upton Park working on the 175. F G Reynolds

The arrival of STLs for route 23 on 1st October 1951 marked the end of Guy operation in central London and made heavy inroads into the class with 34 being withdrawn at Barking on this day alone. Weymann bodied G 35 did not quite make it through to October, having been delicensed along with others in June when replacements in better condition became redundant from route 83 at Alperton. F G Reynolds

The end of Guys on route 23 also brought to an end their presence on odd journeys worked on other services which had been a feature of Barking's schedules for many years. This had included route 148 where Barking's peak hour Guy workings made a change from Seven Kings' usual RTLs. An extremely rare occurrence was for Seven Kings itself to put one of its few Guys on route 148, but G 405 is seen at Dagenham on one such occasion. Alan T Smith

A line-up in Hornchurch garage yard on 16th December 1951 typifies the local fleet during a crucial period of change. New vehicles such as RTL 1233 are arriving to take over from STLs after less than six months on the 175. STL 488 and its compatriots have already begun displacing Guys from six other Hornchurch services, leaving only route 103 in the hands of the utilities. G 122, on the left, will stay at Hornchurch right through to the end of its Guys on 1st June 1952. Alan B Cross

Above **From October 1951 the word ONLY appeared widely on destination blinds to denote short workings, but with one known exception this was applied only to modern, full indicator displays. The only recorded restricted display was on a few Daimlers at Merton and this, in fact, pre-dated the general introduction by four months possibly by way of experiment. The vehicle is Brush bodied D 57, seen in June 1951.** Alan B Cross

Centre **Between October 1951 and January 1952 all eleven unfrozen STDs were taken out of storage at Potters Bar and put to use as staff buses. Heading away from Aldenham on trade plates, past RT 539 on route 18, is STD 102 working the daily return run to Chiswick for staff who have transferred from the old overhaul works to the new. Officially based at Turnham Green, STD 102 worked in this capacity until the end of 1952.** F G Reynolds

Left **On 23rd January 1952 Enfield garage received a surprise allocation of four Weymann bodied Arabs, renewing its acquaintance with a style of body once familiar in the area but which had been lost through transfers and withdrawals. They came from Upton Park to eke out their last few days in exchange for Northern Counties vehicles whose service was required for longer. All were withdrawn on 1st February, and two days before this G 403 is seen outside Enfield garage heading for Forty Hill.** Alan B Cross

A four month moratorium now followed, to be broken on 1st June 1952 by the final demise of Guys at Hornchurch when STLs took over on the 103. Next came the turn of Alperton where the arrival of new RTs for route 83 meant that STLs could be transferred across to eliminate Guys from their last west London foothold, route 79. Twelve were delicensed at Alperton on 1st July, and amongst this small band were included the last Mark I Arabs – both Park Royal and Weymann bodied (including G 45, the last in the fleet to carry the original style, non-glazed emergency window), the unique rebodied G 30, the last of the two Weymann bearerless bodies (G 137), and the unmistakable G 150.

Guys now remained scheduled for service on only three routes worked by the two remaining garages, Enfield (routes 121 and 135) and Upton Park (route 101). The 101 experienced a slow drip-feed of STLs into its massive allocation from November 1951 onwards plus some heavier bouts of Guy withdrawals on 17th June, 1st July and 22nd October 1952, but despite this it was destined to be the last on which the class would serve. At Enfield, in contrast, the Guy situation remained almost static between the coming of the STDs on 1st February and September when the final Guys were swept away upon the arrival of new RTs, a demise which would have come earlier had it not been for a strike at the Park Royal factory where many of the new buses were produced. Between the 3rd and 12th of the month all thirteen remaining Arabs were delicensed. In contrast to the mixture of body shapes and makes which had once characterised Enfield's Guy fleet (which at its maximum had comprised ninety units), this final contingent had been a dull batch carrying only Park Royal style bodies, included amongst which were the last remaining of those supplied by Northern Coachbuilders. Just over three months later, on Christmas Eve 1952, the last twelve remaining Guys at Upton Park were delicensed, bringing an interesting and at times colourful era to an end. The last operational day was December 23rd and the twelve vehicles theoretically available for service were Northern Counties Gs 170, 252, 254, 257, 293, 297, 308 and 309, Park Royal Gs 347, 350 and 432, and Weymann G 392. However, as always in that now far off era, no sentiment was attached to the final withdrawal of a class no matter how large it may have been, so no record was kept of the last Guy in service or, indeed, how many out of the twelve actually ran on the last day. Unlike the utility STDs there was to be no long drawn-out afterlife as staff buses or trainers. Though the class had been largely unloved and unwanted at home, so insatiable had the demand for ex-London Guys become on the second hand market that it was not in the Executive's interest to retain them any longer than absolutely necessary. Even the great majority of those which had been converted into trainers were withdrawn during 1951, and of the eleven which soldiered on in this capacity in 1952 all except one were replaced between May and September. Only G 42 survived in its training capacity to outlive the passenger fleet but succeeded in doing so by only just over a week and was delicensed on 1st January 1953.

For their last year of service Alperton's Guys on route 79 formed a lone outpost for the class in west London. Their withdrawal on 1st July 1952 removed the last oddities from the fleet including Northern Coachbuilders rebodied G 30, seen pulling away from Alperton garage in a puff of exhaust, experimental Park Royal bodied G 150, and the last utility in the fleet to retain an unglazed emergency window, Weymann bodied G 45.
F G Reynolds (2)/Ken Blacker

Even before the withdrawal from service of the last Guys, the beginning of the end for the Bristols and Daimlers had drawn nigh. For the Bristols withdrawal was a gradual process dictated by body condition and only one, B 7, was pressed into alternative use as a trainer – between December 1951 and December 1952 – after being declared unfit for public service. By July 1953 the class had ceased to appear on route 83 as RTs took their place, and because more continued to fall by the wayside STLs were drafted into Southall to cover the shortfall on their last remaining route, the 97. At the end of 1953 fourteen Bristols, representing just under half the original total, remained of which only B 5 was of the 1942 type and this ceased to be active on 1st February 1953. The final day of Bristol operation came on 9th April 1953 by which date the licensed fleet had shrunk to five; Bs 14, 17–19 and 29 were delicensed the next day bringing another London Transport class to an end.

Of the four utility classes only the Daimlers now remained in service and their fate was sealed in June 1952 with the announcement that Daimlers (and STLs) on route 49 would be replaced from September onwards. In fact body condition caused an involuntary start to the withdrawal programme a little earlier than this, in August, and an increasing number fell by the wayside from then onwards purely for this reason. The first replacement vehicles for route 49 came in mid-September and were second hand RTLs from Enfield, but starting from 1st October a stream of new RTs commenced delivery. At Sutton the impact of premature body deterioration proved greater than at Merton even though the fleet was slightly newer, resulting in thirteen Daimler withdrawals between August and October. In November new RTLs began arriving at Sutton for the first time, initially for route 93. By the end of the year 22 Sutton Daimlers, not far short of one quarter of the total batch, had gone. The main end of year event, however, was the replacement in December of the ten lowbridge vehicles at Merton which were withdrawn between the 10th and 18th as new RLHs came to release them from their duties on route 127.

Top **Enfield's final Guy fleet totalled a mere 13 vehicles and these drifted away during the first and second weeks of September 1952. All were similarly styled Arab IIs in new livery as typified by Northern Coachbuilders G 142 seen terminating outside its home garage.** Alan B Cross

Centre **Before the last Guys had gone, the withdrawal programme for Daimlers commenced with route 49 as the first target. On a Saturday in September 1952 when the first RTLs have already begun to arrive, D 126 halts to unload at Streatham Common. Despite carrying modern livery, D 126 had not actually been overhauled for more than three years and, as a consequence, was amongst the early withdrawals.** Ken Blacker

Left **Once Enfield's were gone, only Upton Park retained an allocation of Guys. Although officially allocated to route 101 they were known to stray from time to time. One such occasion occurred on 22nd August 1952 when G 294, with bonnet side open to cool the engine, revived old memories by appearing on route 175. Alongside it at the northern portal of Blackwall Tunnel stands 'tunnel' STL 1841.** Alan T Smith

In 1953 it was downhill all the way for the Daimlers. The body condition of many was becoming precarious prompting the staff, who were genuinely worried, to ask in March if some of the worst could be replaced immediately by STLs stored for the forthcoming celebrations for the coronation of Queen Elizabeth II. This request was refused. They then suggested that Ds could be used on the coronation services instead of STLs but this was rejected because their non-standard controls made them unsuitable for widespread reallocation. However the policy of drafting in new vehicles to both garages as speedily as possible continued to be pursued, but there was a problem in that many of the remaining STLs were proving just as bad as, and in many cases worse than, the Daimlers and this made it difficult to predict a date for the final demise of the utilities. At Merton the steady inroads into the Daimler ranks continued throughout 1953 and barely a month passed in which at least a few were withdrawn; in some months the slaughter was heavy such as in July and September when 36 and 35 were delicensed respectively. For Sutton's Daimlers the position was a little different. Just over half of the fleet had been overhauled fairly recently and could last until the summer at least; the remainder were bad and had to be disposed of urgently. Thus Sutton's Daimler replacement programme took place effectively in two stages with a pause of a few weeks in between. The modernisation of route 93 continued into 1953 and was completed in early February in which month route 156 was also dealt with. In April Sutton's share of route 115 received new vehicles and towards the end of May RTLs began taking over on the 80/A. July and August saw the start of Daimler replacement from routes 164/A although this was a long drawn out process and the final ones were not removed until December in which month the replacement spotlight fell on route 151. At Merton route 49's conversion to RT took several months to complete, but by April the withdrawal of the large Daimler allocation on route 88 was ready to begin followed in July by the 77/A. The completion of the RT takeover on these routes in September 1953 marked the end of utility operation through central London and their fast diminishing presence was now felt only on a handful of suburban services.

Top **The lowest numbered Guy in service at the very end was G 170, seen here in East Ham High Street heading for North Woolwich. Carrying a modern aluminium radiator and overhauled as recently as May 1951, it remained – in common with most Northern Counties bodied Guys – in good condition.** John C Gillham

Centre **After withdrawal of Southall's last Bristols in April 1953, only the Daimlers remained in service to represent the utility classes, and their numbers were diminishing fast. As a final reminder of the Bristol era, B 28 is seen passing its home garage.** J Wyndham

Left **May 1953 saw the replacement of Daimlers on routes 80 and 80A by new RTLs. In this slightly earlier view, taken in February, Merton's D 17 operating on loan to Sutton makes a change from the usual run of Daimlers found on the 80A.** Alan B Cross

The old order and the new. The lowbridge Daimlers were withdrawn between 10th and 18th December 1952 as new RLHs took their place. D 2 stands at Morden looking forlorn, almost as though it knows that in a fortnight's time its work will be at an end. In contrast RLH 75 glistens with newness at the same terminus. Standing beside it is D 16 which is destined to remain in service through to August 1953. Alan B Cross/D W K Jones

D 31 purrs along by the side of the Tate Gallery with a splendid Leyland Tiger from the Ansell's coach fleet following behind, both of them symbols of a fast disappearing era. The ousting of Daimlers from route 88 began in April 1953. G W Morant

Above left **Although the sight of Merton's Daimlers operating on Sutton routes was by no means uncommon, it was very rare for loans to take place in the opposite direction. As an exception to the rule D 257 was found covering a Merton working on route 157 at Raynes Park in September 1952. This was one of the Sutton vehicles not given a second cycle overhaul and thus one of the earlier ones to be withdrawn.** Ken Blacker

Above right **D 192 stands at Cheam on the new shuttle service 262 introduced on 10th June 1953. The fairly typical level of passenger loadings led to the inevitable demise of this operation but not before its Daimler allocation had been replaced by an RT.** Lens of Sutton

Below **Merton's last Daimler route was the 32, its shortest and least busy. Typifying the final era is one-time Green Line D 141 photographed at the St Helier Avenue terminus. This vehicle did not quite last out to the very end, being withdrawn in December 1953.** Lens of Sutton

Sadly no photographers appear to have attempted to record the last days of the utility Daimler era in London. Symbolically D 233 heads away into the distance on the 151 which, along with the one-bus route 262, was the last repository for Daimlers at Sutton. D 233 was of interest in being one of four Daimlers involved in body exchanges upon overhaul in 1949 as described in the next chapter.
Alan B Cross

Route 118 lost its Daimlers in September, route 157 in October and November, and in the latter month a start was made on route 152. By the end of 1953 Merton was scheduled to run Daimlers only on routes 32 and 152 whilst Sutton's remained only for the 151 and 262. The latter, which has not been mentioned before, was a new service introduced experimentally on 10th June 1953 requiring a single vehicle to shuttle between Cheam and Cuddington. The fact that it was designated for Daimler operation was a little surprising at such a late stage in the career of this much depleted class, but it provided an unintended swansong for an era that was almost over.

Of the eleven Merton and thirteen Sutton Daimlers which remained operational at the end of 1953, seven were delicensed on 1st January leaving only seventeen actually available for service at the start of 1954. Utilities last ran on route 152 on the final day of the old year, and it took only a week of the new year to remove them from the other three services too. On the last day of operation, 7th January 1954, D 73 was serviceable at Merton for the 32 with Ds 226 and 250 at Sutton for the 151 and 262. As with the other classes they ran in without ceremony and their passing was not acknowledged in any way. All eyes were on the future and nobody cared that the family of utility double deckers,

which had figured so prominently in the capital's recent transport history, had reached the end of the road.

Unlike the other utility types, no Daimlers suffered the indignity of demotion to training duties after withdrawal from public service; indeed the only instance in which one was put to alternative use was when D 146 was fitted out temporarily as a stores standardisation exhibition unit between March and August 1953. After the demise of the Daimlers the only utilities still occasionally to be seen on London's streets were six of the STDs in their final role as driver trainers. The last of these, STD 107, was delicensed on 1st November 1954 and this really was the end of an era.

After 7th January 1954 all that was left to remind Londoners of the utility era were a few STDs serving out their last days as learner buses. Based for maintenance purposes at Southall, STD 102 looks in need of a little loving attention which is not surprising as it has not received a coat of paint since December 1948.
G W Morant

CHAPTER THIRTEEN

CHISWICK AND THE UTILITIES

London Transport's huge overhauling and coachbuilding works in Chiswick High Road have, like so much else of that once-great organisation's culture and infrastructure, sunk into oblivion in recent times. So thoroughly have the demolition men done their work that nothing tangible remains to even hint at the hive of activity that was once Chiswick Works. In times gone by, on each day of the working week, buses passed through its famous gates from all corners of the fleet, not only on their way to or from overhaul or repair but also when employed on training duties, for this was also the nerve centre for driver and conductor training, and LT's world famous skid patch was located there.

In pre-war days every bus in the fleet visited Chiswick at approximately eighteen month intervals whereupon the body was demounted, enabling both body and chassis to be overhauled and repainted separately before being put together again, though not normally in their original pairing. Because bodies generally took longer to overhaul than chassis it would not have been cost effective for an overhauled chassis to await the availability of its 'own' body; instead it was married to the next compatible body to come off the overhaul line. All the major classes (in the case of double deckers this meant the STs, LTs and STLs) were dealt with in this way and floats of spare bodies were provided from

new to take account of this. London Transport was sometimes criticised for going to the trouble and cost of separating bodies from chassis when few other operators found it necessary or expedient to do so, but answered critics by pointing out that repair of the chassis was made easier, the body undersides could be attended to, and the life of the whole structure was thereby lengthened. In fact this system of overhaul worked extremely well in pre-war years and a high vehicle standard was maintained, but the coming of hostilities caused it to break down with a consequent serious decline in the appearance and general condition of the fleet. The major shortcoming of the system – which had not been apparent in peace time – was its highly centralised nature. When, by government directive, much of Chiswick Works was turned over to war production and ceased to be available for its original purpose, the only alternative was to transfer part of the overhaul programme to a number of bus garages which were not properly equipped for it, resulting not only in a lowering of standards but also in a considerable slippage in the programme as a whole. The separating of bodies from chassis could not easily be carried out in garages, which meant that the length of time which each vehicle was off the road increased; problems in obtaining skilled labour and shortage of materials added still further to the host of

problems which caused wartime overhauls to fall further and further behind schedule.

In between overhauls it was the practice to 'dock' every bus at the parent garage for its engineering group at regular six-weekly intervals when everything needing inspection, adjustment, replacement or repair was attended to. To a degree this was a wasteful procedure in that many units were changed before they were worn out, but it meant that a high standard of reliability was achieved albeit at a cost. This procedure continued, in theory at least, throughout the war, but the general shortage of new and overhauled parts meant that many units now had to be left in service beyond the end of their economic working lives in order to keep vehicles on the road, whilst accident-dented panels and other cosmetic work which would once have been attended to promptly now took low priority.

Above **A typically busy day in the overhaul shops finds work in progress on a variety of vehicles. The Park Royal body from an Arab II, which has been demounted for overhaul whilst its chassis is dealt with in another shop, will be resident at Chiswick for several weeks. D 86, on the other hand, is merely passing through for a quick brown to red repaint. The month is November 1947 and D 86 is destined to return to Chiswick for its full overhaul – and a further new coat of paint – in seven months' time.** LT Museum

A trio of vehicles straight out of the paint shop finds G 184 sandwiched between ST 149 and LT 245. A Barking-based vehicle, this was the first Massey bodied Guy to be repainted into red livery. One of many examples where the programmes for repainting and overhauling were not co-ordinated, G 184's new coat of paint was destined to last a mere ten weeks. The month is again November 1947, and it will be back at Chiswick for its full overhaul on 28th January 1948. At the end of 1947 livery policy changed slightly in that the lower saloon window ledges were henceforth picked out in white instead of red, making G 184 one of the few Masseys to carry the earlier style. LT Museum

The arrival of the utility classes placed an initial burden on engineering resources. The Ministry of Supply made provision for the manufacture of a quantity of spare parts, though generally this was by no means always adequate, and it took time for the engineers to adjust to the vagaries of vehicles to which they were totally unaccustomed. The Guys, in particular, presented very serious problems in their early days but, like the Bristols which also differed from traditional London practice in many design respects, they came to be regarded as extremely robust and reliable vehicles once their initial troubles were sorted out. As far as overhauling was concerned the arrival of the utilities brought a slight respite simply because they were new and would not, in theory at least, require major mechanical or bodywork attention for a few years. However in order to assess the effect of wear and tear on this type of vehicle, and also to formulate the timing and requirements for a future overhaul programme, STD 101 was taken to Chiswick on 8th December 1943 for an overhaul from which it emerged on December 20th. It is not known if the body was removed from the chassis whilst it was there or indeed if it received a complete repaint. Because of serious paint shortage many vehicles were receiving only what became known as a 'touch up and varnish' on overhaul, and STD 101 may have been dealt with in this way.

After the trial run with STD 101 a whole year elapsed before it became possible to overhaul any more utilities. The next one to go into the overhaul shop was STD 103 on 19th March 1945, a day before B 1 was sent in, which being the pilot overhaul for its class

took nearly two months to complete. From May 1945 onwards utilities began to emerge from overhaul on a slow but regular basis, averaging around three per month, and this included the first Guy overhaul to be undertaken on which G 2 was used as the guinea pig, passing through the works between 23rd July and 22nd August. By the end of 1945 all the STDs and early Bristols had received their first overhaul, plus two Guys, a total of 21 utilities having been dealt with during the year.

Morden station, 16th April 1948. A highly resplendent D 24 arrived back at Merton from its first overhaul earlier in the day and has now been pressed into service for the evening rush hour. Out of this batch of 28 Duple bodied Daimlers, 17 have already been overhauled and the remaining eleven are all at Chiswick. None remain in service in their original slatted seat condition. The red painted radiator (instead of black) was a feature of Daimlers overhauled and repainted at Chiswick. Alan B Cross

Chiswick Works was now getting back into full swing. Talks with the Ministry of Aircraft Production in May 1945 had finalised its full reinstatement as a bus repair works following the closure of London Aircraft Production, but even after the whole property was turned back to civilian use it took some time for a full overhaul programme to recommence. Because of wartime neglect it was not possible for overhauls to reach their pre-war intensity and the best that could be hoped for was that each vehicle should be overhauled approximately once every 3½ years; the amount of work to be carried out, on the bodies in particular, meant that each vehicle was spending far longer in the works than had been the case pre-war. The demounting of bodies commenced once again, but because of wartime losses no spare bodies remained for a regular float system to be re-established, so in most cases bodies and chassis rejoined their original partner after overhaul. For the utilities, of course, there had never been any spare bodies anyway.

With many of the utilities there were tasks other than complete overhauling that called for early attention. First of all there were 161 vehicles which required the urgent fitting of illuminated rear registration plates to improve upon the wartime expediency of painting the number on or above the platform windows. The instruction for this to be done came in January 1945, while the war was still in progress, and the government gave operators only until 29th March to comply. London Transport was probably not alone in failing to meet this deadline which later had to be extended by three months to 30th June. The task did not merely involve removing the rear panel and inserting wooden framework to hold an inset registration plate; it also required modification to the wiring system to provide the necessary illumination. It is thought that some were dealt with at Chiswick (in some cases coinciding with their first overhaul) and others at garages. Many ran with both the original and the new registration numbers in place for some time afterwards.

Another government edict of January 1945 was that headlamps could now be used unmasked subject only to normal peacetime regulations except that they still had to be extinguished on the order of a police constable, whilst wartime regulations applicable to side and tail lights were removed altogether. London Transport reacted to this by removing the ungainly headlamp masks fairly quickly but sidelights were unmasked on overhaul for the most part. An action which was considered much more urgent was the fitting of additional half drop windows on the 218 utilities which had been received with only two per deck. The decision to fully equip these vehicles was taken in early August 1945 and an order for sufficient half drops at a cost of £4,220 was placed in October. An additional six opening windows were to be fitted per vehicle (four upstairs and two down) and it was originally intended that the work would be carried out on overhaul. However it quickly became obvious that the overhaul programme was slipping increasingly behind schedule to the extent that it could be as late as 1948 before some vehicles were dealt with, so a

In addition to routine overhauls, the works at Chiswick were required to carry out major repairs arising from accidents. One of the most spectacular to befall the utility fleet occurred on 24th January 1948 when the entire top of Hanwell's G 45 was swept away by the long steel jib of a crane outside Wembley Park station. Fortunately few passengers were injured but the fire brigade was called to rescue those trapped on the upper deck. Within a little over three months G 45 was back in service with a new roof. This bore an extremely close resemblance to the Weymann original, although the coach-builders were presumably unable to locate an opening ventilator for the off-side front window and had plated over the aperture. Evening News/Pamlin Prints

To ease the pressure at Chiswick, and to speed the brown to red repainting programme, a few vehicles were repainted at garages. The non-standard treatment meted out to D 92, notably the omission of a white relief above the cab windows and the black radiator, indicates that this was one of them. D 92 ran in this condition for the first six months of 1948. Alan B Cross

separate programme of window fitment was commenced at Chiswick. This was no small task, for not only did the obvious amount of dismantling take place on each vehicle, but in some instances the existing half drops in the lower saloons had also to be repositioned to give an even spacing of opening apertures.

Between January and August 1946, 51 more Mark I Arabs emerged from overhaul along with G 95 in what was presumably a trial run for the Mark II type including, for the first time, the conversion of wooden seats

into upholstered form. G 95 made its way through the works in June as did STD 101 which became the first utility to undergo a second overhaul. After a short lapse the programme recommenced, and the remaining Mark I Arabs were all dealt with by March 1947, overlapping from February onwards with the G 72-136 batch of Mark IIs. A pilot Daimler overhaul was carried out on D 1 between May and July 1947 in preparation for a regular output to commence from October onwards. In addition to the overhaul

1949 was the peak year for overhauling utilities and as a result much of the fleet looked in good condition, though the appearance of wellbeing was often only skin deep and beneath the surface structural problems were beginning to magnify. Typical of the year's output were STD 111, which emerged from its second cycle overhaul in June, and D 171 whose first (and only) overhaul was completed in November. By this time post-war style side lights were being fitted as a matter of course, and in the case of many earlier bodies, such as that on the STD, the front bulkheads were being rebuilt with the consequential removal of the opening ventilator, a fact which is not clearly visible in this view. J F Higham/John C Gillham

programme itself, a steady flow of repaints began in November 1947 in order to eliminate the many brown vehicles from the fleet. Unfortunately a lack of liaison between the two programmes resulted in many vehicles receiving a repaint only to be painted yet again just a few months, or even weeks, later when called in for overhaul. Such was the case with G 139, one of the first brown to red repaints which returned to Chiswick in January 1948 and became the first of the 1945 deliveries to emerge from overhaul on 10th February (along with Massey bodied Gs 175-7) at the start of a programme for this huge batch of vehicles which took until February 1950 to complete. The latter month was also the same one in which the Daimlers completed their first overhaul cycle. It was towards the end of this cycle that the only instances occurred on the wartime classes of body 'swapping' between vehicles and on both occasions Daimlers were involved. In May 1949 Ds 104 and 107 exchanged bodies during overhaul, but as both carried identical Brush bodies the fact that an exchange had taken place was not outwardly apparent; a similar situation occurred in September 1949 when Sutton's D 223 and D 233 exchanged bodies.

On their first overhaul it was by no means unusual for the utilities to stay in Chiswick for anything between six and nine weeks, the work carried out on them being quite thorough. The chassis were given what was termed a 'heavy' overhaul which in many cases, and particularly with the Guys, could involve lighter weight units being fitted as part of the mechanical refurbishment. A very visible change on many Guys was the fitment of an unpainted aluminium alloy radiator in place of the old black cast iron one, but less apparent were new alloy crank cases, gearcases and back axle worm cases which sometimes replaced the originals. However there was no specific campaign of change for these units (some of which were also fitted at garages) with the result that the Guy fleet ended up carrying a hotch-potch of old and

new units which varied from vehicle to vehicle. The extent to which bodies were stripped down depended largely upon the condition of the framework. Serious deterioration of the timber structure became apparent on many after only a comparatively short period in service due to the use of poor quality, unseasoned timber which had little rot resistance and sometimes seemed to disintegrate from within itself and not just because of water seepage from outside. Such poor quality framing was a far cry from the material specified in pre-war London Transport contracts which insisted upon 'timber seasoned by natural process and entirely free from any shakes, knots, discolouration, sapwood or any other defects'. Sometimes aluminium panels were used instead of steel when re-cladding stripped bodies, as a means of saving weight and reducing corrosion problems, although steel continued to be used exclusively for back platforms and also for wheel arch panels in order to provide strength. On many vehicles the front bulkheads needed reinforcement. In the case of many earlier type bodies built with a hinged ventilator in the nearside window this was removed and a plain glass inserted. Each overhaul was accompanied by a complete internal repaint with disastrous consequences as the pleasant grained wood around the windows and elsewhere was hidden beneath a layer of particularly unattractive light brown paint, and the fresh-looking white lower deck ceilings were covered with a coat of cream.

During 1949 a total of 400 utilities passed through the overhaul shops. This was the peak year and contrasted greatly with the 53 dealt with in 1946, 88 in 1947 and 236 in 1948. The apex was in May 1949 in which month no fewer than 52 were processed after which a gentle decline set in to the extent that, from April 1950 onwards, the monthly output of utilities was often only in single figures. A major reason for the sharp rise which first became visible in 1948 was the commencement of a full scale second cycle

overhaul programme for the earlier utilities which coincided with the ongoing first cycle for the 1945 and 1946 deliveries. Between September 1948 and February 1949 the STDs (with the exception of STD 101) received their second overhaul, which was also destined to be their last. In June 1949 STD 101 emerged after its third journey through the Chiswick overhaul shops and was unique in being the only London utility to be overhauled more than twice. The second cycle for B 1-9 lasted between October 1948 and August 1949 and the replacement of their Gardner engines by AEC 7.7s was carried out at the same time. Overlapping this was the first (and only) overhaul of B 10-29 which emerged from works between January and September 1949.

Guys began to appear from their second overhaul in December 1948. A programme was set up for dealing with the whole of this large class although its wisdom must have seemed a little dubious in view of the condition into which many of the bodies had been found to have deteriorated, necessitating a good deal more rectification work than would normally have been the case on such comparatively new vehicles. Four bodies in the Park Royal batch G 71-136 were found on inspection to be only fit for scrap and this led to a reassessment of others within the batch resulting in several being withdrawn from the programme and designated instead for early withdrawal or conversion to trainer vehicles. The bodies which were acknowledged as having deteriorated worst of all were those supplied by Massey, and after only four had been worked on at a cost which was found to be totally uneconomic, plans for giving a second overhaul to the remainder were abandoned in October 1950. Only six months later the Guy overhaul programme as a whole was jettisoned in line with the revised policy of disposing of the class as quickly as possible. Only 147 out of the 435 had been given a second overhaul, the last of all to emerge from the works being NCB bodied G 151 on 6th June 1951.

The second Guy overhaul programme co-incided with the introduction of London Transport's definitive post-war livery which was designed with future spray painting in mind and therefore had to be as uncompli-cated as possible. It consisted of all-over red relieved only by a single cream band and the usual black mudguards and life rails. An early post-war 'modern' red and cream livery had been applied to the RT family, to huge num-bers of STLs, to a few pre-war STDs and, of course, to Sutton's Daimlers but was destined never to be seen on the other vehicles covered by this volume, all of which retained the more traditional styling of red with off-white win-dow frames and brown roof right through to 1950. On 30th June 1950 G 115 emerged from overhaul as a trial run for the utilities under a new scheme which was introduced fully mid-way through August 1950 and was applied to all overhauls thereafter. In total 55 Guys were overhauled into the new 'all-red' scheme and about 25 more gained it during 1951/2 when a casual repainting programmme was carried out to improve the appearance of some of the shabbiest of the class.

In a fleet as diverse and non-standard as the utilities, the emergence on some vehicles of modifications resulting from structural rebuilding or accident repair was inevitable. On the offside of G 280 only the panel housing the filler cap appears to be the original. F G Reynolds

Below Left **G 19** has been rebuilt with a later type destination screen, making the body appear from the front newer than it really is. J H Aston

Below **Following repair, G 85's side mouldings are retained only in the cab area.** Alan B. Cross

The final second cycle overhaul programme to be carried out on a utility class commenced on the Daimlers in the summer of 1950. Applied on a modest scale at first, it did not get fully under way until March 1951 and even then numbers handled in each individual month fluctuated wildly between four and eighteen. D 1 was the first to be dealt with, and its overhaul in August 1950 was carried out just in time for it to receive the new livery. Some of the vehicles dealt with in early 1952 were subjected to a small experiment to test the effectiveness of hot spray stove enamelling of internal hand rails as a means of stopping the white finish from wearing off as quickly as it was normally prone to do. Unfortunately the new enamel was found to chip quickly and it also appeared to soften and craze through to the bare metal, so this rather belated experiment proved unsuccessful. As with the Guys, the D class overhaul programme was cut short before completion. In the case of Merton based vehicles the last to be accepted for overhaul was D 124 in July 1952 whose overhaul was completed on 26th August; the programme continued three months longer in the case of the newer, Sutton fleet but was truncated with the entry into the Chiswick overhaul shop of D 228 on 30th September. This was not actually the last to appear resplendent from overhaul, an honour which befell D 230 which re-entered service on 26th November 1952. By the time the programme ceased, 204 out of a total 281 Daimlers had been overhauled for the second time. Between December 1943 and November 1952 1,128 overhauls had been carried out at Chiswick on the utility classes.

CHAPTER FOURTEEN

GUYS IN GRAYS

Withdrawal of London's Guys had already begun in earnest when, on Sunday 30th September 1951, an interesting occurrence took place which actually added ten newcomers to the fleet. This was the day on which thirteen Eastern National routes in and around Grays were transferred to London Transport's control together with 28 vehicles of mixed types, including ten utility Guys, and a garage in Argent Street.

It was London Transport's intention to reorganise the Grays area route network on 2nd January 1952, giving staff a three month period to settle into the new ownership before having to cope with the upheaval of a revised route structure. Part of its plan was to restore some of the cross-town facilities which had been lost in the early days of the Board because, at the time, it lacked powers to continue operating them once they had been compulsorily acquired from their former owners. Meanwhile, services continued to run substantially as they had done in Eastern National days using the same route numbers and many of the same vehicles. Although technically on loan to London Transport until the end of the year, all 28 buses were fitted overnight with holders for running number plates and garage stencils, whilst stickers were applied carrying the London Transport fleet name and legal ownership details. In the

event, five elderly Dennis Lancets were not used by London Transport despite being kitted out for operation, and two quite modern Bedford OBs ran only rarely. A number of STLs were drafted into Argent Street right from the start as replacements for the Dennises and Bedfords, but the limited availability of STLs meant that the Guy Arabs, together with a miscellany of Bristol single deckers of various ages, continued running under the new regime much as they had done before.

The ten Guys made up Eastern National's entire stock of such vehicles, the whole of whose working existence had been spent in this outpost of the company's far flung network. All were based on Arab Mark I chassis with 5LW engines and carried Brush lowbridge bodies seating 55. The first three were allocated by the Ministry of War Transport for a theoretical delivery date of May 1942 although in practice they arrived several months later than this; they received fleet numbers 3875-7 and were registered JTW 146-8. Then followed allocations of three, three and one respectively to bring the total to ten. These further seven were delivered as one batch, the first late in 1942 and the remainder in 1943, and became 3878-84 (JTW 233-9). Originally operated in wartime grey, they later received standard post-war Tilling

green and cream livery with black mouldings, and the bodies were extensively reconditioned. Although this reconditioning left them with their basic utility styling, including the 'lobster back' domes and the 'stepped' dash panel which was the main recognition feature of Brush bodied Guys, the appearance of all of them was altered in one way or another and in various combinations. On some the one piece front indicator box was replaced by a two piece arrangement occupying the same total width and depth as the original and reproducing the layout which Eastern National had standardised upon for double deckers in pre-war days, whilst those that retained their original single glass panel had a two piece blind display installed behind it. One vehicle, No. 3877, received a 48inch wide display of the post-war Tilling standard which instantly distinguished it from all the others. Some were fitted with additional half drop windows and in the majority of cases the continuous rain shields were replaced by ones covering the opening apertures only; others received eight sliding ventilators per deck in place of half drops, and from these vehicles the rainshields were removed entirely. On all ten the upper deck front opening ventilators were removed and the metal panelled emergency exits were replaced by glazed ones.

Left **Argent Street garage on 18th November 1951 finds Guy Arab 3879 and STL 731 (just visible on the right) apparently ready for service. Tucked away in the next bay are three more Arabs and three Bristol single deckers.** Alan B Cross

Right **Carrying its original wartime paintwork, Eastern National 3877 loads up in Grays for the busy run to Tilbury. The untidy looking gadgetery below the canopy is an extension to the blind winding mechanism which enables the destination display to be set by the conductor without clambering on to the vehicle. It was much favoured at the time by Eastern National and also by the other Tilling operator in the area, Westcliff-on-Sea.**

Centre **No. 3883, seen at the Fairway Estate terminus on 13th October 1951, sports its new LONDON TRANSPORT fleet name and red painted garage and running number plates. This vehicle now has two separate front indicator apertures and sliding side ventilators as well as a Tilling style radiator cap.** John C Gillham

Bottom **A close-up of 3880 shows the newly applied fleet name and the running number plates in greater detail; it also reveals that the opening windows now fitted are of the type operated by a winding mechanism and not the original pinch-grip type.** Alan B Cross

The thirteen Grays area services taken over by the Executive were numbered 31, 32/A/B, 35, 37A/B, 44, 45, 57, 81, 82 and 85. Several were merely irregular works services but others, such as the 31, 32 group and 37 group, were frequent runs serving the Grays-Tilbury corridor and other local destinations, and it was here that the Guys were mainly employed although they took their turn on the factory runs as required. London Transport's three month period of operation under the old order was marked by a gradual increase in the number of STLs transferred in, but generally these replaced single deckers and the Guys continued in operation through to the end of their hire period. Only two, Nos. 3878 and 3882, failed to complete the course – probably for mechanical reasons – and these were delicensed on 1st December, being transferred for storage to London Transport's main Grays premises in Hogg Lane until they were returned to Eastern National on 27th December. The remaining eight were withdrawn from service on the last day of 1951 and were officially transferred back to Eastern National on the same day. RTs had now joined the Argent Street fleet to augment the STLs and to act as Guy replacements, but the service reorganisation was implemented only two days after the Guys left, and Argent Street garage was closed.

Back in the Eastern National fold, new locations had to be found for the ten Guys for which a further two or three years' life was anticipated. Braintree was a logical choice for some since this ex-Hicks Bros depot already had Guy Arabs of its own inherited from their former owner. The remainder ended their days in a seaside location at Clacton. In August 1954 a total renumbering of the Eastern National fleet resulted in the Guys receiving new fleet numbers 1175-84, but their end was now near. Most were withdrawn for scrap in 1955 and the last two, Nos. 1179 and 1183, were delicensed at Braintree in March 1956.

One other utility vehicle was included within Eastern National's Grays fleet and it became unique in being the only single deck utility ever to carry London Transport as a fleet name. Eastern National No. 3874 was a Bristol L5G but its non-Essex registration number, HHT 459, indicated that it had a more interesting background than usual. In fact, in its earlier days, 3874 had been a most unusual vehicle. It was one of a pair of identical single deckers constructed in 1942 to a design conceived jointly by Bristol and Eastern Coach Works in which a gas producer plant was incorporated into the rear of the bodywork. At the time rigid economy in the use of imported liquid fuel was regarded as vital in the national interest and all operators with more than ten vehicles were expected to convert ten per cent of their fleet to producer gas operation. This target was never achieved on a nationwide scale, but the Tilling group took the matter very much to heart and saw the construction of vehicles with in-built gas producer plants as a natural follow-on from the usual process whereby two wheeled trailers were towed along behind buses to provide their gas power.

HHT 459 (along with its identical sister HHT 460) was licensed in April 1942 to Bristol Tramways in whose fleet it was numbered 2169. However there is no firm evidence that either vehicle ever ran for Bristol, and two months later they were reallocated to other companies in the group, HHT 459 to Eastern National and HHT 460 to Eastern Counties. The pair were constructed on conventional Bristol L type chassis but, to provide the power necessary to accommodate the gas producer system, a Gardner 6LW engine was fitted instead of the usual five cylinder unit, the complete chassis being designated L6GG (the final G standing for Gas). The bodywork was built by ECW at its temporary Irthlingborough works to standard Ministry of Supply specification, this being one of the rare wartime occasions when ECW bodied new rather than reconditioned chassis which was its usual role during this period. The normal front entrance 31 seat utility body was modified by the elimination of the last two rows of seats in whose place was situated a fireproof chamber shut off from the passengers by a steel bulkhead. Within this compartment was situated the gas generating plant, with steel folding doors giving access from the rear for cleaning and refuelling. On the roof were two water tanks which were disguised by a panel resembling a luggage compartment whilst, hidden from view below the vehicle, was the main scrubbing unit.

In September 1944 the government announced that the gas producer programme could be closed down. The tide of war had now turned in favour of the allies and liquid fuel supplies, though far from ample, were now reasonably secure. Although most operators reverted to normal propulsion with alacrity, jettisoning the infamous gas trailers as quickly as they could, the Tilling group was reluctant to abandon the principle altogether. The two Bristol single deckers had shown potential to such a degree that, in November 1944, a request was despatched from the group's headquarters at Crewe House to the Ministry of War Transport seeking authority

A rear view of HHT 459 taken just after completion and before the application of ownership and weight details, shows clearly the steel folding doors giving access to the generating plant and the roof boards hiding the water tanks. A typical utility style 'lobster back' rear dome was fitted when new.

3874 shows the London Transport identity which it may never have actually carried in passenger service. It was photographed in storage at London Transport's own Grays garage on 27th November 1951 in company with unwanted Dennis Lancets. Alan B Cross

for the construction of twelve further vehicles of the same type. Originally the intention was to distribute the twelve around the group's companies, but a modified plan soon evolved whereby Eastern National and Eastern Counties would receive six each. The Ministry proved amenable to the plan and quickly sanctioned the twelve vehicles, but the scheme foundered a few months later because 6LW engines could not be obtained and AEC 7.7 units, which were offered as an alternative, were considered unsuitable.

It is not known when Eastern National ceased using gas propulsion for No. 3874 but when it did so a 5LW engine replaced the larger unit, in effect converting the chassis into a standard L5G. At the same time, or soon afterwards (probably in 1945) the vehicle returned to Eastern Coach Works for the rear end of the bodywork to be rebuilt in a style compatible with the main body design, which included a short reduction in overall length and replacement of the angular back dome with a rounded one. The seating capacity was increased to 33. This was the condition of 3874 when it adopted London Transport identity on 30th September 1951.

Although most of the eleven Grays-based Bristol single deckers were used fairly regularly, at least in the early days of the new regime, this does not appear to have been the case with 3874. It saw little active service with London Transport and may, indeed, not have been used at all. On 1st November 1951 it was delicensed, remaining thereafter in open air storage until 27th December when it made its way back to Eastern National. It finished its time at Chelmsford depot, being renumbered 278 in July 1954 and was finally sold for scrap in November 1956.

A view looking forward inside 3874 in London Transport days reveals some of its spartan wartime construction but also shows that tubular framed seats were fitted, at least in later days. A characteristic Eastern Coach Works embossed plate adorns the flywheel cover. The large fare-board holder attached to the front bulkhead looks like a London Transport addition. Alan B Cross

3877 was immediately recognisable by its wide front indicator display which was of the standard Tilling post-war style but with the upper display latterly painted out. The destination blind which it carried must have been specially made for this bus. R G Westgate collection

Its stint with London Transport over, the former 3883 (now renumbered 1183) stands in the sun at Braintree. Since arrival back at Eastern National the front end has been repanelled above cab level and as a result the front windows and destination apertures are now rubber mounted. Geoff Mills

CHAPTER FIFTEEN

LIFE AFTER LONDON

After the trauma of war and the ensuing catalogue of hardships and shortages which accompanied the last years of the decade, the arrival of the nineteen-fifties held out a fresh promise of much better times to come. On the streets of the capital this promise was seen to be clearly and rapidly heading for fulfilment as the all-conquering RT family swept all the other classes of bus aside, one after another, until even quite new vehicles were in danger of being rendered surplus by the unstoppable quest for total standardisation. The LTs and STs, old stalwarts from London General times, lasted into the nineteen fifties by only a few days, STLs disappeared fast as their bodies decayed beyond repair, and London Transport's management was determined that the utility classes would join the ranks of vehicles to be disposed of as soon as possible and that none would last later than 1953. The Executive's Chiswick-based Supplies officer (who also dealt with disposals) was obliged to make plans for the removal of this large body of vehicles from the fleet.

In the case of older classes such as STLs the question or disposing of huge quantities of redundant and worn out rolling stock had been simply dealt with by selling them all to scrap dealers who, as part of their contract, would return specified mechanical items which were still needed to keep the remaining fleet mobile. In the case of the utilities a whole new approach to disposals was called for in view of their comparative newness and the fact that, mechanically at least, most still had the potential for giving many more years of service even if their existing bodies were worn out. Since nationalisation on 1st January 1948 London Transport had ceased to be its own master on such major matters as fleet acquisition and disposal and was forced to defer to the wishes of the nationalised sector policymakers at the British Transport Commission. Whilst the Commission had been happy for pre-war vehicles to go to the scrap yards in their droves, its policy with regard to the disposal of utilities was more ambitious. In August 1951 the Commission expressed the view that in its own and the national interest "wartime austerity buses fit for further service should be sold... rather than they should be scrapped after such a comparatively short life". The problem was that, at the time, the Commission operated an embargo on selling vehicles for re-use where they might end up competing with the companies which it controlled, which meant in effect that further psv use within Britain was prohibited. How then could London Transport's many hundreds of surplus Guys,

Daimlers and Leylands be disposed of for further service when such an embargo existed? The Commission suggested that they might be sold abroad, or otherwise used in this country by building contractors and such like, or perhaps sold for non-passenger use such as mobile homes, but it was obvious to everybody, London Transport included, that the scope for sales such as these was minimal. It was a different matter where Bristol-built utilities were concerned. The nationalised Tilling group's slightly penny-pinching attitude to rolling stock renewal left not the slightest doubt that any surplus Bristols would all be rapidly snapped up by group companies for further use and even rebodying, as indeed proved to be the case.

Edgware garage yard was a collecting point for redundant Guys where they could be examined by prospective purchasers. The three Northern Counties vehicles, Gs 224, 172 and 225, were bought by the Ministry of Supply in July 1952; the chassis of Massey G 313 and Park Royal Gs 77 and 84 passed to Edinburgh Corporation three months earlier for conversion into almost new vehicles. All six had been withdrawn from service when Enfield garage received an influx of STDs on 1st February 1952. J Wyndham

★ BUSES ★ CHASSIS ★ ENGINES ★

FOR EXPORT & HOME TRADE (in specially approved circumstances)

A.E.C. REGENT

56-Seater
Double-Decker Buses

fitted 7.7 direct-injection Diesel engines. All in clean condition and good mechanically. Unladen weight 6 tons 10 cwts.

£285

All Vehicles can be landed Ostend or Dunkirk at a small extra cost for collection and driving to European and North African destinations.

GUYS

1946 fitted 5 L.W. Diesel Engines,

also

DAIMLER

C.W.A.6 1946/7
56-seater
BUSES & CHASSIS

£450

Moquette or Leather Seating. Bodies by Duple, Park Royal and Brush. DIESEL. ENGINE: A.E.C. 7.7 105 m.m. bore, 95 b.h.p. direction injection. TRANSMISSION: Fluid flywheel and preselective gearbox. REAR AXLE: Floating. TYRES: Front 36in. x 8in., rear 9in. x 20in. ELECTRICAL: 24 volt. UNLADEN WEIGHT: 7 tons 6 cwts. (fitted 56-seater double-decker bus body).

CHASSIS MEASUREMENTS

LENGTH: 26ft. 6in. (or could be shortened by 3ft. 10in. by cutting off end of chassis behind rear spring hanger for shipping). WIDTH: 7ft. 6in. HEIGHT: Chassis 5ft. 8in. (to top of radiator). MAX. HEIGHT (bus): 14ft. 4in. MIN. HEIGHT (bus): 14ft. 1in. Every vehicle carries a Certificate of Fitness, in some cases until 1957.

A FEW OF THESE VEHICLES AVAILABLE FOR THE HOME MARKET

A.E.C. Single-Decker Buses fitted 8.8 D.I. Diesel engines, 30/33/34 seaters. Rear Emergency Door.   EXPORT **£450**

GARDNER

5 L.W. Diesel engines, £250. Also 4 and 6 L.W. or fitted unit construction gearbox, £275. A.E.C. 7.7, £250. 8.8 Diesels £200. Complete all accessories. Packing and delivery Docks £20.

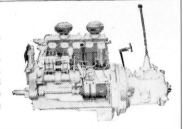

A.E.C. 37-seater, fitted 7.7 D.I. Diesel engine. Park Royal Bodies, unladen weight 6 tons 5 cwts. Rear Emergency Door.   EXPORT **£450**

CHASSIS

Daimler or Guy. All Diesels, ideal for haulage. **£375**

Leyland and Daimler fitted 5 L.W. Gardner. **£300**

A.E.C. fitted 7.7 Diesel. **£275**
All Diesels. Unladen weight 4 tons 15 cwts.

SPARES FOR EVERY MAKE OF PASSENGER VEHICLE.

★ PROSPECTIVE BUYERS may appoint their own Consulting Engineer at road test and expert examination of vehicles and units is welcomed.

RE-ARRANGEMENT OF SEATS WOULD INCREASE CARRYING CAPACITY OVERSEAS. AMPLE STANDING ROOM.

FULL-FRONTED A.E.C. 35-seater Single-Deck Buses fitted 7.7 direct injection Diesel engines. Unladen weight 6 tons. Emergency door opposite side.   EXPORT **£450**

W. NORTH OF LEEDS LTD. 94 VICAR LANE, LEEDS, YORKS., ENG.

Telephone: Leeds 26248 & 23482.   Telegrams & Cables: Busnorth, Leeds.

W North advertised its stock of ex-London vehicles widely. At £450 a Park Royal Guy, depicted here, would command a much better price than an STL. North's mark-up on the utilities was handsome indeed as they had mostly been acquired for a mere £165 apiece.

The first disposals were authorised as early as May 1950 but covered only two vehicles, Gs 73 and 113, whose bodies had been found at overhaul to be totally beyond salvation. These were removed in the same month and burnt at Chiswick but an endeavour to sell their chassis as runners was not successful and they were dismantled, also at Chiswick, in March 1951. At least one other delapidated body, that of G 98, had also been burnt there by now, but with many other Guys about to be rendered surplus and no obvious market for them immediately available, the Executive began selling vehicles to scrap merchants George Cohen & Sons Ltd for cutting up at the Penhall Road, Charlton, tram scrapping depot. First to go, on 3rd May 1951, was G 127 and it marked the start of a long line of utility disposals which was not finally completed until September 1955. Cohen's contract covered fifty Guys, mostly Park Royal and Massey bodied, and was complete by November. The price paid for each vehicle was a mere £27, or £24 in the case of three which were bodyless, meaning that each body represented a scrap value of just £3. These low sums reflected the problem that all BTC-controlled companies faced in realising good second hand prices when much of the market was closed to them by the Commission's edict, and there was much frustration that municipal and BET operators, who usually had no restrictive sales policy, were at the same time realising inflated prices because the number of buses which they could supply to the second hand market fell far short of demand.

June 1951 saw the first sale of a London utility for further passenger use when G 35 passed to Sabena, the Belgian state airline, followed by G 405 in October. They were purchased for the transportation of tourists at Brussels airport and the sale was significant for two reasons; G 35 was the first of very many London utilities to make a new career overseas, and the £250 received for it was a clear pointer to the much more satisfactory and realistic sums obtainable if the second hand market could be successfully tapped in preference to scrapping. When L. W. Vass of Ampthill, Bedfordshire purchased G 149 speculatively in September 1951 it was with the hope of opening up a new market in Australia for which Vass purchased a further five Guys in 1952. Alas, the scheme fell through and the vehicles were left to moulder in Vass's yard, and equally unsuccessful was a much more ambitious request for no fewer than one hundred Guys from a firm called Overseas Vehicles (Disposals) Ltd who intended to export them to an agent in Melbourne. Inordinately more successful, in the long run, was W. North of Leeds Ltd from whose yards at Stourton and Whinmoor on the outskirts of Leeds many Guys and Daimlers were destined to head abroad for further service. North's original approach, in July 1951 was merely to purchase two Guys; the deal was done and proved to be the prelude to many more. So successful became the relationship with North's that from May 1952 onwards they were appointed as the main contractor for purchasing surplus London vehicles of all types including STLs and several obsolete single deck models which had previously proved practically unsaleable.

North's were particularly keen to get their hands on the Guys and Daimlers which they knew were eminently marketable, but in taking all the other types too they were able to drive down the price for utilities from £250 in July 1951 to £165, giving them a very good mark up each time one found a new home. Particularly impressive was their handling of the Daimlers; they purchased all except one and were successful in finding new operators for all but about eleven of the 280.

The deal with North's provided the chink which gradually opened the door permitting London Transport and other BTC subsidiaries to sell vehicles unfettered on the home market. London Transport badly needed a new disposal source to replace Cohen's and was very eager to secure a large scale contract with North's who were both efficient and paid a fair price. However North's stipulated that they should have freedom to dispose of up to ten per cent of double deckers on the home market for re-use as psv's. Under pressure, possibly from the new Conservative government as well as from London Transport, the British Transport Commission relaxed its rules in December 1952 to permit this. A principle of sorts had, in any case, already been established when, as a special one-off concession, the Commission permitted the direct sale of sixty Guys to Edinburgh Corporation earlier in 1952. However, complete freedom for nationalised companies to dispose of vehicles as they wished did not come until January 1959, long after all the utilities had left the scene.

Facing page **Penhall Road scrapyard. Massey G 180, having served latterly as a staff room at the temporary Brixton premises pending the full commissioning of the tram depot as a new bus garage, now joins the trams rendered redundant by the January 1951 stage of the conversion programme. Apart from its windscreens E1 class car 1361 is still almost complete, but not for much longer. Feltham 2124 awaits transportation for further service in Leeds. In the later view, showing the specially installed tram traverser track, four Guys are in evidence and also several STLs. The two Guys nearest the camera, Northern Coachbuilders G 199 and Weymann G 393, have already been shorn of many windows and panels.** F W Ivey/Alan B Cross

Above **Australia was the hoped-for destination but Vass's yard at Ampthill was as far as it got. Ten years after settling in there G 94 is still clearly recognisable though much of the body framework has rotted and fallen away through the passage of time.** Alan B Cross

Although London Transport regarded its huge fleet of utilities as obsolete there were many operators who took a more cost conscious view of life with the result that, of the 756 vehicles which comprised the B, D, G and 3STD2 classes, an astonishingly high proportion totalling well in excess of 600 went on to passenger carrying duties elsewhere after leaving the capital. The great majority of these were handled by North's. Particularly astonishing was that some 22% of the utilities embarked on a new career abroad, a fact which did not escape the notice of or please some sections of the manufacturing industry. The Society of Motor Manufacturers & Traders was not slow to assert that the shipment of so many used vehicles overseas reduced

potential for new sales and lowered the industry's prestige. A more vociferous complainant than the SMMT was Sidney Guy whose view was that exporting second hand chassis not only reduced sales of new vehicles but was inconsistent with the government's constant exhortations to manufacturers to tap export markets to the maximum, in addition to depriving industry of the scrap which could be used in the production of new exports. He was also very worried about the damaging effect on Guy's reputation of so many old Arabs being exported, especially as it was widely known that they were not being replaced by new Guys. These worries came to the fore when their agents in India, trying to clinch a sale to West Bengal State Transport, cabled

"Leylands insinuating LT no longer buying Guy buses on account inferior quality. Please cable refutation". Guy Motors themselves subsequently considered purchasing 131 of London's surplus Arabs with a view to completely reconditioning them for sale overseas carrying the same guarantee as new chassis, but abandoned this idea in October 1952 because the prevailing condition of the export market did not appear to justify the amount of capital which would be locked up. The manufacturers' fears that a flood of used vehicles would reduce export potential for new ones were probably totally unfounded, for most of the surplus London utilities which were purchased for service abroad went to operators who were short of ready cash and would almost certainly not have been able to purchase new vehicles even if they had wanted to.

As we have already seen, nearly all of the 281 Daimlers found new homes, as did all of the Bristols. Of the Guys, fifty were scrapped by Cohen's before a second hand market was established, but all but about forty of the remainder were re-used in one way or another, and even those which North broke up would have provided a fund of spare parts, Gardner engines being particularly valuable at the time both for road transport and marine purposes at home and abroad. At the other end of the scale none of the eleven 'unfrozen' STDs were re-used at psv's. This was not a great surprise because the second hand market for pre-war style Leylands had never been very strong and even the demand for their engines, good as they were, was insignificant compared with that for AEC 7.7s and, particularly, Gardners.

Ironically, although they were the first utility class to be withdrawn from passenger service, the STDs were the last to remain in London Transport ownership, latterly as trainers. This probably reflected the absence of a strong second hand market for them and the consequent lack of pressure from North's for their early release. The last Bristol, B 29, left London Transport ownership on 13th May 1953; the last Guy, G 336, went on 4th September 1953 followed by the final Daimlers, Ds 95 and 228, on 16th February 1954. Most of the STDs (all, in fact, except STDs 110 and 111) were still in stock at this time. This last of this angular, characterful and now very decrepit utility breed finally left London for North's on 16th September 1955, and taking part in the final run to the Leeds scrapyard were STDs 102, 109 and the vehicle which had started off the whole utility era back in October 1941, STD 101. Within a comparatively short space of time London utilities could be found amongst fleets in three out of the four main operating sectors; state owned, municipal and independent. Only the BET companies remained aloof but even here one of them almost succumbed. In May 1952 Maidstone & District sought to purchase four Guys direct from London Transport, and the deal was approved only to fall through in June. Later on, however, the deficiency was rectified by chance when two of the group's subsidiaries, East Yorkshire and Potteries Motor Traction, absorbed small private operators and the ex-London vehicles which their fleets contained.

Looking solid albeit a little drab in all-over green, G 158 travels under the trolleybus wires in Reading as it works a service for atomic energy workers organised by the Ministry of Supply. The LONDON TRANSPORT enamel radiator badge has been removed to reveal the original GUY insignia.
Alan Nightingale collection

THE MINISTRY OF SUPPLY GUYS

On 1st July 1951 the first real withdrawals of any significance took place to reduce the number of Guys active within the fleet. About 25 had fallen by the wayside before this, in dribs and drabs and usually because of body decay. In most cases these early withdrawals had not been pre-planned but were the result of a dreaded 'PSV 71' certificate having been slapped upon them by Ministry of Transport examiners meaning, in effect, that without very considerable financial outlay they could not be recertified to run again. The remainder, which still totalled in excess of four hundred, continued to exercise a considerable presence on the London bus scene, either in passenger service or as trainers, until this first, July 1951 onslaught into their ranks. By happy coincidence, in the same month London Transport received an enquiry as to whether a quantity of surplus vehicles, in good condition, could be made available fairly quickly from a source which was prepared to pay a good price. This source was the Ministry of Supply which had played such a prominent role during the war years in procuring the manufacture of new buses and which now needed to buy some back to fulfil a specific role. Department No. 29 at the Ministry was responsible for the upkeep of a 'pool' of vehicles from which other departments could draw if necessary, and a fleet of buses was now needed for the transportation of government workers. The Ministry had its own internal

policy in regard to the provision of staff transport which was that, where available, public services should be used and augmented if necessary. If unavailable, suitable transport should be hired, but if this was not possible the Ministry would buy vehicles and run the services itself. A number of sites in various parts of the country were considered to be of a 'sensitive' nature and it was mainly to serve these that the Ministry wished to acquire 29 double deckers capable of lasting for at least the next two or three years during which time the prospect of being able to obtain new vehicles appeared remote.

London Transport quickly obtained approval from the British Transport Commission to dispose of 29 Guys (later increased to 32) for the excellent price of £400 each. As this was well in excess of the going rate for second hand utility vehicles it entitled the Ministry to choose the very best vehicles from a selection of 36 which the Executive's engineers recommended as having good life potential. As was to be expected, most carried bodies by Northern Counties but one of the metal-framed Weymann experimentals was included as were two with timber framed Massey bodies which had been very extensively reframed late in 1950. The Ministry's engineers made their choice in March 1952 and the 32 vehicles changed hands, after being mechanically serviced, between May and July of that year.

The Ministry's fleet consisted of:
Northern Counties: G 154, 156, 158, 159, 162, 169, 172, 219, 224-226, 228-230, 232-234, 237, 245, 246, 248, 249, 269, 271, 274, 276-279
Weymann: G 138
Massey: G 175, 176

It is rumoured that a few were shipped for service in Nigeria but no further details of this have come to light. The great majority were given a coat of the Ministry's standard rather drab dark green paint and entered service at several sites including the Windscale nuclear power station in Cumberland, the Atomic Energy Research Establishment at Harwell, the Atomic Weapons Research Establishment at Aldermaston and the secret research premises at Fort Halstead, Kent. Being part of a 'pool', there was no fixed allocation of vehicles to routes and they were transferred from one location to another as required. The mileage operated was only moderate and maintenance was good, factors which must have contributed to the majority of the fleet lasting far longer under the Ministry's banner than the two to three years originally planned. In fact Weymann-bodied G 138 and around ten of the Northern Counties specimens served very nearly a full decade. They were finally disposed of in about April 1962 when a fleet of eleven brand new AEC Regent Vs with particularly ungainly Park Royal bodies was purchased to replace them.

GUYS FOR SCOTTISH OMNIBUSES

Over a span of eighteen months beginning in November 1951 and ending in May 1953 a total of 140 redundant Guy Arabs was sold for service with subsidiary companies within what was loosely termed the Scottish Bus Group. These acquisitions, in batches of 60, 50 and 30, were all handled through Scottish Omnibuses Ltd, one of the group's constituent companies, and marked the largest number of former London utilities to be sold to a single operating organisation. Policy at the time dictated that all vehicles rendered surplus to the requirements of companies under the British Transport Commission umbrella should first be offered to others within the organisation before being disposed of externally, and as a result of notifying the impending mass withdrawal of Arabs London Transport received an enquiry from James Amos, the head of the Scottish Bus Group, for fifty, subsequently increased to sixty.

The two companies primarily interested in running these vehicles were Walter Alexander & Sons Ltd and the Western SMT Company Ltd and the managing directors of these, Walter Alexander junior and William Sword – both well respected 'characters' in the transport world – travelled down to London in September 1951 to discuss the matter. A deal was agreed in November whereby sixty Guys would be supplied at £185 each less tyres, and collection began in the same month.

The first Scottish batch embraced a miscellany of bodywork, there being 24 with Park Royal/Northern Coachbuilders bodies, 23 Weymann, 8 Massey and 5 Northern Counties. Their new owners were well aware that, in many cases, the bodies were close to the end of their natural lives and a few were totally inoperable as they stood, having been withdrawn because of PSV 71 'stops'. The plan was to rebuild or rebody many, but in the meantime to identify the best ones for operation in their original condition as a short term measure. On this purely temporary basis eight joined the fleet of Scottish Omnibuses Ltd in December 1951 and received the attractive light green livery which still retained the old diamond SMT from pre-nationalisation badge days as a fleet name. Nos. E 23-30 in the SMT fleet were former Guys G 329, 334, 341, 343, 211, 344 (all Park Royal), and G 365, 366 (Massey). These were joined in September 1952 by E 31, Weymann-bodied ex-G 409 transferred in from the Alexander fleet. Inter-fleet transfers amongst Scottish companies were traditionally a fairly common occurrence from which the ex-London Guys were not immune.

The green SMT Guys were all withdrawn in 1953 and their bodies sold for scrap in October. Their destiny was to be extensively rebuilt into almost new single deckers for both the parent fleet and Highland Omnibuses Ltd and we shall follow this

process in chapter 17. The same fate befell Gs 116 and 204 which joined the Highland fleet direct and donned its rather depressing dark red livery early in 1952. They were, in fact, the first vehicles to be acquired subsequent to the formation of this latest nationalised bus company where they joined a variety of other Guy Arabs, both double and single deck, receiving fleet numbers E 87 and 88. In August 1952 a trio was formed with the transfer from Alexander's of E 89, formerly G 375. The withdrawal of the SMT and Highland vehicles for conversion into single deckers left both fleets without 'genuine' ex-London Guys, and although none ever returned to the former, Highland collected a miscellany of oddments from time to time as we shall see later. For the rebuilding programme into single deckers the withdrawn vehicles were joined by eleven vehicles which had arrived in Scotland unfit for immediate use and had lain in store pending reconditioning; these were Park Royal bodied Gs 79, 82, 88, 103, 108, 216-218, Massey Gs 360 and 363 and Weymann G 411.

Whether or not it was intentional is unknown, but the best vehicles out of the original sixty all seem to have gone to the Alexander fleet whose contingent of seventeen was as follows:

RO 631-635: G 168, 171, 242-244 (Northern Counties)

RO 636-647: G 378, 379, 406, 423, 387, 375, 409, 414, 424, 407, 371, 380 (Weymann)

Unlike companies in the English nationalised sector inherited with the Tilling group, Scottish operators were not confined to standardised livery colours and styles with the result that all the ex-London Guys, except for Highland's rather dismal looking vehicles, received bright, flattering liveries. In the case of the Alexander fleet there were, in fact, two colour schemes in use. The old established blue and ivory livery was the most widespread and looked very handsome indeed, even on the most basic utilities, thanks to the black edging and white lining out which it employed. However on town services in Perth and Kirkcaldy where the company's buses had replaced municipally-owned trams in the early nineteen-thirties, the blue was substituted by an equally rich and pleasant red. London Guys could be found in due course in both colours as they were employed in the two former tramway towns and, in blue, in Dunfermline.

The Guys which passed to the Walter Alexander fleet were particularly well turned out and maintained. Weymann G 387 is seen in Kirkcaldy. G 373 was one of the Western Guys which almost certainly never received their allocated fleet numbers until after they had been rebodied by Alexander in 1953. Most of the utility bodies rendered surplus by the rebodying programme were scrapped but one of the Weymanns was in sufficiently sound condition to reappear, in due course, on a 1942 Arab I chassis. John Fozard/S N J White

Although they may not have realised the significance at first, Alexander's engineers soon became aware that the five Northern Counties bodied vehicles were in a far better condition than all the others. Inevitably news spread throughout the group and the possibility of acquiring more of these was discussed. Western SMT's management was particularly interested, and in August 1952 the former G 243 was transferred to Western for evaluation purposes where it took fleet number Y 919. Despite having the largest quota of ex-London Guys, Western was unfortunate in being allocated only composite bodied vehicles, many in very dubious condition. Its fleet of 22, acquired in November and December 1951, consisted of:

Y 988-996, 1006: G 381, 384, 420, 373, 376, 400, 412, 418, 429, 369 (Weymann)

Y 997-1001, 1009: G 78, 81, 91, 97, 112, 75 (Park Royal)

Y 1002-1005: G 361, 364, 367, 368 (Massey)

Y 1007, 1008: G 196, 201 (Northern Coachbuilders)

In most or maybe all cases the Western fleet numbers were not actually carried until after the original bodies had been removed in late 1952 or 1953, when all except three (Y 988-990) were reconditioned mechanically and despatched to Alexander's workshops at Falkirk for new 53-seat lowbridge bodies to be fitted. Once part of the same group as Western SMT and the other bus operating companies, Walter Alexander & Sons (Coachbuilders) Ltd was now under separate ownership having escaped the net of nationalisation, but in its new independent role a stronger bond than ever was developing as, more and more frequently, Scottish operators including those in the nationalised sector turned to the company when ordering new bodies. Formerly happy to construct double deck bodies containing more than a trace of Leyland influence, Alexander had now developed a very different, handsome four bay style not unlike current Massey practice in its rounded lines. Unfortunately it was destined not to last long as the lightweight era lay just around the corner, but it was applied to all nineteen ex-London Guys. A subtle approach was adopted in the cab design which was aligned to the radiator position, eliminating the snout effect. The front mudguards were also reshaped in modern style by cutting away at an angle the forward sweep to create an effect not unlike that of the then current Arab Mark IV in its exposed radiator version. Surprisingly the original Park Royal body from G 112 was re-used in 1953 on Western's R 257, a Daimler CWA6, on which it replaced the original Brush utility body and gave a further four years service.

The London Guys, in whichever form they ended up, represented a sufficiently useful addition to the Scottish fleets to encourage the purchase late in 1952 of a further fifty at the same price as before. A special request was made to London Transport that as many as possible should have Northern Counties bodies, and James Amos wrote, "there is some competition between my companies as to who gets the Northern Counties bodywork, which is a compliment to Northern Counties". In fact the competition was solely between Alexander and Western SMT who were to share all fifty. Before collection from London began in February 1953 a follow-on contract for a further thirty was agreed, this time at the higher price of £267.10s.0d per bus. The increased charge was due to the fact that the thirty vehicles concerned had already been sold to North's for more than the £185 per bus previously paid by the Scottish companies and had to be re-acquired by London Transport; indeed sixteen had already been despatched to Leeds and were sent direct on to Scotland from there, the remaining fourteen departing direct from London.

By no means all of the Western Guys rebodied by Alexander had seen service in Scotland prior to rebodying. Here a line-up of ten Massey and Park Royal style vehicles at Kilmarnock – mostly with engines and radiators removed – awaits mechanical modification including shortening of the front chassis members. Not all, in fact, are Western vehicles; some are destined to be single deckers for Highland Omnibuses. Alan B Cross

The designated reception point for all eighty Guys was Alexander's premises at Larbert Road, Falkirk, and all had arrived there by May 1953. Western had agreed to take 43 of them, of which 25 were to be Northern Counties bodied. These were numbered by their new owner in a single batch Y 1022-1046 comprising, in strict numerical sequence, Gs 157, 160, 165, 167, 170, 221, 235, 236, 238, 240, 241, 252-254, 256, 257, 273, 281, 282-284, 287-290. They joined the erstwhile G 243 and many similar, and in some cases identical, vehicles already in the Western fleet which had been purchased new by the company or acquired in June 1950 with the takeover of Youngs' Bus Service of Paisley. Next into service were Y 1048-1055 (G 11, 42, 47, 49, 372, 128, 178, 267), but not before they had been fitted with 1947-built Croft bodies removed from elderly Leyland TD1 and TD2 chassis.

These Leylands had originated with a miscellany of operators such as Eastern National, Keighley Corporation, Maidstone & District, Plymouth Corporation, Yorkshire Woollen and Glasgow Corporation but had arrived with Western via the Caledonian Omnibus Co. Ltd, formerly the only Tilling-owned company in Scotland, which had been merged into the Western fleet on 1st January 1950. Caledonian, which was noted for the ancient nature of much of its fleet, had fitted the new 53-seat lowbridge bodies. Having come from elderly Titan chassis, the Croft bodies were shorter than those normally fitted to wartime Arabs and a step was inserted below the windscreen to meet the radiator. This worked satisfactorily in the case of the four mark I Arabs, but on the Arab IIs it was necessary to set the radiator back to the Arab I position whilst shortening the mudguards to suit; however this left the chassis frame and headlamps protruding from the front of the vehicle in a very ungainly way.

After the eight Croft conversions Western was left with ten vehicles (G 118, 129, 130, 193, 263, 316, 317, 374, 392, 404) still unused. These were subsequently rebuilt into virtually new buses whose London origin was completely obscured, and their story in this form is described in Chapter 17.

Western's Northern Counties bodied Guys worked hard in their new environment and survived until 1957/8; the Croft vehicles with early post-war Croft bodies outlasted them until 1961 whilst the earlier acquisitions carrying 1952/3 Alexander bodies stayed longer still, the final ones being withdrawn in 1964. However it remained easy to find ex-London Guys still with their original bodies after 1958 by visiting the Alexander fleet where rebodying of utilities was not in fashion. Alexander's 1953 intake of London Guys consisted of 37 vehicles of which fourteen were Northern Counties bodied. The newcomers were numbered by their new owner from RO 696 upwards in what appeared to be a completely random fashion but which possibly indicated the order in which they entered Scottish service. Their London numbers were as follows:

G 66, 139, 147, 151, 292, 294, 304, 296, 310, 117, 19, 101, 146, 148, 152, 291, 298, 299, 301, 311, 140, 293, 297, 308, 309, 198, 356, 330, 349 (RO 696-724).

G 376 in its new guise as Western GY 992 looks resplendent with its new Alexander body. Although the chassis front end has been rebuilt, and new mudguards fitted, opportunity has not been taken to fit a modern, low radiator as practised by various other operators when reconditioning wartime Guy Arabs. The letter G prefixing the fleet number denotes the garage to which the vehicle is allocated, in this case Greenock (Ladyburn). Photobus

Western's Northern Counties Arabs gave good service whilst retaining their original bodies, some of which received sliding windows in place of their original half drops. G 157 stands in Carlisle garage. D A Jones

Even with its front end truncated, the chassis of G 372 is still too long for the Croft body formerly on a Leyland TD1 or TD2, hence the deep ledge below the windscreen. Alongside it at Gretna stands one of the two Caledonian Bristol K5Gs which had entered service on loan to London Transport when new in 1949 along with many other Tilling group Bristols; Caledonian was absorbed by Western on 1st January 1950 so they never actually ran for their original owner. D A Jones

After the entry into service of RO 724 interest in the class appears to have waned and the remaining eight were either scrapped for spares or resold to fairground showmen. These were G 142, 144, 332, 337, 340, 347, 350 and 432 which would have occupied fleet numbers RO 725-732 had they survived although not necessarily in the same order.

In May 1961 a major reorganisation saw the splitting-up of the huge Alexander empire into three self contained companies, W. Alexander & Sons (Midland), (Fife) and (Northern). No fewer than 27 of the former London Transport Guys were still in service at the time, all with their original bodies. All except one of the Northern Counties vehicles were, naturally enough, included in this total, but so, too, were ten others including an Arab Mark I. These were outwardly still in remarkably good condition and had presumably been heavily renovated by Alexander's without altering their external features. There were no Guys in the Alexander (Northern) fleet but seventeen Londoners were inherited by Midland, who adopted the old Alexander blue livery, and ten by Fife whose colour was the ex-Alexander red. The fleets were as follows:

Midland
MRO 646 (ex G 371) Weymann
MRO 696 (G 66), 722 (G 356) Park Royal
MRO 697 (G 139), 698 (G 147), 699 (G 151), 721 (G 198) Northern Coachbuilders
MRO 701 (G 294), 711 (G 291), 712 (G 298), 713 (G 299), 714 (G 301), 715 (G 311), 717 (G 293), 718 (G 297), 719 (G 308), 720 (G 309) Northern Counties

Fife
FRO 638 (G 406), 639 (G 423), 640 (G 387) Weymann
FRO 631 (G 168), 632 (G 171), 633 (G 242), 635 (G 244), 702 (G 304), 703 (G 296), 704 (G 310) Northern Counties

However time was now running out and new Bristol Lodekkas were making their mark on the former Alexander town services. The Fife Arabs formerly in Dunfermline and Kirkcaldy had all departed by March 1963 with the exception of the former G 310 which is believed to have lasted through to 1964. Midland's Perth fleet was subjected to inroads from August 1962 onwards and was wiped out by May 1963 except that, here too, a sole survivor existed in the form of ex-G 308 which, in December 1963, was sold to Highland.

The impecunious nature of most of Highland's operations meant that the company relied heavily on elderly vehicles handed down from other group companies, and as a considerable portion of the double deck requirement was for low mileage workers' transport to and from the Douneray nuclear power station in Caithness, almost time expired vehicles such as the ex-London Guys were ideal. After Highland's three original London Guys left for rebuilding in 1954 there was a three year gap before any more reached the company's Inverness headquarters. Next to arrive were Northern Counties bodied ex-Gs 273 and 281 in October 1957. These had been amongst many rendered surplus by a huge influx of Bristol Lodekkas and Leyland PD3s into the Western SMT fleet but which still had a few years' potential life left in them. At Highland they became fleet numbers E 31 and 30. The same pattern was

repeated in 1963 when another massive intake of new vehicles, this time Albion Lowlanders, found Western SMT disposing of more London Guys. On this occasion the former G 367-369 carrying ten year old Alexander bodies became Highland's E 7, 8, 6. Last of all, in December 1965, came E 9 from Alexander (Midland) in the shape of ex-G 308, still in its original Northern Counties form.

Above **RO 719 was one of the 37 London Guys added to the Alexander fleet in 1953. Seen at Perth in Alexander (Midland) days, the former G 308 still looks very smart. It carries the red livery long associated with Perth city services whilst the Bristol Lodekka, emerging from the depot behind it, is in blue.**
Alan Nightingale

G 281 moved from Western to become Highland's E 30 in October 1957, where it was destined to remain, serving the northernmost tip of mainland Scotland, for nine years. Sliding windows have been fitted and a platform door is useful in the harsh weather conditions often prevailing.
Alan Nightingale

Many Highland vehicles journeyed each day from Wick and Thurso to the nuclear industry's fast breeder reactor plant at Douneray on the bleak Caithness coast where they would lay over in long rows between workers' shifts. In September 1964 Alexander rebodied G 368 and unrebodied G 273 join a very heavily rebuilt former SMT lowbridge Arab on the Douneray run.
Ken Blacker

This vehicle, along with the erstwhile G 273, ceased operation in 1964, but the last original bodied Londoner in Scotland, G 281, soldiered on through to 1966. Of the rebodied vehicles G 367 also left Highland's service in 1966 whilst Gs 367 and 368 brought the Scottish Bus Group's ex-London Guy era to a close after more than fifteen years when they were withdrawn in May 1967.

MUNICIPAL UTILITIES

Britain's extensive municipal transport sector provided a fruitful outlet for no fewer than 187 of London's utilities, or nearly a quarter of the total, many of which were supplied through North's of Leeds. Sixty Guys which were so totally refurbished by Edinburgh Corporation as to become unrecognisable as former London buses are described later, but the remainder retained their identity, if not their original bodies, through what was to prove in many cases a long and worthwhile municipal career.

The first novel viewing of a London utility running under Corporation control came about in February 1953 when the former G 319 entered service with what seemed at the time to be a most unlikely owner, Lancaster Corporation. For a Lancashire operator, this municipality had an unusually mixed fleet which was by no means as heavily biased towards the native-built Leylands as was usually the case, but it had never before purchased second hand double deckers apart from ex-demonstrators acquired direct from their manufacturers. The Corporation already had Guy utilities of its own but these had all been rebodied with new Guy or Crossley bodies and no traditional utilities remained in the fleet. G 319 was one of a pair obtained from North's in February 1953, the other being G 153; two more (G 326, 395) joined them in March and all four had entered Corporation service by September. Lancaster's numbering system at the time was simply to use the numerical section of the registration number, resulting in anything but a sequential scheme. Thus the London Guys became Lancaster 97 (G 153), 105 (G 326), 174 (G 395) and 459 (G 319). With the exception of G 395 which was Weymann built

they all carried Park Royal style bodies (G 153 actually being by Northern Coachbuilders), and though Lancaster's ruby red and broken white livery was not unlike the traditional London style the rather more extensive use of white, together with their new Lancaster-style front indicator displays, altered their appearance very considerably.

Unlike Lancaster's own former Guy utilities the four Londoners were not rebodied and appear only to have been purchased as a stop gap. When they finally left the fleet no apparent direct replacements were obtained for any of them. Two were withdrawn from service early in 1956 but were still in good enough condition to find further employment with independent operators. The remaining two (the former G 153, 395) left Lancaster in the spring of 1957.

If North's sales schemes had gone according to plan a much larger fleet of ex-London utilities than Lancaster's would have seen municipal service within the county of Lancashire, for in the spring of 1953 an arrangement was made whereby no fewer than fifty Daimlers would be sold to Manchester Corporation. Indeed two, Ds 210 and 242, were actually delivered to the Corporation's Hyde Road premises in April. Much to the annoyance of North's sales staff an incautious remark by a senior London Transport official to an equally influential member of the Council's transport committee to the effect that the vehicles were fit only for scrap resulted in cancellation of the deal at the eleventh hour, and the two Daimlers were returned to London.

At the same time that Lancaster Corporation was obtaining its ex-London Guys from North's the corporation transport department at Burton-upon-Trent was doing likewise. Burton's operations had traditionally been bedevilled by a proliferation of low railway bridges requiring the extensive use of single deckers, although a re-linking scheme of 1943 had allowed the limited use of double deckers; now further double deckers were needed to replace smaller vehicles on operations where roadways had been lowered to provided greater headroom. Burton's existing fleet of 32 double deckers consisted, with one exception, of Guy Arabs of both wartime and post-war origin, so it was hardly surprising that, when further vehicles were needed at fairly short notice, second hand Guys were an obvious choice. Six were purchased and North's were able to supply all late examples (G 324, 339, 346, 351, 415, 434) of which G 415 stood out from the others in being Weymann bodied rather than Park Royal. They were allocated Burton fleet numbers 67, 65, 69, 70, 66 and 68 respectively. Although they arrived in Burton between February and April 1953 the Corporation took the wise decision to send them away for reconditioning prior to entering service. They had not been purchased as some sort of short term expediency, indeed it was expected that they would serve out their full nominal life span. Fortunately the reconditioning did not alter their external appearance and even the original London front indicators were retained with the bulk of the aperture masked out to accommodate the new operator's rather meagre standard destination display.

The first to enter service in Burton's rather drab maroon and cream livery was G 324 in July 1953 and all six were in use by November replacing Guy single deckers which, though only roughly a year newer, were much more modern looking vehicles with bodies completely post-war in style. The London Guys seemed perfectly at home in their new surroundings and blended in almost inconspicuously with the native fleet, many of which were physically almost identical to them. The usual body deterioration associated with utilities resulted in a certain amount of further rebuilding work being carried out by the Corporation after a few years' service whilst the former G 434, having collided with a low bridge, received a new and non-matching top deck in April 1955. A new, slightly lighter livery of madder and cream, with more of the latter than before, cheered the fleet's appearance from about 1960.

Inevitably fatigue dictated the commencement of withdrawals in due course, but this did not come about until April 1964. The last of the six, the former G 346, was delicensed in March 1967 by which time it was 21 years old. At this late stage utilities in anything resembling original condition were very rare indeed and it is fortunate that a sister vehicle withdrawn a couple of months earlier, G 351, was acquired for preservation and exists to this day.

The addition of a newcomer to the ranks of municipal bus operators was a very great rarity in the post-war era, but this is what occurred when Hartlepool Borough Council began running four buses on a service into neighbouring West Hartlepool on 1st August 1953. To add to the interest the initial fleet comprised four ex-London Bristol utilities looking pristine in a light blue and cream livery.

Above G 434, alias Burton-on-Trent 68, demonstrates the new top deck received after a low bridge accident. The original outline is still retained but rubber mounted windows with radiused corners transform its appearance.
Alan Nightingale

Left The trolleybuses have gone and the blue livery of Hartlepool Borough Council, a new operator on the bus scene, adorns Duple bodied B 14. Newly overhauled for the Council by United Automobile Services, even the insides of the mudguards have been repainted silver, perhaps indicating the thoroughness with which the work was carried out. D A Jones

The only 'unfrozen' Bristol in the Hartlepool fleet was B 5. Now in anything but pristine condition, bulging below the lower deck windows indicates that all is far from well with the body structure.
John Fozard

Hartlepool's one-route operation was not introduced without acrimony between the Borough Council and the larger West Hartlepool County Borough with whom the service was co-ordinated by order of the Traffic Commissioner. The two had, in fact, co-operated for many years with tram and trolleybus operation, and though Hartlepool had never operated vehicles of its own, it had shared in the ownership of some of the trolleybuses which had all been operated by West Hartlepool as manager. In 1946 the two councils agreed to replace the joint trolleybus service by motor buses and this took effect on 2nd April 1953. Unfortunately for Hartlepool Borough Council it was discovered that motor bus powers which it had acquired as early as 1925, but not exercised, only gave it authority to run on routes other than the trolleybus route. This meant that it was excluded from the replacement motor bus service which, whilst a new parliamentary Act was obtained, was worked solely by West Hartlepool. Having had the road to themselves West Hartlepool decided that they would prefer to keep it that way and appealed against the granting of a licence to its neighbour, but justice prevailed and West Hartlepool was forced, against its wishes, to share the service on an equal basis. Fortunately relationships later improved to the extent that each began to accept the other's return tickets.

With a fleet as minuscule as four vehicles it was clearly not worth while for Hartlepool to set up an operating base of its own so arrangements were duly made for the local major Tilling group operator, United Automobile Services Ltd, to manage and run the operation on its behalf. United was left to seek suitable vehicles and naturally opted for Bristols. Through its Tilling connections it learnt that four of the ex-London fleet originally allocated to fellow group members were surplus to requirements and arranged to purchase them on Hartlepool's behalf. One was a Park Royal bodied vehicle from the 1942 batch, B 5, latterly allocated to Crosville, whilst Duple bodied Bs 13 and 14 had come via Lincolnshire Road Car and B 28 from Brighton Hove & District. Upon acquisition the four Bristols were taken to United's central works in Darlington where they were overhauled mechanically and the worst body timbers were replaced. To enable them to be immediately distinguished from the red liveried West Hartlepool fleet a bright blue and cream livery was applied. Although the fleet numbered only four vehicles it was apparently felt worthwhile to allocate fleet numbers in an H (for Hartlepool) series, H 1-4 being respectively the former B 13, 28, 14 and 5. Unfortunately at this stage United had to opt out of its agreement to manage the service. These were times of full employment and militant union power, and United's staff refused to co-operate unless they received municipal rates of pay and conditions which were traditionally more favourable than those applying in the company sector. Aware that acquiescence to the demand might result in expensive repercussions in other towns where United vehicles operated alongside municipals, the company refused, leaving Hartlepool Borough Council to conclude a replacement agreement with local independent operator Bee-Line Roadways (Tees-side) Ltd.

Bee-Line's payment for running the service was arranged on a mileage basis and included the provision of all management and staff; it also carried out all vehicle maintenance at its depot in York Road, West Hartlepool. Although it had no conventional stage carriage services of its own Bee-Line was a substantial undertaking by independent standards and ran its own double deck fleet, many numbers of which provided internal transport within the huge ICI works at Wilton near Redcar. The company had extremely well equipped workshops and stores and carried out all its own major mechanical work except for crankshaft grinding and cylinder boring. When necessary, Bee-Line provided replacements for the Hartlepool vehicles and also ran duplicates as required using its own double deckers in their dual green livery, and these were often ex-London Daimlers of which they owned eight. Hartlepool's ex-London Bristols were replaced in 1956 by a quartet of handsome Roe bodied Regent Vs which formed the entire fleet for its remaining eleven years.

Another, more southerly municipal operator to acquire London utilities in the furtherance of trolleybus replacement was Southend-on-Sea Corporation Transport. Back in 1946 the Corporation had concluded an agreement with the local Tilling group operator, Westcliff-on-Sea Motor Services, to introduce a co-ordination scheme for Southend and the surrounding area, but their plans were thwarted by the existence of two quite substantial local independents, Benfleet & District and the City Coach Company. After these were acquired by Westcliff in 1951 and 1952 respectively co-ordination was again contemplated but the continued existence of the Corporation's trolleybuses was regarded as a stumbling block to the flexibility which the scheme demanded. To hasten their demise the Corporation sought to purchase eighteen ex-London Daimlers from North's. Six suitable candidates were acquired between March and June 1953, but a quest for the remainder early in 1954 unearthed only seven more which were considered to be good enough. North had by this time sold most of the ex-London stock and, indeed, Southend Corporation took the last few. Meanwhile in anticipation of obtaining all eighteen the Corporation had placed an order for this quantity of new bodies from Massey and subsequently purchased five new Leyland PD2 chassis for the five bodies which were surplus.

The thirteen London Daimlers bought by Southend Corporation provided inexpensive rolling stock for trolleybus replacement. Only the chassis were required, but D 241's cab structure was left temporarily in situ for the journey to the Corporation's London Road depot where it stands alongside a venerable AEC-English Electric trolleybus recently withdrawn from service. Some of the bodies were left behind in a Council yard near Shoeburyness where they were subsequently broken up. Ken Blacker

The new Massey bodies were 55 seaters and were of the low height type favoured by the Corporation because of a low railway bridge in the High Street. Like all Massey products of the time they were easily distinguished by their well rounded outline, the frontal curve in particular being more pronounced than on any other concurrent make of body, and they fitted well into the Southend fleet where Massey bodied Daimlers were already in use. They differed from earlier vehicles, however, in having metal rather than composite frames and were built to an unusual intermediate width of 7ft 9ins. Like all Massey-built vehicles of the time they exuded quality, both inside and out, and although the smart polished wood interiors were now succeeded by a modern finish, the gold-coloured anodised window surrounds contrasting against a rexine finish and attractive blue moquette seats provided a very satisfactory alternative.

Fleet numbers 263-275 were allocated to Ds 27, 149, 275, 241, 246, 159, 202, 71, 136, 52, 53, 95 and 228 respectively. From April 1954 onwards they began to drift into service as and when they arrived back from Wigan and all thirteen were in use by July. At this time one trolleybus service still survived but the vehicles and overhead wiring were now in a very run down condition and electric traction ceased altogether on 28th October 1954. The co-ordination scheme was planned to start on 2nd January 1955 and in anticipation of this the thirteen new bodies incorporated Tilling-style three piece indicator displays to accommodate the multiplicity of routes which would be operated by the Corporation henceforth. They were the first in the fleet to carry the new layout although all earlier vehicles were quickly converted. New blinds were not available for the first few months so only part of the indicator display was used and a third of the screen was blanked off.

Approximately half of the batch ended their Southend careers upon arrival of some partic-ularly ungainly new Albion Lowlanders in 1963 and the demise of the remainder came two years later when Leyland PD3s, carrying Southend's last new Massey bodies, took their place. The former D 27, which was sold ahead of the others in 1962 for conversion into a mobile road safety exhibition with the local constabulary, survived long enough to outlive all the others and to become a preservation project.

Whereas the Bristols at Hartlepool and Daimlers at Southend had found second owners as a result of trolleybus scrapping policies, the largest municipal fleet of ex-London vehicles was purchased specifically for tramway replacement. The scene was Belfast where a decision to scrap the tram system in favour of trolleybuses had been adopted before the war but, as in the case of London, hostilities had brought a temporary halt to the programme resulting in the trams surviving much longer than originally intended. Unlike London Transport, Belfast Corporation had resumed conversion using trolleybuses, and although new BUTs were still being delivered in 1953, even in this stronghold of electric traction a move towards motor buses was becoming apparent. Some had already replaced trams very successfully, and when it came to finding replacements for the City's last and busiest tram service, the Queens Road route, motor buses were decided upon. This was not so much due to any anti-trolleybus bias but because of objections to overhead wiring which could hinder movement of high loads passing to and from the shipyards from time to time.

In order to ease its financial position the Corporation had resorted to purchasing some second hand trolleybuses from Wolverhampton Corporation in 1952, and the success of this led to an ambitious scheme to buy no fewer than one hundred second hand motor buses for the Queens Road route. Daimlers were an obvious choice as the Corporation already had many, and a contract was concluded with North's to supply one hundred former London vehicles as and when they became available at a price reported to be £300 each. The intention was to remove the bodies, overhaul the chassis and fit new bodywork, and even when all this was done the transport department expected to make a substantial saving of £150,000 in capital cost against buying an equivalent number of new vehicles. Furthermore the tramway conversion could be carried out at an earlier date by this means, thereby achieving a further saving as the trams were now proving very costly to run.

An initial vehicle, D 196, was supplied to the Corporation in September 1953 and many more followed in October and November with the final large batch being received in February 1954. The Belfast and former London fleet numbers are shown in Appendix 3. As a temporary expedient all but eighteen – basically the oldest ones – were placed into service still with their original bodies after receiving the Corporation's red and white livery and standard front indicator display. The trams made their final runs on Saturday 27th February 1954.

Between January 1955 and November 1956 the hundred buses were despatched one by one to the local coachbuilders, Harkness Coachworks Ltd, for new bodies to be fitted. Harkness had long supplied bodywork for the Corporation's bus and trolleybus fleets, and though the design had evolved over the years a distinctive Belfast style ran through them all. Harkness purchased the metal framework on which its bodies were based from various outside sources; in post-war years Metal Sections of Oldbury was its favoured supplier. Before being sent to Harkness each chassis was stripped of its body and extensively overhauled, including the fitment of automatic chassis lubrication. The dropped rear extension to the chassis frame was re-moved as redundant, the platform area of the Harkness body being hung off the main frame and therefore self supporting. Although they all looked identical, differences beneath the skin meant that eighty were constructed on Metal Sections steel frames whilst, in order to produce a worthwhile saving in weight, ten had Metal Sections aluminium frames and the final ten had alloy framework supplied by Park Royal. After rebodying, the London Daimlers blended totally into the Belfast fleet although their London registration numbers remained as a means of instant recognition.

The whole fleet remained intact for many years, the first inroads being made when the former Ds 132 and 135 were lost in August 1969 through the terrorism campaign which had commenced in the previous year and afterwards resulted in the loss of numerous buses throughout Northern Ireland. However, after more than fifteen years' service in Belfast, the London Daimlers were now becoming obsolete and a withdrawal programme began towards the end of 1969 as new Daimler Fleetline single and double deckers came in to take their place. The final vehicles were sold, mostly for scrap, in November 1970 with the exception of the one-time D 93 which passed in March 1971 to the Irish Transport Trust for preservation.

Two phases of ex-London Daimler operation in Belfast. D 139 still carries its original Duple body, modified to carry the Corporation's standard indicator display, as fleet number 519. After rebodying, D 146 (now Belfast 487) shows off the typical Belfast styling of its new Harkness body as it traverses Donegall Square.
A M Wright/Ken Blacker

BRISTOLS AND THE TILLING GROUP

Although it did not intend to take them out of service immediately, London Transport obtained authority in July 1951 to withdraw its fleet of 29 Bristols, and in due course their forthcoming availability was circulated to potentially interested parties within the British Transport Commission. There was never any doubt that they would be snapped up by Tilling Association members, as indeed proved to be the case. In general the age profile of Tilling fleets tended to be markedly higher than those in the BET or municipal sectors and the opportunity to obtain relatively new second hand Bristols was too good to miss. The 29 vehicles were divided between three companies in the group, Crosville whose fleet of ancient Leyland TD1s and TD2s was legendary, Lincolnshire which was traditionally one of the weakest performers in the group from a financial point of view, and Brighton Hove & District. They were allocated fifteen, nine and five respectively, with the whole of the 1942 batch, B 1-9, destined for Crosville. The first Bristols departed from London in December 1952, two months before a deal was finally sealed setting a price of £185 on each vehicle, whereafter some continued to run at Southall although technically sold, and the last ones did not reach their new owners until May 1953.

As Crosville was destined to take the largest share, it was perhaps only fitting that it should be the recipient of the first ones to be released, Bs 8 and 9. Crosville's fifteen Bristols were allocated fleet numbers MB 160-170, 193-196 (B 1-9, 16, 17, 12, 23, 24, 27) but MB 164 (B 5) was not in fact received. It was diverted, together with vehicles from the other two recipients, to United for operation on behalf of Hartlepool Borough Council. Of the remaining fourteen, six (the former B 2-4, 6-8) were destined to lose their original Park Royal bodies prior to entering service. The replacements were also utilities, but lowbridge 55-seaters by Strachans which had been removed from some of Crosville's own Bristol Ks when these had received new ECW bodies. A further transformation took place when, between February 1954 and May 1956, all except MB 194 (the former B 12) were given standard post-war ECW lowbridge bodywork of 1948/9 vintage which had formerly graced ancient AEC Regent and Leyland Titan chassis. At the same time the eight vehicles of the 1942 batch were rebuilt with low, PV2-type radiators, and in their revised form the ex-London Bristols became indistinguishable from the multitude of standard Bristol/ECW K-types commonplace in so many parts of the country. Only MB 193 retained Duple bodywork to the end, but this was the body formerly on MB 169 (B 16) fitted in February 1954, and not its own.

In 1958 Crosville revised its vehicle classifications with the result that the MB code, which denoted Bristol K6As and derived from

Only two out of the eight 'unfrozen' Bristols entered Crosville service still carrying original Park Royal bodywork. The former B 1 has no destination blinds, but this was not uncommon on Crosville at the time when much reliance was placed on paper labels to indicate a vehicle's destination. John Fozard

B 9 was the other 'unfrozen' Bristol which entered Crosville service carrying its original body, but like the rest of the batch it received a lowbridge Strachans utility body in due course. Ken Blacker

In its final guise only the registration number distinguishes B 7 from any other Tilling group standard Eastern Coach Works bodied Bristol K. John Fozard

a system introduced many years earlier, was replaced by DKA, although the former numbers were retained. In the following year a phased withdrawal commenced which was not completed until about October 1962. Even then ten of the batch remained on passenger carrying duties in Wales, but now under the ownership of Atomic Power Construction Ltd for the transportation of workers at the new Trawsfynydd plant where some could still be found in use until as late as 1965.

Lincolnshire's allocation of nine ex-London Bristols was, in May 1953, reduced to seven with the loss of Bs 13 and 14 for use in Hartlepool. The remainder received fleet numbers 979-983, 993, 994 in order of their arrival between January and April 1953, their former London identities being B 10, 20, 25, 26, 15, 11, 21. Before entering service they received the same Tilling green and cream livery as the Crosville vehicles. After only a few months a general fleet renumbering took place which resulted in the batch becoming 2106-2112, but now in strict registration number sequence. All seven retained their original bodies throughout their stay with Lincolnshire, and although a certain amount of reconditioning took place the basic relaxed austerity appearance was never altered. They proved a good investment and lasted, with one exception, through to 1960. After withdrawal No. 2108 (ex B 15) was retained by the company as a tree lopper and remained in stock until December 1972, well into the National Bus Company era.

Brighton Hove & District had one bus (B 28) removed from its allocation to work in Hartlepool and was left with Bs 22, 18, 19 and 29 which became Nos. 5997-5999 with their new owner. These very high fleet numbers were a legacy from the old Thomas Tilling days when a common numbering system was used for the fleets in both London and Brighton. The first digit was officially removed under a renumbering scheme of April 1955 although in practice some vehicles continued carrying their old identity for up to five years later. Brighton Hove & District was unique amongst Tilling companies in being allowed to opt out of the group's standard Tilling red or Tilling green colour schemes, and the London Bristols looked very attractive in the brighter red and cream livery which the company shared with Brighton Corporation under a co-ordination scheme in which the two operators participated. Their vehicles also shared a common two-piece destination screen arrangement which was fitted to the London vehicles prior to entering service. The four vehicles kept their original bodies only until the closing months of 1954 when they were removed and scrapped, the last being 5999 (B 29) which was dealt with in December. The chassis were then despatched to Lowestoft and in March and April 1955 they reappeared carrying new four-bay Eastern Coach Works 60-seat bodies. This gave a new, ten year lease of life which ended under an influx of new Bristol Lodekkas in 1965. Even then the four vehicles still carried valid Certificates of Fitness and were in sufficiently attractive condition for three out of the four to find further, albeit short term employment with independent operators.

B 25 looks remarkably sprightly as Lincolnshire 2111. Its Duple body remains largely unaltered apart from the fitment of new front windows and a Clayton-type front indicator box of the style favoured by Lincolnshire before standard Tilling screens became the norm. John Fozard

At Old Steine, Brighton, B 19 terminates on a sunny day and B 18 is seen in the rain, both in the red and cream livery of Brighton Hove & District. Although the original Duple bodies were only retained temporarily, they were smartly repainted and received standard Brighton front indicators. ECW built very fine new four-bay bodies for them in 1955. John Fozard

'INDEPENDENT' UTILITIES

A glance, today, at photographs of ex-London utilities in the service of independent operators might give the impression that their use by operators in this sector became widespread. In fact this was not so. Certainly North's sold them as widely as they could within the limits imposed upon them by the British Transport Commission's strict guidelines governing the future employment of sold double deckers (which North's exceeded anyway!), but by chance a few major pockets developed leaving other areas, even ones where independents were prolific on stage carriage work, with few or maybe none at all. Most of those which went to the independent sector were Daimlers. Despite Guy being the more numerous of the two makes only four of these passed, in the first instance, to independent operators as against more than sixty Daimlers, although a few others came later as a result of subsequent disposals.

In order to see London's utilities running for independents in the middle and late 1950s Yorkshire was the county to visit. The fleet of 24 amassed by the Ledgard concern is described later, but in the same county T. Burrows & Sons Ltd of Wombwell worked three (D 84, 86, 153) on their trunk Leeds to Rawmarsh service, meeting up at Wakefield and Barnsley with D 98 run by W.R. & P.B. Bingley of Kinsley, a member of the three-operator United Services consortium. A little to the south, in Doncaster, Leon Motor Services Ltd of Finningley placed Ds 172 and 176 on their daily runs to Misson and Finningley with Tuesday and Saturday extensions to Wroot, and when D 172 was sold in May 1956 it was immediately replaced by D 278 from the Bee-Line fleet at West Hartlepool. In the East Riding, J. Wilson & W. Hughes' White Bus Company at Bridlington had Ds 152, 167 and 177 for their service to Flamborough although they never got around to putting the last of these on the road before selling out to the BET subsidiary East Yorkshire Motor Services in November 1955.

Top and Centre **T Burrows & Sons' long, busy Leeds-Rawmarsh route via Wakefield and Barnsley was worked by a miscellany of double deckers, old and new. In Leeds central bus station D 84, now carrying Burrows' red livery as its no. 81, works the following journey to another Londoner, STL 1796. Later, in Wakefield bus station, D 86 disports its new 8ft wide Burlingham body which sits a little uneasily on the narrower chassis. All three London Daimler chassis received these new Burlingham bodies in 1957, two of standard height and one (D 84) in low-bridge style.** R H G Simpson/Alan B Cross

Right **The old Glasgow Paddocks bus station in Doncaster has long since gone as have most of the small independent operators who once served the town. Leon's remains, however, and D 172 was a member of its mixed but largely fairly elderly fleet in 1954.** D A Jones

158

At a later date P.W. Cherry & Sons, who ran locally in Beverley, found employment for G 319 in 1956/7 after Lancaster Corporation had finished with it. On contract services within the county were Greyhound Coaches Ltd of Sheffield's D 96 and F.W. Balme's D 173 at Otley.

In County Durham, a notable Mecca for independent stage carriage operators, Trimdon Motor Services Ltd added eleven London Daimlers to its large, mixed and – at the time – multi-coloured fleet during 1953 (D 8, 10, 34, 42, 60, 77-9, 97, 242, 270). Ds 10 and 42 soon passed to Transport Motor Services (Bishop Auckland) Ltd, a newly formed TMS subsidiary set up to work the recently acquired Favourite Direct service linking Bishop Auckland with Stockton and Middlesbrough. In the same part of the county G.E. Martindale took G 34 which could occasionally be found on one or other of his two short stage carriage runs between Ferryhill and the nearby village of Ferryhill Station, but was more usually confined to contract work. About a decade later the one-time Bs 19 and 29 joined Martindale from Brighton Hove & District and were modern looking members of the fleet with their 1955 ECW bodies, but lasted at Ferryhill only from the autumn of 1965 to about May 1966. Bee-Line has been mentioned earlier in this chapter; they had Ds 31, 32, 81, 90, 240, 260, 278 and 279 at their West Hartlepool base. Apart from a seasonal service from Thornaby to Seaton Carew via Middlesbrough the Daimlers were used almost exclusively on Bee Line's extensive range of contract services although they sometimes deputised for or duplicated ex-London Bristols on the service worked on behalf of the Hartlepool municipality. Two of the Hartlepool Bristols (the former Bs 13 and 28) actually joined the Bee Line fleet when displaced by new AEC Regents in 1956 and stayed for about a year, passing to the local contract operations of Curry of Fencehouses (B 13) and Rogers of Redcar (B 28).

Balme Coaches of Otley purchased D 173 in 1953 and kept it until 1959; it was used purely on contract work as Balme held no stage carriage licences. It is seen here along with a Yorkshire Woollen District Leyland PS1 and numerous Leeds City Transport AEC Regents. John Fozard

In the nineteen-fifties Trimdon Motor Services was not the smart, modern outfit it became in its later days. Duple bodied D 10, seen at Sedgefield in October 1953, has obviously been hurriedly pressed into service but at least its London advertisements have been removed – just! D 10 passed soon afterwards to Transport Motor Services. John C Gillham

Bee-Line's D 278 shows the blind display used when covering duties on the Hartlepool Corporation contract service, and also a strange new front window and dome arrangement, presumably acquired as a result of an earlier accident. In this distinctive form it later ran for Leon's from 1956 to 1958. R F Mack

Left **One of six London Daimlers in the Brown's Blue fleet, D 179 is seen at the depot in Ibstock. It now has sliding windows and a platform door.**
Right **Untidy rebuilding of the front windows, and the off-centre positioning of the destination box, are features which combine to give an unsatisfactory frontal aspect to D 261. It served Gibson Bros of Barleston for several years and was not finally disposed of until 1960.** Robin Hannay

The unmistakable G 150 passed through two ownerships after leaving London but neither made any visible changes to its Park Royal metal framed body. In its earlier guise it is seen at the Tunstall terminus carrying Rowbotham's pale blue livery, and subsequently in red and cream at Mow Cop, shortly after being taken over by PMT early in 1959. C Carter/John Fozard

In the Midlands the only real focal point for London utilities was Leicester where St Margaret's bus station saw the frequent departures of Markfield-based Brown's Blue Coaches Ltd, who were the owners for five or six years of Ds 19, 74, 161, 165, 169 and 179, whilst from Western Boulevard Gibson Bros of Barleston's Comfort Service Ds 30 and 261 departed on two routes to Market Bosworth for about the same period of time. In the Staffordshire Potteries district, renowned for its many independent operators, only W.S. Rowbotham & Sons of Harriseahead was tempted by purchasing the unique G 150 for its run between Tunstall and Mow Cop. The Rowbotham business was sold to Potteries

Motor Traction on 1st January 1959 whereupon G 150 joined the ex White Bus of Bridlington Daimlers in becoming a rare example of an ex-London utility within a BET fleet. To the south of the county Harper Brothers (Heath Hayes) Ltd included D 238 amongst its busy fleet serving Cannock and the surrounding area for almost four years. In Gloucestershire Warners Motors Ltd of Tewkesbury employed Gs 335 and 356 on contract work for nearly a decade whilst G.J. Miller & Sons of Cirencester owned D 101 until their Farringdon service passed to Bristol Tramways in January 1955 and the Daimler moved on to spend a couple of years with A.H. Kearsey of Cheltenham. Later,

when the era of third hand sales arrived, E.G. Palmer's Fordham & District fleet in Cambridgeshire became the home for onetime White Bus D 167, G.R. Holder's Charlton-on-Otmoor Services in Oxfordshire purchased ex-Lancaster Corporation G 326 and J.W. Lloyd & Son Ltd of Nuneaton used the former Ministry of Supply G 169 for a short while on contract work, but probably never on its Rugby-Barby stage carriage service. There were also a few other cases of ex-London utilities working contract services, such as the former White Bus and East Yorkshire D 152 which returned to the London area to join Margo's Coaches at Bexleyheath, but mostly these were short lived.

Looking somewhat barren without its front indicator box, and sporting a chromium plated radiator, much rebuilt D 101 passes through Cheltenham in Kearsey's grey livery. R F Mack

Another Guy to enjoy a post-London career with two operators was G 326 although the change of ownership did not come about through business acquisition as had been the case with G 150. Park Royal G 326 found itself surplus to Lancaster City Transport's requirements and ran for Charlton-on-Otmoor Services from April 1956 until becoming a store shed a couple of years later. Alan B Cross

Left **Life after Western SMT. JNU 556, owned by Paton Bros and seen in their Renfrew yard, carries a Northern Counties body of London origin. Ostensibly the chassis of the Paton vehicle is ex-Chesterfield Corporation, but it is not clear whether the body has actually been transferred from one chassis to another or whether a registration plate swap has taken place.** Ken Blacker

Right **G 143 ran for the Dodds branch of AA Motor Services, still with its original Northern Coachbuilders utility body, for a full eight years before receiving a second hand, post war ECW body in 1961. It is seen in original guise at AA's Ayr bus station.** W J Haynes

No London utilities whatever passed to independents in Wales but a handful reached operators in Scotland, adding to the large numbers employed there by the nationalised operators not to mention the sixty Guys completely renovated by Edinburgh Corporation. First to cross the border was G 143 when it donned the green livery of AA Motor Services Ltd of Ayr, its actual owner in this three-fleet co-operative being Dodds of Troon with whom it stayed for many years, later acquiring a modern though second hand Eastern Coach Works body. The first Daimler in Scotland was D 268 which joined the fleet of William Stokes & Sons of Carstairs who probably employed it on miners' or works services rather than on their two Lanark-Lesmahagow stage runs. Then came D 79 which, after a very short spell with Bee-Line, passed to the Tumilty-owned section of AA. When D 172 was sold by Leon's it reached the extensive Baylis contract fleet based at Creca near Annan, whilst D 260 ended up on similar work for Yuille's of Larkhall after the end of its service with Bee-Line. Finally G 236, once with Western SMT, ended its days employed on contract work with Northern Roadways Ltd of Glasgow.

Pride of place within the independent sector, by virtue of its high profile, was undoubtedly the 24-strong fleet of ex-London utilities carrying the name of Samuel Ledgard. The extensive network of services within the Leeds-Bradford-Ilkley triangle of the West Riding gave the impression that Ledgard was a major territorial operator, although in fact this honour was held by the Tilling group's West Yorkshire Road Car Co Ltd to whom the Ledgard concern was for long a major thorn in the side. From their five depots at Armley, Bradford, Otley, Ilkley and Yeadon, Ledgard's blue vehicles served many of the same places and in some instances covered the same routes as West Yorkshire's ubiquitous Bristols.

G 143 in its modified form is seen at Dodds' Troon garage sandwiched between another rebodied utility (ex-PMT) and an Arab III. Ken Blacker

Tumilty's D 79 worked the AA service in the heavily rebuilt condition into which quite a number of operators transformed their utilities in preference to completely rebodying them. No doubt much of the original Duple timber framework has been replaced; the windows are now rubber mounted and a curved rear dome has been installed. Alan Nightingale collection

Three stages in the lives of Ledgard's Daimlers. D 274 passes through Leeds still very much in 'as London' condition. The original Ledgard livery of all-over blue except for a green roof has been brightened by the addition of a central white band. D 237 has had its opening front windows removed and the destination box repositioned; it also carries platform doors principally for use on the Bradford-Harrogate service. Finally D 199 arrives at Otley with new opening windows throughout and a frontal aspect which, shorn of its half drop windows and London indicator box layout, looks more like a utility now than it did in London. R F Mack

In 1952 Samuel Ledgard died and the business plunged into an era of instability when suddenly deprived of his expertise and hands-on management style, and its misfortune was compounded by heavy death duties which placed a severe strain on its financial resources. The various strands of the business were reorganised under the titles Executors of Samuel Ledgard, Executors of Samuel Ledgard (Bradford) Ltd and Executors of Samuel Ledgard (Ilkley) Ltd and a badly needed fleet renewal programme began early in 1953 with the purchase of fourteen double deckers. In former times the preference had always been to obtain new vehicles but, in the straitened circumstances now prevailing, this was not possible and the next best thing was to buy six year old Daimlers from North's. In order to find the money to pay for them more than forty disused buses and lorries, some of which had not run since well before the war, were sold for scrap.

Between February and April 1953 one Duple and thirteen Park Royal bodied ex-London Daimlers passed from North's to Ledgard (D 178, 220, 227, 234, 236, 239, 263, 271, 272, 274, 276, 277, 280, 281). First into service, in April, were Ds 220 and 236, and all were in use by November except for D 271 which, when licensed in April 1954, bore the registration number JUB 649 from one of Ledgard's own Daimler CWA6s. The real JUB 649 had meanwhile appeared at the end of 1953 carrying D 271's identity and a reconditioned pre-war Brush single deck coach body transferred from the company's only Maudslay SF40. Each vehicle was overhauled and repainted before entering service under the Ledgard banner, and whilst the only external alteration of a physical nature made at this time was the removal of the projecting rear indicators from the Park Royal bodies and their replacement by a flat panel, these same bodies were transformed internally by replacement of their typical London brown, yellow and green decor with a wood grained finish which had the effect of making them look much more like utilities than before.

This influx of London Daimlers was clearly a success and it came as no surprise when nine more were bought between February and May 1954. These were all Sutton type vehicles (D 199, 210, 211, 213, 214, 230, 231, 233, 237) of which there were now 22 in the fleet. Though past their prime, they were considerably newer than the first single deck acquisitions by the company's executors which also came in 1954 and were pre-war Leyland Tigers made redundant by United Automobile Services. All the Daimlers were in operation with Ledgard by May 1955, five of this batch having received platform doors as did two of the previous year's acquisitions when they were overhauled a year or two later. In 1956 the final London Daimler arrived in the fleet, but on this occasion the source was Bee-Line at West Hartlepool. The one-time D 126 was the oldest and also the only Brush bodied ex-London Daimler to carry the Ledgard name.

The large London contingent worked hard in Ledgard service for the remainder of the decade and all but two lasted through to 1960. Over the years, however, various changes in appearance took place as and when the bodies needed further reconditioning, involving alterations to the front indicators, opening window arrangements and livery styles. Such was the extent of these alterations that, in their final form, many of the Park Royal bodies bore little immediate resemblance to their distinctive appearance of former Sutton days. The influx of a further generation of second hand double deckers from 1960 onwards heralded a rapid end, and the last of the 24, D 234, was withdrawn in February 1962. However the break in dependence on ex-London rolling stock was only temporary and starting from 1963 onwards a much larger contingent of London Transport types – RT, RTL and RLH – became the backbone of Ledgard's operations, but that is another story.

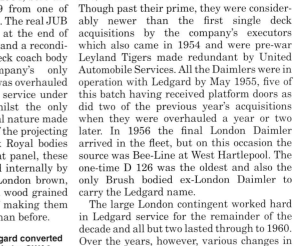

Ledgard converted a Daimler CWA6 into a single decker using a 36-seat Brush coach body dating from 1935 and formerly on a Maudslay SF40 chassis, and called it HGF 948. This was, in fact, the chassis of Ledgard's own JUB 649 whose registration number was transferred to D 271. R L Kell

CHAPTER SIXTEEN

LONDON UTILITIES OVERSEAS

London and its suburbs marked a far cry from the destinations that were to beckon more than 150 of the utilities after their life in the capital was over. In wartime days, and in the almost equally austere times immediately afterwards, few would have dreamt that many of the buses newly in service would, a little more than half a decade later, be running in exotic places, not only in Europe but on the continents of Asia and Africa too.

The precise number of London utilities shipped overseas will almost certainly never be known for sure, especially since most went through dealers reticent about disclosing details of their activities for commercial reasons. Nor will the exact history of many of these vehicles once overseas ever be complete, especially where operations in Africa are concerned, and this chapter records the story as best it can be pieced together. Sales have been positively traced to seven countries and it is known that there were tentative approaches from others. Ventures mooted in Australia have already been mentioned, and in July 1952 North of Leeds was busily working on a scheme to export twenty reconditioned Guys to India. Some may well have gone to overseas customers incognito as bare chassis, and if they did so it is highly unlikely that we shall trace details of them at this late stage.

Sabena's guided tours of Brussels airport by double deck bus were a popular feature of the nineteen-fifties but the number of ex-London Guys used on them is not known precisely. The vehicle featured in both views is G 35, the first in Sabena ownership. W J Wyse

The first overseas wanderings were within Europe, and these started tentatively enough in 1951 with the purchase by Sabena Airlines of Gs 35 and 405 in June and October. They were obtained direct from London Transport for guided sightseeing tours of Brussels' Melsbroek airport, for which they were much better suited than the two former Bradford Corporation lowbridge, open staircase Leyland TD1s which had been bought in November 1945 to inaugurate the facility. In due course at least two more ex-London Guys arrived with Sabena and it has even been recorded that the number in stock rose to six, but these were not purchased direct and almost certainly went via North's. The identities of these additional Guys have not been established. The original Sabena purchase was followed right at the end of the year by the first of numerous overseas deals by North's when Weymann bodied G 36 was sold to the Yugoslavian operator AutoPrevos of Sarajevo in whose fleet it became No. 91 in January 1952. London Transport was unaware at the time that a market for such vehicles could exist in a country such as Yugoslavia and was surprised to receive a report in early May that a Guy had been seen in Belgrade in very delapidated condition bearing LT markings. (G 36 had either been

The first London Guy in Yugoslavia was G 36 which joined the Auto-Prevos fleet in January 1952. Now minus advertisements but otherwise in full London condition – even to the extent of the Upton Park-applied fleet number on the roof – it was photographed in Sarajevo on 21st August 1952. This vehicle demonstrates that it was one of the few early London utilities never to receive a glazed emergency window. John C Gillham

Mirror images in Sarajevo. This unusual scene, taken – it is thought – in 1956, contrasts a Guy still in original condition with another on which the platform and staircase have been reversed to suit the rule of the road. In view of the later style Park Royal (or Northern Coachbuilders) bodywork fitted, it is presumed that these are two of the vehicles purchased for the Sarajevo-Ilidza route. N N Forbes

loaned to the capital from Sarajevo or, more likely, the wrong location was quoted; there is no record of any ex-London vehicles in the capital at this time). However any doubts that may have lingered about the suitability of time-expired Guys for further use in Yugoslavia were dispelled when, on 30th June 1952, Yugoslavia's commerical attaché in London visited 55 Broadway with a request to buy ten. The Executive's informant in Yugoslavia may have been scathing about the condition of G 36 but in Yugoslavian eyes it was a godsend. The attaché, Mr Kopetanic, was offered ten (or twelve if he wanted, but this was presumably beyond his remit) and he quickly arranged for the President of Sarajevo Council, who happened to be in London at the time as a guest of the London County Council, accompanied by a Minister from the Embassy, to see the buses. Eight were in store at Poplar trolleybus depot and on the strength of seeing these they decided to purchase all ten even though it was stressed to them that the bodies of seven were, by London standards, beyond economic repair. They were a mixed bunch consisting of five with Park Royal bodies (G 100, 111, 122, 131, 135), one Weymann (G 37), one Massey (G 177), the unique Duple bodied G 43 and, as if thrown in for good measure, two with

Northern Counties bodies (G 286, 300). The latter were, in fact, the only ones of this type to escape abroad. The three gentlemen saw no problems in driving the vehicles across Europe, preferably using London Transport drivers but, failing this, at least with one of the Executive's mechanics on hand. Operating a fleet of double deckers in Sarajevo would be an experiment, they said, and if successful, new double deckers would be bought.

The ten vehicles had barely departed when a request arrived from the mayor of Ilidza municipality, a holiday town near Sarajevo, enquiring about terms and delivery arrangements for ten to fifteen "two decked" buses wanted for transport between the two towns. London Transport signalled its willingness to set fifteen aside for immediate delivery at the same price as before – £300 per bus – only to learn that the initial urgency had waned. Owing to an immediate and serious shortage of hard currency, the Yugoslavian government had prohibited the importation of buses until 31st March 1953. Perhaps in an acknowledgement of the purchaser's cash plight the final sale price for the fifteen vehicles, which departed in April and May 1953, was reduced to £220 each. Even then credit had to be extended as the cash to pay for them (plus ten

10T10 single deckers) was not available until later in the year. Nearly all of this batch were Park Royal bodied or, in one case, a Park Royal lookalike by Northern Coachbuilders (G 23, 56, 57, 60, 69, 70, 80, 110, 145, 327, 333, 342, 355) with the balance made up by Massey G 359 and Weymann G 426. As with the earlier export order the bodies on many of these were extremely poor but they were put into service in 'as received' condition and appear to have run successfully despite their unsuitability for right-of-the-road running.

Sarajevo's ex-London double deckers did not go unnoticed by other Yugoslav operators. In June 1953 the government agency, Jugoimport, enquired as to the possible purchase of sixty vehicles for service in Belgrade, although in this case single deck bodywork was preferred, and in the same month Zagreb Electric Tramways asked for twenty Guy double deckers. However the supply of Guys was now exhausted. Although strictly speaking outside the scope of this history, it is interesting to complete the story by recording that in 1955 one further Guy double decker was sent from London to Yugoslavia; this was London Transport's only Arab Mark III, G 436. It was sold as part of a bulk lot along with 65 Leyland PD1s which formed the batch STD 112-176.

Locally-built dual-entrance bodywork was carried by the ex-London Guys in Las Palmas. A modern guy badge was displayed on the topmost of the many bars forming the dummy radiator grille, but nothing was immediately visible to show its London origin. Instead of carrying the normal APJG livery of blue and yellow, GC 8579 is in the grey, blue and white of Spantax, the charter airline, to whom it is on hire. Andrew Johnson

Forty years ago the Spanish-administered archipelago lying in the Atlantic Ocean off the north west coast of Morocco, known as the Canary Islands, was only just beginning to develop as a popular tourist destination for British holidaymakers. Although some had been resort islands since the late 19th century, the package holiday boom had hardly started when the sale by North's of some ex-London Guy chassis for operation there was agreed in March 1952. It is not possible to be precise as to how many vehicles were actually involved. In an interview given to the trade press in April 1954 the owner of North's, Mr L. W. Elvins, stated that about forty Guy chassis had been despatched to the Canary Islands, the first six having been ordered without inspection with more contracts quickly following. Not all of these, however, may have been London vehicles, and the number quoted may well have been inflated for commercial reasons. The true number of London Guys involved may, in fact, have been no more than twenty. The island for which they were destined, Gran Canaria, was the most populous of the group and contained the busy capital, Las Palmas, whose network of local bus services was provided by the co-operative organisation APJG (Asociasion Patronal de Jardineras Guagas). It was APJG who purchased the majority of the Guys, placing about eighteen into service from 1952 onwards. The only ones positively identified are Gs 25, 38, 62, 64, 428 and 433.

The Canary Islands of the nineteen-fifties and sixties were home to a wide variety of British built buses, mostly purchased second hand, which provided a great deal of interest in the days before the ubiquitous Spanish-built Pegasos ousted them all. The blue-painted APJG fleet contained a typical mixture apart from the Guys, pride of place amongst them being three STLs which initially retained their double deck bodies largely unaltered except for a reversed platform and staircase. For operation in Las Palmas the Guys were given new locally-built full-fronted single deck dual entrance bodies seating 29 or 30 on which the Guy radiator was hidden behind a grille. Almost certainly they were exported in chassis form after being overhauled by or on behalf of North's, and in their new guise they could easily have been mistaken for completely new vehicles except that, perhaps surprisingly, their right hand driving positions were retained.

Although the majority of ex-London Guys were to be found on local service in Las Palmas, where they covered three major numbered routes and several lesser, unnumbered ones, four are known to have operated outside the capital in the small fleet of Transportes Sardina-Galdar whose service covered the four miles of road linking the two northerly villages named in its title. Two of the four were ex-APJG (one being the former G 62) but the source of the other two (Gs 9 and 399), which carried the same type of dual entrance single deck body, has not been confirmed. Former APJG Guys also joined other small fleets on the island when their days in Las Palmas were over. Empresa P. Tovar, operating routes from Guia to La Puntilla and El Palmitad, had the former G 62 and one other whilst Transportes Pardilla of Telda, whose service ran between La Pardilla and Telda, acquired three including G 38.

A press release in June 1952 was the first intimation to most people that ex-London Guys had travelled as far as southern Africa. "Double deckers will shortly run for the first time in Southern Rhodesia" it announced, adding that "Trans-Rhodes Services" based in the city of Salisbury had purchased ten Guys and also five 10T10 type single deckers. (Today Southern Rhodesia is better known as Zimbabwe and Salisbury has become Harare). Readers were informed that the Guys would probably run on the Cranborne and Mabelreign routes and later to Mount Hampden and that they cost £20,000, though even allowing for shipping charges this inflated sum could not have been correct. The importer of the London vehicles was a Mr Johnston of Que Que who owned Johnston's Motor Transport and registered Transrhodes Services (Pvt) Ltd for the purpose of commencing operations in Salisbury complementary to those already provided by Salisbury City Council.

Destination Africa. With most of its identifying marks removed, G 385 is ready for its long shipment to Durban en route for Southern Rhodesia. This was one of three Weymann bodied vehicles to join the Transrhodes fleet. R F Mack

Above Left **A Massey bodied Guy seen in 1956 carrying Salisbury United livery. Sliding windows have been added on each deck to improve ventilation. Its London identity is not known but it may have been either G 266 or G 357, both of which Massey Guys are known to have operated in Southern Rhodesia.**

Above Centre and Right **The Guys of the KBS Mombasa fleet were placed into service with little modification apart from enclosure of the rear platform. Park Royal D 54 was formerly G 86 and Weymann D 55 was G 386. Both have all windows fully open, windscreens included, but even this provided inadequate cooling in the searing heat of the Kenya coast.** Alan B Cross

Although news of their impending entry into service did not leak until June, the vehicles had in fact been bought from North's in March 1952, the time lapse being due to the need to arrange shipping and the length of the voyage. The ten Guys were shipped to the port of Durban in South Africa and driven the 1,500 or so miles northwards from there to Salisbury. The Guys purchased in the deal were Park Royal type Gs 132, 134, 192, 203, 320, 325; Massey G 266 and Weymann Gs 370, 385 and 413. The five 10T10s mentioned in the British report do not appear to have materialised, but in April 1953 a further six Guy double deckers were obtained, this time from another dealer, Comberhill Motors of Wakefield. In what appears to have been an unusually complex arrangement they were sold by North's to Comberhill but it remains a mystery why the supply chain was lengthened in this way. Four of the six are known to have been Gs 141, 328, 357 and 425 and the other two were almost certainly Gs 181 and 408 but this has not been confirmed.

In February 1954 the Salisbury United Omnibus Co Ltd was formed to act as successor to the Transrhodes operations. This was part of the British owned United Transport group which, at the time, still had J.H. Watts at the helm although his home based Red & White interests had now been sold to the state. In the same month Transrhodes was sold to United Transport (Africa) Ltd and its vehicles formed the basis of the new Salisbury United fleet, which subsequently took over the municipal buses on 11th September 1954. Salisbury United ran on a franchise from Salisbury City Council who granted it a monopoly of stage carriage operations within a 26 mile radius of the Central Post Office. Of the sixteen London Guys only fifteen are believed to have entered service, the other being used as an office at the depot. Under the then current system of racial segregation, the Guys were all employed on 'African' services, the 'European' fleet consisting entirely of single deckers. The full history of the London Guys whilst in Southern Rhodesia is by no means clear but it would appear that most if not all were still running with their original bodies in 1956, mostly as 55-seaters, but by the beginning of 1958 only two were recorded as still being double deckers; these were

probably Gs 192 and 357. The remainder had been rebodied by a South African company, Blanckenburg, as saloons. One of the batch was destroyed when it collided with a train at a level crossing, although it is not known if it was then still a double decker. At least one single decker, the former G 328, was transferred in about October 1956 to Blantyre, the chief town of Nyasaland in the highlands of central Africa, where another United Transport subsidiary, Nyasaland Transport Co Ltd, was the principal operator with a fleet of Albions and Guys. Independence came to Nyasaland in July 1964 and the owning company became United Transport (Malawi) Ltd. Under its ownership G 328 was rebodied yet again in 1965 with a new 47-seat single deck body by the MCW-related Bus Bodies (S.A.) Ltd.

United Transport also had extensive interests in eastern Africa. Through a holding organisation entitled the Overseas Motor Transport Co Ltd, they controlled important operations in Kenya, Tanganyika (now Tanzania) and Uganda including city services in the Kenyan capital, Nairobi, and the country's major port, Mombasa. Kenya Bus Services Ltd of Nairobi and Kenya Bus Services (Mombasa) Ltd were in the news in late 1991 when the BET group sold its United Transport interests in Kenya to the fast growing Stagecoach organisation, which had already purchased extensive operations in Malawi two years earlier. Back in 1952, however, the two companies were in the news for the entirely different reason that they were negotiating to purchase redundant London Transport Guy utilities to augment their hard pressed fleets.

United Transport purchased numbers of Albions and Leylands for its east Africa operations, but the staple diet of its fleets consisted for many years of Guys whose ruggedness suited them to the great variety of operations over the range of altitudes and climatic conditions which they were required to cover, not to mention very many miles of poor road surfaces. Large numbers of new Guys were purchased, mainly single but also a few double deckers, and it was therefore not surprising that, when new Guys could not be obtained quickly enough, used ones were sought. For this purpose Overseas Motor

Transport approached Guy Motors in May 1952 stating that they required six Arabs for use in Kenya and Tanganyika, and their enquiries led them finally to North's. It is not known if six were actually purchased at the time or if any went eventually to Tanganyika (where their destination would have been the Dar es Salaam Motor Transport Co Ltd), but two are known for certain to have been obtained from North's in July 1952 (Gs 391 and 323) and these became Nos. 18 and 19 in the large KBS Nairobi fleet. Three further Guys (G 331, 338, 354) were purchased for the same fleet a year later becoming its Nos. 1-3. Kenya Bus Services (Mombasa) Ltd, which operated as an entirely separate entity despite having directors in common with the rather larger Nairobi company, also gained a small fleet of five London Guys, this time in a single delivery early in 1953 when Gs 396, 90, 86, 386 and 209 joined the fleet as D 52-56 respectively.

Their arrival coincided with the start of the violent Mau Mau uprising which was to pave the way for the ending of Kenya's colonial status in December 1963, but the ex-London Guys in both cities survived this and gave good service both in the tropical heat of Mombasa and in the more equable climate of Nairobi. They were pressed into service by the two operators in more or less the same condition in which they had arrived, but in most cases new locally built bodies were fitted in about 1956/7 which, in common with the operators' other double deckers of the time, were mostly though not entirely of the centre entrance type. An early casualty was G 86, a Mombasa bus, which was scrapped in June 1957 after colliding with a low bridge. Some of the remaining Mombasa vehicles are believed later to have been rebodied for a second time as single deckers.

The true number of ex-London Guys exported by North's to destinations in Africa, and the use to which they were put after arrival, will probably never fully be known. A photograph from North's archives shows an unidentified Mark I chassis prepared for shipment to the port of Sekondi in the Gold Coast (nowadays Ghana) early in 1953. It is by no means improbable that other Guys besides this one found a new existence in western Africa.

The largest concentration of ex-London utilities was also the furthest away. The Indian Ocean island of Ceylon – one of the world's most beautiful – had gained independence in February 1948 but was in the Commonwealth and much of the old British tradition still remained. This included the use of double deck buses and trolleybuses in and around the capital, Colombo. In times gone by bus services in the island had been totally unstructured and unregulated resulting in cut-throat competition and abysmal vehicle standards, but the havoc became such that a series of controlled territorial monopolies was formed in 1942 forcing operators to combine and transform themselves into private limited liability companies. Under a further government ordinance of 1951 they were compelled to become public companies. It was into this setting that some one hundred London double deckers arrived in 1952/3 to inject much needed rolling stock into an arena of great shortage. According to government statistics of 1954, 2480 buses were required on the island but only 1889 were licensed to cope with a huge post-war travelling boom.

The initial decision to purchase London double deckers seems to have come about in a strange way, indeed almost by chance. Mr K.B.L. Perera, a Vice President of the All-Ceylon Omnibus Companies Association, appears to have mentioned in passing to the Traffic Commissioner for the Northern Area, Mr S.W. Nelson, that he was seeking a small number of Guy double deckers to send back to the island. Perhaps he had been unsuccessful in finding any in the north of England; in any event Mr Nelson referred him to London Transport who passed his enquiry on to North's. The resultant deal was further complicated in being handled through Comberhill Motors who, in May 1952, obtained six Guys from North's and shipped them out to Ceylon.

Five of the batch were destined for the Colombo Omnibus Co Ltd, one of the country's biggest operators. Its fleet of some 130 vehicles covered a busy network centred principally on the eastern suburbs of Colombo, but the company was also licensed to run the only cross-city motor bus link. Their five London vehicles were Park Royal Gs 6, 46, 55, 74 and Massey-bodied G 358 which initially ran in their original form as double deckers but with an enhanced seating capacity of 58, although later G 74 (at least) received a new single deck body.

Photographed in pre-Transport Board days, before driving and maintenance shortcomings wrought havoc with their appearance, three Ceylon Daimlers show the differing degrees of modification applied prior to entering service. D 61 (IC 2132) is still virtually in London condition; behind it stand two of the Guy Arab IIIs bought new by South Western, the front one of the two now in London style livery. D 38 (IC 2103) has a new indicator box, whilst the front windows, and also many on the sides, have their upper halves permanently unglazed to provide better ventilation. Improved ventilation on D 203 (IC 2094) has been achieved by fitting double the number of half drops, presumably cannibalised from another Park Royal body of the same type.
J B Atkinson/Brian Blackburn/R F Mack

The sixth vehicle of the May 1952 batch, G 416, was destined for the South Western Omnibus Co (1952) Ltd whose monopoly on the Galle Road corridor southwards along the coast from Colombo had enabled it to become the island's largest operator. Double deckers were no stranger to this company; in fact very early in the post-war era it had taken some of the Guy Arabs which the Ministry of War Transport had been unable to dispose of at home due to lack of demand. G 416 is believed to have been fitted with a new 35-seat single deck body built locally by the Swadeshi Industrial Works before entering service in about August 1952. Although it probably did not run for South Western as a double decker, it acted as a precursor for many that did.

The London Arabs had not been on the road in Colombo for long when, late in October 1952, North's received an urgent request for twelve buses from South Western. Guys would have been preferred because of their crash gearboxes, but all that North could offer immediately were twelve Daimlers which, to suit them to Ceylon conditions, required 6:1 ratio differentials to be fitted. At the time of sale, North's Mr Elvins happened to mention casually to South Western that further buses may become available in due course. Only a month later he found out to his amazement that the company had chartered a ship capable of carrying fifty buses which was already on its way and wanted to fill it. North's had nothing like this number in stock and had to turn to London Transport for help. They responded to the urgency, and when the ship sailed in January 1953 fifty double deckers were indeed on board; 39 Daimlers and 11 Guys. A large proportion of the contingent, 22 in all, consisted of Sutton-type Daimlers, but some items of interest were included amongst the remainder, notably eight out of the ten lowbridge Daimlers (including all four of the second batch), Northern Coachbuilders rebodied G 30 and metal-bodied Weymann G 137. This process was repeated in December 1953 when a further fifty double deckers were despatched to the South Western fleet, but in this case all were Daimlers.

Most of the one hundred ran initially in the condition in which they were received, but the bodies of many were subsequently rebuilt to varying degrees and, in true Ceylon style, most quickly took on an air of genteel delapidation. For several years South Western's large open depot at Ratmalana, near Mount Lavinia, rang to the sound of London double deckers. However, from an administrative viewpoint things were about to change radically. A new government elected in April 1956 was pledged to nationalise all major elements of the island's economy, and on 1st January 1958 Ceylon's bus companies were merged overnight into the Ceylon Transport Board. The only privately owned buses permitted thereafter were confined to private hire, occasional and works services, and services for institutions' own employees. The Colombo Omnibus Company's Guys and South Western's Daimlers and Guys thus found themselves in the same huge fleet which, though successful overall in its early years after an initial bout of chaos, later became much reviled and was a loss maker right from the start. Between 1958 and 1968 the CTB

Photographs of ex-London Guys in Ceylon are comparatively rare. G 76, operating from the Transport Board's Maharagama depot, is either working route 7 to Slave Island or route 88 to Fort, depending on which destination board you believe Alan B Cross

Below Standing in the central bus station in Colombo in April or May 1972, immediately before the country was renamed Sri Lanka, is D 266. The significance of its grey livery and S12 on the windscreen is not known. Of particular interest is the body which is clearly not the original and has presumably been built locally. By 1978 D 266 had become a Transport Board lorry. The RTL standing alongside it illustrates the lamentable condition into which many (probably most) double deckers deteriorated. John Shearman

Back home in Britain the instances of London utilities ending their working days as lorries were fairly rare, but it was a common occurrence in Sri Lanka where at least 36 Daimlers and Guys suffered this fate. Having been sold by the Transport Board, D 36 is now owned by a transport contractor in Colombo. Note the crew cab behind the driver. John Shearman

fleet was augmented by no fewer than 1,273 members of the RT family purchased direct from London Transport and for some years these ran alongside the Guys and Daimlers, several of which later acquired new single deck bodies. Many continued operating in the Colombo area well into the middle or late 1960s, and some even lasted into the 1970s to witness the re-titling of the organisation as the Sri Lanka Central Transport Board.

Several Guys and many Daimlers later became lorries, both in the Transport Board fleet and with private contractors. A few could still be seen in and around Colombo in this form as late as 1980 by which time the bus industry had turned almost a full circle and private operators were once again permitted in the hope that they would make good many of the deficiencies of, and lack of adequate investment in, the Transport Board.

CHAPTER SEVENTEEN

IMPROVING THE BREED

It has been remarked earlier that the wartime Arab chassis was regarded in many quarters as being almost indestructible, and as if to add credence to this assertion no fewer than 94 of them, representing over twenty per cent of the original London Transport fleet, were rebuilt by subsequent owners to such an extent as to become almost indistinguishable from new vehicles. These rebuilds took on a variety of shapes, styles and sizes but all had in common the fact that they in no way outwardly resembled the utility background from which they had originated; they were given totally new identities, and in their new guise almost all of them achieved a longer span of working life than they had done in their original form.

First to reconsider reconditioning Arab chassis on a major scale was Edinburgh Corporation Transport. The Corporation's transport manager, W.M. Little, had for some time been anxious to scrap the city's extensive tramway system and had proposed in June 1950 that, as a start, the conversion to diesel buses of a quarter of the network should be authorised. Much of the track was in a very poor condition and the Ministry of Transport had refused powers to borrow the full sum required for renewals. The first conversion in this limited programme took place on 1st June 1952 and, in anticipation of its success, the Corporation's transport committee recommended only a month later that the system should be scrapped in its entirety, a policy approved by the Council on 25th September. Well before this date Mr Little had anticipated this outcome and set in motion steps to obtain large numbers of buses with which to replace the trams. His enquiries for vehicles led him to Guy Motors and the possibility that they might acquire a substantial quantity of second hand Arab chassis which would be

completely renovated and then passed on to the Corporation for rebodying. Guy had London Transport in mind as the source for these chassis and in November 1951 submitted an offer for the purchase of sixty. A major problem now arose. London Transport was more than happy to sell the chassis but was prohibited from doing so by the British Transport Commission's edict that vehicles must not be sold for re-use on stage carriage work. To break the logjam, London Transport enlisted the help of James Amos, the powerful boss of the Scottish Bus Group, in an endeavour to persuade the Commission to bend its own rules on this occasion. At stake would be the loss of £275 for the sale of each bus against the scrap value which was realistically all that would be achieved otherwise. In a sense Amos's support was surprising in that one of the group's companies, Scottish Omnibuses Ltd, worked in the same territory as Edinburgh Corporation, but in fact there was no enmity or even direct competition between the two and Scottish Omnibuses stood to gain from tram withdrawal in that it would inherit the Musselburgh route over which the Corporation had no bus powers. In due course the BTC acceded to the joint approach and Lord Hurcombe himself approved the deal on the stipulation that the vehicles would be sold direct to the Corporation and not via Guy's, and that they would not be resold by the Corporation and would be used by them only on stage carriage work and not private hire unless the latter was carried out on behalf of BTC companies.

It was the Corporation's intention to scrap the bodies from the sixty Arabs and overhaul and modernise the chassis at a cost of between £600 and £800 per bus depending on condition and the amount of work which needed to be carried out on each one.

Although Edinburgh's own Guys were powered by 6LWs, it was decided to retain the five cylinder units in the London chassis but to redress the power balance by fitting new lightweight bodies. It was the Corporation's intention to cut away the front chassis extension and to reposition the radiator immediately in front of the engine. This was partly for visual effect but was also a legal necessity as the Corporation had decided to give each vehicle a completely new identity including reregistration, and by altering their status in this manner the original wartime concession permitting them to exceed the legal maximum length no longer applied. In view of the high price being paid per vehicle the Corporation was allowed to select its own choice from those which had already been taken out of service and during March 1952 its engineers made of list of sixty suitable vehicles, all of the Mark II variety. London Transport's own engineers had earlier toyed with the idea of withholding all Northern Counties bodied Guys from the sale list and relicensing them for service to replace others, but did not get around to doing so with the result that 26 out of the Edinburgh contingent consisted of these.

Above left **Who would have expected a London utility to feature in a full page advertisement for new buses in March 1953? But that is exactly what happened here. Of course, Duple made no mention of the fact that the vehicle depicted was based on a second hand chassis – in this case G 84.**

Above right **Even after Leyland style 'tin fronts' had been fitted, the ex-London Guys still retained their redundant nearside front pillar and dummy windscreen, but sliding windows were added to improve ventilation inside the saloons. One-time G 163 is seen nearing the end of its days in the Scottish capital.** Alan Nightingale

The sixty Guys were all collected from the yard of Edgware garage between 9th April and 16th May 1952. Their bodies were removed and scrapped and the chassis were extensively overhauled and allocated new chassis numbers 195201-60. Meanwhile the Corporation had placed an order for the construction of new bodies with a surprising source, Duple Motor Bodies Ltd, who were not normally favoured by Scottish municipal operators and whose impact on the double deck market had been minimal in post-war years. The completed vehicles, when they finally arrived on the Edinburgh scene, were in fact shapely looking and as far removed from the utility concept as could be.

Because of low engine power, lightness was the keynote of the new Duple bodies. These were, in fact, Edinburgh's first lightweights and their sparse internal fittings were in complete contrast to all that had gone before. Even opening windows were omitted from the saloon sides making the bodies more spartan in this respect than even the most basic utilities. The four bay metal framed bodies were 8ft wide and had a total weight of only 2tons 6½cwt; the complete vehicle weighed only 6tons 14cwt 1qr in most cases. As in their previous incarnation they remained 56 seaters, but because a Birmingham style straight staircase was fitted the seating split was revised to 25 in the lower deck and 31 in the upper. Although anything but sumptuous internally, the external appearance gave little indication of the lightweight nature of the Duple design. A most unusual embellishment was a dummy full front incorporating an unglazed nearside 'windscreen', with a large aperture in the nearside bodywork above the front wheel which gave easy access to the engine compartment and presumably also helped to trap quantities of road dirt. This same frontal design was copied a year later by Alexander when rebodying sixteen of Edinburgh's own Daimler utilities but was abandoned for the huge fleet of very plain MCW Orion-bodied Leyland PD2s which subsequently formed the bulk of the tramway conversion fleet.

The sixty London Guys became 301-60 in the Edinburgh fleet and received new registration numbers JWS 581-640. No. 301 (the erstwhile G 84) was built at Duple's Hendon factory as a pre-production prototype for delivery late in November 1952, and the remainder followed on between February and July 1953. The second of the class, No. 302, was also built at Hendon but the only work carried out there on the remaining 58 was the construction and fitting of the lower deck shell. The rest was done at the Kegworth, Leicestershire works of Nudd Bros & Lockyer which had recently been taken over by Duple and was subsequently renamed Duple Motor Bodies (Midland) Ltd.

In their handsome madder and white livery the sixty vehicles performed sterling work on tram conversion duties and provided an interesting facet of the Edinburgh bus scene for several years. In 1958/9 all were rebuilt with the then outmoded but still standard (for Edinburgh) Leyland-type 'tin' fronts – now actually made in glass fibre – in place of the original stylish but less practical Duple arrangement with its rows of distinctive hor-

A 'new' single decker under construction in SMT's Edinburgh works. The chassis has been lengthened and a new style low radiator has been fitted; now the timber framed body shell is almost complete except at the front end. The substantial steel truss panels along each side can be clearly seen.

The styling of the new SMT bodies was plain, but neat and functional, although by the time of their construction the employment of a half-cab layout on new single deckers had virtually ceased. Even so, they could easily have been mistaken for completely new vehicles had it not been for the retention of the old conical-shaped Guy back axle. K 75 was the first of the batch. A J Douglas

izontal aluminium strips. This was done for ease of maintenance but did not altogether ruin the unusual nature of the vehicles as the dummy nearside windscreen arrangement was retained. Passengers benefited too, as opening side windows were now installed in both saloons rectifying a defect which had made both the London Guys and also the later Leyland/Orions very unpopular. One of the batch, No. 314 (once G 77), received a Gardner 6LW engine in 1963 which involved fitting a projecting bonnet to accommodate its greater length. In later life the batch was relegated from front line duties and could be found mainly on peak hour work, and forty were sold at the end of 1967. The remaining twenty departed in March 1969 after a creditable working life of almost sixteen years in the Scottish capital. True to the Corporation's word at the time of purchase, none were sold to other operators and, with one exception which survives to this day, the scrap yard was their immediate fate.

Edinburgh's batch of sixty was not the first class of heavily rebuilt London Arabs to reach the highways of Scotland. The Scottish Bus Group, whose support in lobbying the BTC had helped in paving the way for the Edinburgh sale, had already commenced a rebuilding programme of its own although this was on a smaller and more protracted scale than the Edinburgh scheme, and the resultant vehicles could hardly have been more different. Over a period of about two years from September 1952 onwards a programme of converting 23 London Arabs into single deckers for rural operation was pursued in a fairly leisurely manner.

The original stimulus for the scheme can be traced back to February 1952 and the formation of Highland Omnibuses Ltd. This new, nationalised concern was created to amalga-mate the old Highland Transport Co Ltd, which had become fully state owned in the previous September, with the business of MacRae & Dick Ltd of Inverness, purchased by the BTC in November 1951, and the Inverness area services of Walter Alexander & Sons Ltd. The new concern's main operating territory consisted predominantly of sparsely populated areas which provided poor returns on bus operation, and much of the acquired fleet was badly run down and in need of heavy overhaul or complete replacement. A few second hand buses (including the three ex-London Guy double deckers mentioned earlier) were drafted in during the first year to help out but better quality vehicles were badly needed. Highland ran at a substantial loss and funds did not exist to purchase completely new vehicles, so for the first three years of the new company's existence it was necessary to rely on rebuilt ex-London Arabs to provide its only affordable source of 'new' rolling stock.

Although Highland was managed locally from Inverness it was controlled by Edinburgh-based Scottish Omnibuses Ltd, whose idea it was to create new low-cost buses for use in the Highlands by rebuilding old double deckers. The initial programme embraced ten vehicles for 1952/3 delivery and utilised chassis which had been amongst those bought in November 1951 by Scottish Omnibuses but which had remained unused. Each chassis was completely stripped in the Company's workshops at Marine Gardens, Edinburgh, and as the wheelbase was to be increased to 18ft 5ins to enable a 30ft long body to be fitted, the frame was cut at a point just forward of the gearbox (which was retained) and a 2ft 2ins extension piece inserted. The inserted portion was exactly the same profile as the original Guy frame and was electrically welded into position, the patch then being reinforced with a channel section bolted over the frame and extending well beyond the insertion in either direction. An extra tubular cross member was then placed behind the first universal joint of the lengthened front propellor shaft and a new steering box bracket was fitted plus new arms to correct the steering geometry. The chassis frame was again cut behind the rear bulkhead mounting bracket, this time to fit a new extension designed to allow for a large rear luggage locker and at the same time give adequate ground clearance. As the 5LW engine was retained the front chassis extension was removed and the bonnet and radiator were lowered by 4ins to give better vision to the driver, the resultant front end now resembling that of a post-war Arab.

The bodies were also built in the company's workshops. Although it had not been the practice of Scottish Omnibuses or its predecessor to build new bodies on a fully regular basis, the company constructed batches from time to time and had contributed to the wartime Bedford OWB programme, following this by some coaches on Bedford OB chassis which closely resembled Duple's Vista design. Reconstruction and general overhaul work were the coachbuilding department's other and more regular sources of employment. For the Highland single deckers a straightforward general purpose design was required with particular emphasis on ease of construction and simplicity of maintenance. Because of the nature of many highland roads the width was kept to 7ft 6ins and a seating capacity of 39 was specified with an entrance at the front. All seats faced forward; there were full length parcel racks, and interior heating was provided as well as a sliding roof panel for the occasional summer days when, even in the far north, the weather could turn warm enough to justify its existence. The main body structure consisted of teak although cross bearers were in oak with metal flitch plates, and there were full length steel truss panels along each side. The resultant vehicle was plain and functional, but was also very outdated since underfloor engined single deckers were now the norm and very few half-cab single deckers were still being built. However the interior with its traditional polished wood mouldings, moquette covered tubular seats with leather edgings, and effective heating was warm and welcoming. From a passenger's point of view the vehicles rode impressively smoothly and quietly but from the driver's aspect they were far from sparkling performers and their length sometimes proved awkward on twisting highland roads. Despite being nicknamed 'kangaroos' by the staff, Highland's new single deckers proved to be reliable and versatile additions to the fleet.

The ten Guys comprising the initial 1952/3 delivery received fleet numbers K 75/82/84/85 and registration numbers JWS 122-131. As with the Edinburgh fleet the old chassis numbers were discarded in favour of a new series commencing at SMT 1. The vehicles out of which they were created were originally Gs 79, 82, 88, 103, 216-8, 360, 363 and 411, but as parts were interchanged during rebuilding it is not possible to identify with accuracy the

original identity of any individual vehicle. Two further chassis, the former Gs 108 and 211, were converted in 1953 to become Ks 93 and 87 (KSC 918/9). Unlike all the others G 211 had already run in Scotland in its original, double deck form carrying Scottish Omnibuses' green SMT livery, the supply of unused chassis having now been exhausted.

Following on the success of the twelve conversions, Scottish Omnibuses decided in 1953 upon an extension of the programme to produce eleven more vehicles in the coming year. The figure of eleven equalled precisely the fleet of ex-London Transport Guys still running with their original bodies, eight with SMT and three with Highland. In London days the eleven vehicles had been Gs 116, 204, 329, 334, 341, 343, 344, 365, 366, 375 and 409. On this occasion five of the 'new' single deckers were destined for Scottish Omnibuses itself in whose fleet they were numbered D 1-5; registered LSC 91-5 they had chassis numbered SMT 13-17. In appearance they were in stark contrast to the company's other main deliveries of the year, ECW-bodied Bristol LSs and Park Royal/AEC Monocoaches, but the SMT fleet had some quiet territory of its own such as the border country and the Guys had a role to play. In their cheery green and cream they looked brighter and more attractive than in Highland's sombre dark red. Following on in both registration and chassis number order (LSC 96-101; SMT 18-23) came Highland's final delivery of six, K 95-100. These differed from all the others in having full coach standard seating, to accommodate which a whole row was eliminated to produce a seating capacity of 35. Despite their austere external appearance they formed the backbone of Highland's coach fleet until more suitable vehicles came along.

After just over seven years the five SMT vehicles were withdrawn in January 1962 and sold for a further eighteen months' use carrying workers at the Llanwern power station. Highland's allocation lasted longer, being gradually taken out of service between 1963 and 1966. A pair of them, Ks 76 and 78, passed in 1963 to Norman Smith of Grantown on Spey who ran in harmony with Highland,

and K 78 even returned 'home' in December 1966 when Smith's business was purchased, although it was now mechanically defunct and never re-entered service. By the time of their demise all but two had lasted for a decade or more with Highland; they had been a cheap and successful substitute for new vehicles at a difficult time and the expense involved in their transformation from urban double decker to rural single decker must have been repaid many times over.

The final rebuilding to be carried out north of the border on a batch of ex-London Guys took place in 1954. The operator responsible on this occasion was Western SMT from whose extensive stock of Arabs ten were selected for modernisation. None had previously operated in Western colours, having been in store since they were purchased in 1953. They had previously carried a miscellany of Park Royal, Massey and Weymann bodies none of which could be contemplated for further use and were scrapped. The chassis were completely overhauled at Western's works in Kilmarnock even to the extent of fitting new, low driving positions and fashionable Birmingham style 'tin' fronts purchased from Guy's. When this work was completed they were despatched to the Northern Counties factory at Wigan for the fitment of new 8ft wide 53-seat lowbridge bodies.

Northern Counties was producing at the time a very handsome and curvaceous four bay style of body on which the front dome swept stylishly down to incorporate the front windows; there was an attractive outward flare to the lower panels and the whole ensemble was, if anything, complemented by the Guy new look front end. In 1953 Western had taken delivery of a batch of seven identical looking bodies on new Arab IV chassis and the ten London rebuilds were almost indistinguishable from these, the only clue to their very different origin being the retention of the old conical shaped rear hub which had

Western SMT's Guy conversions were handsome vehicles which gave long, valuable service. Johnstone-based JY 1060 was already several years into its Western career when photographed in Paisley in August 1962. The chassis was originally that of G 263. Alan Nightingale

long since been replaced on newer models by a more conventional flat-headed unit. Internally the bodies were typical examples of their era with dark red enamelled finish but the seating layout, with 26 in the lower saloon and 27 upstairs, was comfortable and on the upper deck positively spacious. Under Western's fleet numbering system, the batch of ten occupied the series Y 1056–65, each number being prefixed by the depot code placed before the class letter Y (which, incidentally, was the last letter of the name Guy); thus a vehicle allocated to Johnstone depot would be numbered, for example, JY 1056. The new registration series was FSD 454-463 and the chassis were renumbered in the series RB (for rebuild) /51/1 to 10. Former London fleet numbers were G 130, 129, 118, 193, 263, 316, 317, 374, 392, 404.

The rebuilt Guys carried Western's attractive red and cream livery for a life span of thirteen years, and indeed they lasted just as long as the brand new Guys of a year earlier. They were not speedy performers and were kept off the prestigious long distance routes which were a long-standing feature of Western's double deck operation, but they served well on local runs in the Glasgow and Paisley areas. After withdrawal by Western one vehicle, 1060, joined a pair of 1955 Arab IVs and a miscellany of Leyland PD1s and 2s and Albion Lowlanders despatched north to Highland in 1967 in whose fleet it became E 1 and served for a further year without being repainted into Highland colours.

For the final major Guy rebuild we turn the clock forward for a full decade and look to the south coast where the Gosport & Fareham Omnibus Company, a statutory undertaking based at Hoeford near Fareham, ran under the fleet name Provincial. This compact but idiosyncratic fleet had long been managed by one of the bus industry's 'characters', H. Orme White, who was not averse to astutely purchasing second hand vehicles and subsequently heavily rebuilding them out of all recognition. Commencing in 1957 he had instituted a policy of rebodying Guy Arab chassis with a distinctive and unique style of full front body, and a year later began equipping these rebuilt vehicles with German-built

Deutz air cooled engines. In all the company produced eleven air-cooled Guy double deckers (plus one single decker) between 1958 and 1967 of which the penultimate one, created in 1965, was based on a now aged ex-London Transport chassis.

G 276 had been one of the Northern Counties Arabs sold in 1952 to the Ministry of Supply from whom it had passed in 1959 to a contractor in Gosport. Its normal life span completed, the chassis was made available for disposal and presumably proved irresistible to Orme White who purchased it in May 1963. The staff at Hoeford set about their now familiar task of reconditioning the chassis and fitting the new engine. Air-cooled engines had never been favoured in Britain despite their theoretical advantages of savings in weight and the reliability which could be gained through the absence of radiator, water pump, thermostat and joints, because the disadvantages of greater noise and uneven cooling had usually been regarded as too high a price to pay. Indeed there was little choice when it came to acquiring air cooled engines and Provincial had to turn to Klockner-Humboldt-Deutz A.G. of Cologne to obtain a six cylinder unit suitable for bus application. This company, which had begun research into air-cooled diesels in 1935 and had completed its first one during the war, in 1942, was able to supply its model F6L514 indirect injection 7.98 litre unit which, for Provincial's use, was derated from 125bhp at 2300rpm to 94bhp at 1750rpm. Installation required rotating the engine about 20 degrees out of the vertical in order to fit it into the available space and it was linked to a single dry-plate German-built Fichtel & Sachs clutch. The original rubber-mounted Guy gearbox was retained.

The bodywork for all of Provincial's Guy rebuilds was provided by Reading & Co Ltd of Portsmouth and was a peculiar mixture of outdated side and rear design with a modernistic full front which included a hinged panel for engine access. The lower saloon was framed in teak but the upper deck employed light alloys which produced a saving of some 6cwt over the weight which a fully timber-framed body would incur. The customary seating capacity of 56 was achieved and the

saloon interiors enjoyed a cheerfully florid look thanks to the style of moquette and seat back coverings employed, but the upper deck was marred by being single panelled on the roof in the style of wartime utilities, leaving exposed roof hoops and untidy trunking panels for the lighting. The company was an early exponent of hopper-type opening windows which were rightly considered less draughty than the customary sliding ventilators, and a novel feature was that a compartment for large items of baggage was provided inside the cab above the nearside wheel arch. In order to minimise the clatter associated with air-cooled diesels the engine compartment was double skinned throughout with a thick layer of glass fibre between the inner and outer panelling. In the case of the ex-London vehicle the lower deck was actually assembled by Provincial at Hoeford using parts supplied by Reading, who subsequently fitted the upper structure in their own works.

Despite many gloomy predictions, Provincial's Deutz engined Guys ran very quietly and without noticeable vibration. The engines were four-point rubber mounted and this no doubt helped. As was to be expected the amount of engine repair work was reduced although spare parts, on the occasions when they were required, proved very expensive, and a similar fuel return was achieved to a Gardner 5LW. The biggest problem, which the company endured for several years, lay with the clutch which was not really suited to the frequent stop-start work typifying most of Provincial's operations.

The erstwhile G 276 was numbered 33 in the Provincial fleet and registered CHO 449C, making it the only ex-London utility ever to receive a new-style number with letter suffix. In this instance the original Guy chassis number was retained. The vehicle was renumbered 61 in December 1970, but by this time big changes were under way. Orme White had retired in December 1966 and the Deutz conversion programme was brought to a close in the following year with the completion of work then in hand. In March 1969 the parent company, Provincial Traction Co Ltd, came into the ownership of the Wiles motor group and on 1st January 1970 the bus operations were sold to the National Bus Company who placed control of the Provincial operations under Hants & Dorset at Bournemouth. As was to be expected, big fleet changes quickly came about under NBC ownership and withdrawal of the air-cooled Guys commenced soon after they took control. CHO 449C was itself withdrawn in 1972; it had been the last London utility to remain in service within Britain and its demise broke the final link in the chain stretching back thirty years.

G 276, posing as Provincial's No.33, stands at Gosport Ferry in the company of a pair of more conventional Guy Arabs. Below the dummy radiator is a Deutz badge, indicating that the vehicle was powered by an air-cooled engine. Ken Blacker

APPENDIX I – FLEET SUMMARY

Fleet No.		Registration		Type	LT Body No.	Bodybuilder
STD	101	FXT	405	Leyland TD7	476	Park Royal
	102–111	FXT	428–437	Leyland TD7	486–495	Park Royal
B	1–9	FXT	419–427	Bristol K5G	477–485	Park Royal
	10–29	HGC	235–254	Bristol K6A	1079–1098	Duple
G	1–31	GLF	651–681	Guy Arab I	496–526	Park Royal (a)
	32–42	GLF	682–692	Guy Arab I	527–537	Weymann
	43	GLF	693	Guy Arab I	538	Duple
	44–50	GLF	694–700	Guy Arab I	539–545	Weymann
	51–71	GLL	551–571	Guy Arab I	546–566	Park Royal
	72–84	GLL	572–584	Guy Arab II	567–579	Park Royal
	85	GLL	600 (b)	Guy Arab II	580	Park Royal
	86–100	GLL	585–599	Guy Arab II	581–595	Park Royal
	101–136	GXE	541–576	Guy Arab II	596–631	Park Royal
	137, 138	GXV	793, 794	Guy Arab II	693, 694	Weymann
	139–149	GYE	83–93	Guy Arab II	727–737	Northern Coachbuilders
	150	GYE	94	Guy Arab II	738	Park Royal
	151–153	GYE	95–97	Guy Arab II	739–741	Northern Coachbuilders
	154–173	GYL	293–312	Guy Arab II	777–796	Northern Counties
	174–193	GYL	313–332	Guy Arab II	797–816	Massey
	194–205	GYL	333–344	Guy Arab II	817–828	Northern Coachbuilders
	206–218	GYL	345–357	Guy Arab II	829–841	Park Royal
	219–257	GYL	358–396	Guy Arab II	842–880	Northern Counties
	258–268	GYL	397–407	Guy Arab II	881–891	Massey
	269–311	GYL	409–451	Guy Arab II	892–934	Northern Counties
	312–318	GYL	452–458	Guy Arab II	935–941	Massey
	319, 320	GYL	459, 460	Guy Arab II	942, 943	Park Royal
	321–357	HGC	100–136	Guy Arab II	944–980	Park Royal
	358–368	HGC	137–147	Guy Arab II	981–991	Massey
	369–430	HGC	148–209	Guy Arab II	992–1053	Weymann
	431–435	HGC	210–214	Guy Arab II	1054–1058	Park Royal
D	1–6	GXE	578–583	Daimler CWA6	632–637	Duple (low height)
	7–13	GXE	584–590	Daimler CWA6	638–644	Duple
	14–34	GLX	900–920	Daimler CWA6	645–665	Duple
	35–38	GLX	921–924	Daimler CWA6	666–669	Brush
	39–61	GXV	770–792	Daimler CWA6	670–692	Brush
	62–73	GYE	51–62	Daimler CWA6	695–706	Brush
	74–92	GYE	64–82	Daimler CWA6	708–726	Duple
	93–95	GYE	98–100	Daimler CWA6	742–744	Brush
	96–126	GYL	261–291	Daimler CWA6	745–775	Brush
	127	GYL	292	Daimler CWD6	776	Brush
	128–131	HGC	255–258	Daimler CWA6	1099–1102	Duple (low height)
	132–172	HGC	259–299	(c)	1103–1143	Duple
	173–181	HGF	800–808	(c)	1144–1152	Duple
	182–281	HGF	859–958	Daimler CWA6	1205–1304	Park Royal

(a)   G 30 rebodied by Northern Coachbuilders (LT body No. 707)
(b)   Originally allocated registration FXT 441 but amended before entering service
(c)   D 138–140, 142, 150, 155, 160, 162, 163, 171, 180, 181 type CWD6, remainder CWA6

Sadly only four of London's utilities have been preserved, and only one of these still carries bodywork from its London days. Thanks to John Lines, G 351 was kept when its days with Burton-upon-Trent Corporation were over, and it is now housed at the Cobham Bus Museum. Seen on an early Historic Commercial Vehicle Club London to Brighton run, the distortion in its body framework was, even then, only too apparent.
S Clennell

APPENDIX 2 – MONTHLY SUMMARY OF NEW VEHICLES LICENSED FOR SERVICE AND INITIAL ALLOCATIONS

December 1941	STD 101 (GM)
May 1942	STD 102, 103 (GM)
	B 1–6 (HW)
June 1942	STD 104 (GM)
	B 7–9 (HW)
July 1942	STD 105, 106, 109 (GM)
August 1942	STD 107, 108, 110, 111 (GM)
December 1942	G 1, 2, 8, 13, 14, 32 (AR)
January 1943	G 3, 15, 16, 18, 19, 22, 33 (AR)
February 1943	G 4, 17, 20, 21, 24–26, 29, 35, 36, 38, 39, 41, 42 (AR)
April 1943	G 7 (AR)
June 1943	G 10, 30, 34, 40, 54, 59, 65 (AR), G 5, 6, 9, 11, 23, 27, 28, 37, 48, 57, 60–64, 66 (HW)
July 1943	G 12, 31, 43–47, 49–53, 55, 56, 58, 67–71, 73–75, 77 (HW)
August 1943	G 72, 76, 78, 79 (ON), G 80, 81, (AR)
September 1943	G 82, 84–92 (ON)
October 1943	G 83, 93–96 (ON)
November 1943	G 97–100 (ON)
January 1944	G 101–106, 108 (ON), G 107 (HW)
February 1944	G 109–111, 113 (HW), G 112, 115 (BK)
March 1944	G 114 (HW), G 116–136 (BK)
May 1944	D 1, 3–6, (AL)
June 1944	D 2 (AL)
August 1944	D 7, 9 (AL)
September 1944	D 8, 10–20, 22–24 (AL)
October 1944	D 21, 25–34 (AL)
January 1945	G 137 (ON)
February 1945	D 35–39 (AL)
March 1945	D 40–57, 70, 74, 79–83 (AL)
April 1945	D 58–62, 64, 65, 84 (AL)
May 1945	G 138, 174 (ON), G 175–180, 182, 184 (BK)
	D 63, 66, 69, 71, 72. 75–78, 87, 89, 91 (AL)
June 1945	G 139, 154, 156, 157, 159, 181, 183, 185–190 (BK), G 155 (ON)
	D 67, 68, 73, 85, 86, 88, 90, 92–96, 100 (AL)
July 1945	G 140–142, 145, 148, 149, 171, (ON), G 143, 144, 146, 147, 151, 152, 170, 172, 173
	220, 222–226, 229, 259–261 (GM), G 158, 160–169, 191–193 (BK), G 221 (U), G 219, 258 (RD)
	D 97–99, 101–113, 115, 117, 118 (AL)
August 1945	G 153 (ON), G 194 (AR), G 195, 227, 228, 230–242, 262–268, 312–314 (GM),
	G 243, 269, 315–318, 358, 359 (RD)
	D 114, 116, 119–126 (AL)
September 1945	G 150 (ON), G 196–205, 244–249, 270–278, 360–376, 378 (RD)
October 1945	G 206, 207, 210–218, 252, 280–286, 377, 386, 389, 390, 392–400 (E), G 208, 251,
	279, 385, 391 (BK), G 209, 250, 379–384, 387, 388 (RD)
	D 127 (AL)
November 1945	G 253, 290–292, 406, 415, 419, 421 (U), G 254, 289, 401–405, 407–414, 416, 417 (BK),
	G 287, 288 (E)
	D 128–131 (AL)
December 1945	B 11, 13 (HW)
	G 255–257, 293–300, 319–327, 332–334, 418, 420, 422–428 (U), G 429 (ON),
	D 132 (AL)
January 1946	B 10, 12, 14–29 (HW)
	G 301, 304, 306, 328–331, 335–342, 346, 430 (U), G 302, 303, 305, 343–345 (BK)
	D 138–140, 142 (AL)
February 1946	G 347–353 (U)
	D 150, 155, 160, 162, 163 (AL)
March 1946	G 307–310, 354–357, 431–433 (U)
	D 133–137, 141, 143–149, 151–154, 156–159, 161, 164–170, 172–179 (RE), D 170,
	171, 180, 181 (AL)
April 1946	G 311, 434, 435 (U)
May 1946	D 182–195 (A)
June 1946	D 196–203, 205 (A)
July 1946	D 204, 206–219, 221, 222 (A)
August 1946	D 220, 223–240 (A)
September 1946	D 241–248 (A)
October 1946	D 249–271 (A)
November 1946	D 272–281 (A)

The official codes quoted denote garages as follows: A – Sutton, AL – Merton, AR – Tottenham, BK – Barking, E – Enfield, GM – Victoria, HW – Hanwell, ON – Alperton, RD – Hornchurch, RE – Romford, U – Upton Park.

APPENDIX 3 - LONDON DAIMLERS IN BELFAST

Belfast no.	London no.	Registration		Belfast no.	London no.	Registration		Belfast no.	London no.	Registration	
450	D 11	GXE	587	484	D 125	GYL	290	518	D 135	HGC	262
451	D 12	GXE	588	485	D 138	HGC	265	519	D 139	HGC	266
452	D 13	GXE	590	486	D 140	HGC	267	520	D 142	HGC	269
453	D 15	GLX	901	487	D 146	HGC	273	521	D 156	HGC	283
454	D 16	GLX	902	488	D 150	HGC	277	522	D 162	HGC	289
455	D 17	GLX	903	489	D 154	HGC	281	523	D 164	HGC	291
456	D 18	GLX	904	490	D 157	HGC	284	524	D 186	HGF	863
457	D 20	GLX	906	491	D 182	HGF	859	525	D 195	HGF	872
458	D 22	GLX	908	492	D 183	HGF	860	526	D 197	HGF	874
459	D 23	GLX	909	493	D 184	HGF	861	527	D 200	HGF	877
460	D 37	GLX	923	494	D 185	HGF	862	528	D 69	GYE	58
461	D 40	GXV	771	495	D 187	HGF	864	529	D 73	GYE	62
462	D 45	GXV	776	496	D 188	HGF	865	530	D 108	GYL	273
463	D 48	GXV	779	497	D 189	HGF	866	531	D 116	GYL	281
464	D 51	GXV	782	498	D 190	HGF	867	532	D 120	GYL	285
465	D 54	GXV	785	499	D 191	HGF	868	533	D 121	GYL	286
466	D 58	GXV	789	500	D 192	HGF	869	534	D 133	HGC	260
467	D 62	GYE	51	501	D 193	HGF	870	535	D 134	HGC	261
468	D 63	GYE	52	502	D 194	HGF	871	536	D 137	HGC	264
469	D 64	GYE	53	503	D 196	HGF	873	537	D 141	HGC	268
470	D 66	GYE	55	504	D 56	GXV	787	538	D 147	HGC	274
471	D 67	GYE	56	505	D 59	GXV	790	539	D 151	HGC	278
472	D 72	GYE	61	506	D 75	GYE	65	540	D 201	HGF	878
473	D 76	GYE	66	507	D 92	GYE	82	541	D 215	HGF	892
474	D 87	GYE	77	508	D 94	GYE	99	542	D 217	HGF	894
475	D 89	GYE	79	509	D 104	GYL	269	543	D 219	HGF	896
476	D 93	GYL	98	510	D 106	GYL	271	544	D 221	HGF	898
477	D 99	GYL	264	511	D 107	GYL	272	545	D 224	HGF	901
478	D 103	GYL	268	512	D 110	GYL	275	546	D 226	HGF	903
479	D 105	GYL	270	513	D 113	GYL	278	547	D 250	HGF	927
480	D 111	GYL	276	514	D 114	GYL	279	548	D 254	HGF	931
481	D 112	GYL	277	515	D 115	GYL	280	549	D 259	HGF	936
482	D 118	GYL	283	516	D 119	GYL	284				
483	D 124	GYL	289	517	D 132	HGC	259				

APPENDIX 4 - GUYS PURCHASED BY EDINBURGH CORPORATION

Edinburgh	London		Edinburgh	London		Edinburgh	London		Edinburgh	London	
301	G 84		316	G 251		331	G 272		346	G 197	
302	G 223		317	G 285		332	G 275		347	G 215	
303	G 353		318	G 250		333	G 388		348	G 222	
304	G 345		319	G 163		334	G 161		349	G 402	
305	G 119		320	G 264		335	G 247		350	G 419	
306	G 305		321	G 270		336	G 258		351	G 104	
307	G 303		322	G 164		337	G 205		352	G 173	
308	G 265		323	G 398		338	G 208		353	G 213	
309	G 120		324	G 430		339	G 166		354	G 227	
310	G 306		325	G 302		340	G 185		355	G 313	
311	G 239		326	G 202		341	G 321		356	G 255	
312	G 314		327	G 206		342	G 231		357	G 403	
313	G 280		328	G 212		343	G 210		358	G 421	
314	G 77		329	G 220		344	G 214		359	G 155	
315	G 377		330	G 295		345	G 121		360	G 382	

APPENDIX 5 - LONDON UTILITIES PURCHASED BY THE SOUTH WESTERN OMNIBUS COMPANY (1952) LTD, FOR OPERATION IN CEYLON

Shipped in May 1952   —   G 416

Shipped in January 1953   —   G 30, 72, 76, 83, 85, 96, 105, 109, 125, 137, 435

       D 2, 3, 5, 6, 9, 29, 100, 128, 129, 130, 131, 166, 168, 170, 171, 180, 181, 225, 229, 232, 235, 243, 244, 245, 247, 248, 249, 251, 252, 255, 256, 257, 258, 262, 264, 265, 266, 267, 273

Shipped in December 1953   —   D 21, 24, 25, 26, 33, 35, 36, 38, 43, 44, 46, 47, 49, 50, 55, 57, 61, 68, 70, 80, 82, 83, 85, 88, 102, 109, 117, 123, 127, 143, 144, 145, 148, 155, 164, 174, 198, 203, 204, 205, 206, 207, 208, 209, 212, 216, 218, 222, 223, 269